RETAILING IN ENGLAND
DURING THE INDUSTRIAL REVOLUTION

Retailing in England during the Industrial Revolution

by

DAVID ALEXANDER

UNIVERSITY OF LONDON

THE ATHLONE PRESS

1970

Published by
THE ATHLONE PRESS
UNIVERSITY OF LONDON
at 2 Gower Street, London WC1

Distributed by Tiptree Book Services Ltd
Tiptree, Essex

Australia and New Zealand
Melbourne University Press

U.S.A.
Oxford University Press Inc
New York

© *David Alexander*, 1970

ISBN 0 485 11116 0

Printed in Great Britain by
WESTERN PRINTING SERVICES LTD
BRISTOL

To
SYDNEY PETTIT
and
RODNEY POISSON

PREFACE

THE INDUSTRIAL REVOLUTION is one of the most intensely studied periods of British economic history. Innumerable general histories have been written in addition to monographs and articles dealing with agriculture, industry, foreign trade, transport, banking, and demography; but remarkably little has been written about internal trade, either wholesale or retail. R. B. Westerfield's *Middlemen in English Business*, written as long ago as 1915, remains a principal source on eighteenth century distribution. More recently, and in addition to an emerging periodical literature on the subject, A. Adburgham's *Shops and Shopkeeping* has provided insights into the high class retail trade of the nineteenth century, while D. Davis' *A History of Shopping* has traced retail trading over several centuries. But a fundamental question with respect to nineteenth century distribution remains unanswered. In his monumental *Economic History of Modern Britain*, J. H. Clapham argued that the essential features of the nineteenth century distribution system emerged in the first half of the century; but this interpretation was challenged by J. B. Jefferys in *Retail Trading in Britain*, who countered that the changes in distribution between 1750 and 1850 did not amount to a transformation, and that the system as a whole 'still bore the marks of a pre-industrial economy'.

One objective of this study is to attempt a resolution of the conflict between these hypotheses: they remain hypotheses, in my opinion, since neither scholar examined distribution in depth for the period 1800 to 1850. But a more fundamental question must be posed: what is the *social* function of the distribution system in a country going through the early phase of industrialization? If this question is asked, then the issue of whether distribution lagged behind other sectors of the economy in the early nineteenth century will be placed in its essential context. That is, *technical* efficiency and *economic* efficiency do not necessarily coincide. This issue has been raised with respect to 'dualism' in underdeveloped economies and the 'Second Industrial Revolution' or Electronic Revolution in developed nations. In 1961 David J. MacDonald, President of the United Steelworkers of America, testified before the House Subcommittee on Unemployment and the Impact of Automation, that he had been assured by electronic technologists that it was possible 'to create all the goods that Americans can consume and can sell with one-tenth of our current work force', but that 'it would mean scrapping . . . a great deal of existing industrial plants . . . which would not be economically feasible.' A similar issue confronted industrializing Britain in the early nineteenth century; and it will be argued here that while it may be true that the distribution system, as some historians have argued, was woefully 'backward', paradoxically, this measure of backwardness was economically and socially efficient.

The preparation of this study has been greatly assisted by research grants from the Canada Council, the Central Research Fund of the University of London, and the London School of Economics and Political Science. The staffs of the British Museum, the Public Record Office, and many Libraries and Record Offices throughout Britain were always generous in their assistance. My special thanks are due to Professor A. H. John of the London School of Economics, who supervised an earlier version of this study as a Ph.D. thesis, and has since encouraged and assisted me in many ways. I am also indebted to Professor B. S. Yamey of the London School of Economics, and Professors H. C. and L. H. Mui and C. Wadel of the Memorial University of Newfoundland who have read the manuscript and offered most helpful advice. Thanks are due to my wife Anne for preparing the index.

Memorial University of Newfoundland   D. A.
St John's, 1969

CONTENTS

LIST OF TABLES

ABBREVIATIONS

B.3. 123. . .   Abbreviation for reference to the files of the
                     Court of Bankruptcy, Public Record Office
B.P.P.   *British Parliamentary Papers*
Econ. Hist. Rev.   *Economic History Review*
J. Econ. Hist.   *Journal of Economic History*
J. Stat. Soc. London *Journal of the Statistical Society of London*
General View of . . . Abbreviation for reference to the Board of
                     Agriculture County Reports, typically styled,
                     General View of the Agriculture of the County of. . .

PART I

Retailing and the Economic and Social Context

I

Aspects of a Changing Retail Market

IT HAS BEEN argued that a distribution system is only a mechanism for the exchange of goods and services between producers and consumers. Accordingly, what is crucial to a society, and therefore crucial for analysis, is the structure of production and consumption units.

This argument reveals a remarkable lack of curiosity about the organization of social systems and the complexities of interaction among parts of those systems. It is obvious that all distribution systems are not structurally the same. They differ because the kind of distribution service required is a function of the size and distribution of the population, the structure of production units and the level of individual and local self-sufficiency, the availability of transport and communication services, the size and distribution of income, and many other factors. These economic and social variables, from a technical point of view, determine the kind of distribution system which is necessary and possible for any given society. From the entrepreneurial point of view, these factors are determinants of the *niches* available for exploitation, the assets which must be brought to bear to exploit niche opportunities, and what is very difficult to determine, the expectations of consumers with respect to the entrepreneur: what services do they expect from him and what form of entrepreneurial exploitation is acceptable to them in terms of social expectations? Not all of these factors can be discussed immediately, but this chapter does provide at least a preliminary discussion of the impact of population, transport and living standards on the distribution system.

1. *Population and Urbanization*

The scale of distribution services needed to service an economy is a function of the size of the population, but not of size alone.

The population of England and Wales in 1700 was about 5.5M. In the next fifty years the population rose to just under 6.5M, and when the first census was taken in 1801 England and Wales contained about 9M people. By 1851 this population had almost doubled itself to just under 18M people.[1] If the *per capita* demand for distribution services was a constant factor over these 150 years (an assumption which is in fact not valid), then population growth alone would have required a distribution service which had expanded by more than a factor of 3.

The demand for distribution services is also a function of the distribution of population and the degree of occupational specialization and self-sufficiency implied (historically if not necessarily theoretically) in a particular population distribution. The growth of population in England and Wales was associated with a shift in concentration from the South to the Midlands and North,[2] and a significant increase in the number of people living in large towns and cities.[3]

The Greater London conurbation doubled in size between 1801 and 1851 from 1.1M people to 2.6M.[4] In 1801, London aside, there was no town in England and Wales with a population over 100 000, and only five towns (Liverpool, Manchester, Birmingham, Bristol and Leeds) with populations over 50 000. But by 1821, Liverpool, Manchester and Birmingham were all over 100 000, with, in 1831, the addition of Leeds and Bristol, in 1841 with Sheffield, and in 1851 with Bradford. In 1821 there were 8 towns with populations over 50 000, but by 1851 there were some 24. In 1801 there were 42 towns with populations ranging between 10 000 and 50 000; and in 1851, despite the spectacular growth of London and the provincial cities over 100 000 and the big towns between 50 000 and 100 000 there were still some 35 towns with populations in this range, including several in South Wales.[5] By any standard these figures are impressive testimony of rapid urbanization. But looked at in another way, it has been suggested that in 1801

---

[1] B. R. Mitchell and P. Deane, *Abstract of British Historical Statistics* (1962), Population and Vital Statistics, tables 1 and 2.

[2] See A. Redford, *Labour Migration in England* (1926).

[3] See W. Ashworth, *The Genesis of British Town Planning* (1954).

[4] Mitchell and Deane, *Abstract*, table 6.

[5] Ibid., table 8.

only a fifth of the population of England lived in an urban setting, whereas by 1851 this figure had risen to one half.[6] In 1801 about 17 per cent of the population of England and Wales lived in towns or cities of over 20 000 people, as compared with about 38 per cent in 1861.[7]

In what ways would one expect rapid urbanization to affect the demand for distribution services? In a predominantly rural, non-industrial society, a large proportion of the population is to some extent self-sufficient with respect to food, fuel and even clothing. The few needs for manufactured goods requiring specialized skills may be satisfied by barter or direct purchase from local craftsman,[8] or by attending local and regional markets and fairs. The need for specialist distributors (wholesalers, retailers and providers of transport services) is correspondingly low. In other words, the economic and demographic structure of the society offers comparatively few *niche* opportunities in distribution, and the vertical growth possibilities of the entrepreneurial unit is constrained.

In such an economy, then, aggregate distribution costs are insignificant. There is little fixed capital invested in distribution facilities (market sites and shops); information services (advertising of all kinds) are almost eliminated by the proximity of producer and consumer (where they are distinct); processing costs are usually indistinguishable from production costs; holding costs are reduced by bespoke demand; and transportation costs are confined largely to the movement of essential foodstuffs, luxury goods and raw materials. Of course, this does not make for a consumer's paradise: the absence of economies of scale in production and the high distribution costs on those commodities which must be imported from abroad or other regions mean the society enjoys a generally low-level material culture.

In England, personal, local and regional self-sufficiency began to break down in the late seventeenth century, accelerating in the late eighteenth and nineteenth centuries. Not only

---

[6] J. Burnett, *Plenty and Want* (1966), p. 1.

[7] Ashworth, *Town Planning*, p. 8.

[8] See for example, G. M. Foster, 'Folk Economy of Rural Mexico', *Journal of Marketing* xiii, no. 2, (1948).

did the growing population require more distribution services, but as the society industrialized, as occupational specialization became more pronounced and population was distributed increasingly in urban settings, personal subsistence activities became increasingly less important and the *per capita* demand for distribution services rose. R. B. Westerfield has shown that in early eighteenth century England there emerged a large body of middlemen whose principal function was to distribute imported commodities, to assemble stocks of agricultural produce, raw materials and manufactured goods for export and for internal re-distribution.[9] Much of this activity was focussed on the London market and the export and import facilities of the Port of London. The metropolis was uniquely dependent upon supplies of agricultural produce and manufactured goods assembled by middlemen from an ever increasing area beyond the city.[10] With the mushrooming of towns and cities in the late eighteenth and nineteenth centuries, however, London's dependence upon middlemen ceased to be unique. The characteristics of distribution for rural, non-industrial societies ceased to be true over much of England: distribution costs for the economy rose, and the *niches* available for exploitation by entrepreneurs expanded in number and, as we shall see, changed in character, in terms of skills employed and the settings in which distribution took place.

The conversion of urban central areas into a more workable environment for buyers and sellers was one crucial feature of the changing setting in which distribution took place. A more efficient use and control of central streets was essential if the distribution system was adequately to service a population increasingly dependent upon it. Scarce capital and local government inexperience meant that town centres in the nineteenth century rarely matched the increasing demands placed upon them, but the main requirements were recognized and acted upon with varying degrees of enlightenment.

Paving and lighting Acts passed in Parliament date back to the sixteenth century, but a growing stream of more compre-

[9] *Middlemen in English Business* (1915), pp. 124–5.
[10] F. J. Fisher, 'The Development of the London Food Market', *Econ. Hist. Rev.*, 2, (1934–35).

hensive urban improvement measures dates from the late eighteenth century. Almost 400 local and private town and market improvement Acts were passed by Parliament between 1785 and 1850 affecting urban areas outside Greater London. The scope of the early Acts was restricted largely to matters concerning paving, lighting and the removal of nuisances. For example, the Dover Act of 1778 empowered commissioners to direct the laying of pavements, to arrange for the cleaning of streets and the erection of lamps. Unfenced cellar doors, projecting shop signs, windows and steps, unattended carts and stalls, wandering livestock and slaughtering in the streets were all new offences under the Act.[11] Limited measures of this kind were the initial step in establishing efficient use of central areas.[12] In the nineteenth century this type of limited Improvement Act was extended to include regulation of gas installations, control of smoke, establishment of fire brigades and fire hydrants and the regulation of street widths.[13] Many of the Acts allowed authorities to remove ruinous buildings and to plan for the future straightening and widening of streets.

A second type of Improvement Act was concerned with major alterations in the street pattern of central areas. In Manchester and Liverpool in the late eighteenth century the press of commercial activity necessitated the demolition of large parts of the medieval central area. Bristol, Birmingham, Sheffield, and a few smaller towns such as Wolverhampton and Durham undertook similarly ambitious programmes of improvement.[14] Fashionable resort towns, like Bath and Cheltenham, were assiduous in seeking powers to remove

[11] 18 Geo. III, c. lxxvi.

[12] Whether or not these powers were used depended upon the initiative of the commissioners and the courage of constables. The impression is that enforcement, for most of the early nineteenth century, was not very rigorous. For the case of Birmingham, see C. Gill, *History of Birmingham* (1952) i.

[13] Thus, the 1829 Act for Aston established that on streets up to 10 yards wide, bulks and sashes were not to extend more than 12 inches from walls, and on streets under that width they were prohibited. Violators were to be fined and required to alter the structure. All new and rebuilt streets were to be a minimum of 14 yards wide. 10 Geo. IV, c. vi.

[14] Manchester—16 Geo. III, c. lxiii; Liverpool—26 Geo. III, c xii; Bristol—28 Geo. III, c. lxvii; Birmingham—41 Geo. III, c. xxxix; Sheffield—24 Geo. III, c. v, s. 2; Wolverhampton—17 Geo. III, c. xxv; Durham—30 Geo. III, c. lxvii.

unsightly buildings and alter street patterns to secure a less congested flow of traffic.

A third aspect of urban improvement involved the removal of wholesale and retail markets from the principal streets. Market relocation in the larger cities with fast growing populations began in many cases before 1815, even in the case of smaller towns like Ramsgate, Lewes, Abergavenny, Newark, Bridgwater, Bedford, and Chichester. Typically, the preambles to these Acts make reference to 'a large and increasing Population', point out that the markets are 'quite open (and) exposed to Rain and Wind' and suggest that traffic congestion is a danger to life and an impediment to trade.[15]

By 1850 the central core of the major provincial cities, and many of the larger towns, had ceased to be medieval and were recognizably modern. They were invariably dominated by offices, warehouses and retail shops commanding high rents. A discernable commercial district existed in Manchester as early as 1800,[16] but the foundation of modern Manchester began with the widening of Market Street in the 1820s.[17] In 1839 a local historian noted that,

Within the last few years Mosley-street contained only private dwelling-houses; it is now converted almost entirely into warehouses; and the increasing business of the town is rapidly converting all the principal dwelling-houses which exist in that neighbourhood into mercantile establishments and is drawing most of the respectable inhabitants into the suburbs...on land purchased at so high a rate new buildings have generally been erected; and...a more than usual number of warehouses are raised on a limited space, the towering height of which make up for their contracted width.[18]

In this respect Manchester's experience was not unique. At Halifax in 1820 a grocer noted that Crown Street was 'the centre of the town' and 'As far as I recollect, all (the buildings) are shops on both sides'. He pointed out that a shop site on any other street would not be so commercially valuable.[19] In

[15] Exeter in 1820, 1 Geo. IV, c. lxxviii. See chapter II for a fuller discussion of market improvements.
[16] J. Aston, *The Manchester Guide* (1804) p. 272.
[17] Anon., *A Gossip about Old Manchester* (1888) p. 23.
[18] Anon., *Manchester as it is* (1839) pp. 200–1.
[19] *B.P.P., Select Committee on the Shop Windows Duty*: Mins. of Ev., 1819 (528) ii, p. 13.

the same year a draper at Birmingham, whose shop was 'many hundred years old', testified that a few years previous he had paid an annual rent of £30; but the shop being located on what was now considered a valuable site, the rental had been raised to £120 a year. The draper had purchased the shop for £3000 and spent another £1000 on repairs. But he added that had 'it not been for the purpose of situation as a retail trade, I would not have given £500 for the whole...'.[20]

The emphasis upon modern central areas and good shopping facilities, which is to be found in periodicals and guidebooks, is remarkable. Journals like the *Tradesman*, published between 1808 and 1816, and the *British Almanac*, carried regular lists of 'provincial improvements'. Guidebooks did not hesitate to draw comparisons between central streets in provincial towns and those in London; nor did they fail to condemn any signs of backwardness and inactivity. The streets of Newcastle, for example, were described in 1817 as being 'wide and well built; the shops large and remarkably elegant' and the town was noted as having 'a bustle and appearance of business' which was not 'exceeded on this side of London'.[21] By 1827 the shuttered shop windows in Newcastle had been replaced with glass, and the heavy overhanging balconies removed.[22] By contrast, Shrewsbury in 1824 was described as having streets 'irregularly disposed ... narrow and steep, and all very indifferently paved'. The writer heavily instructed the town to adopt 'a well considered plan of progressive improvement, such as has been put in practice in almost every other place of equal size and consequence...'[23] In Chester, where the retail market was probably much livelier, shopkeepers converted the old Rows into attractive, modern structures: the shop fronts were described as 'filled with plate-glass, and with all the brilliancy of the most modern art and taste'.[24] Southampton in 1831 was described as 'well lighted with gas, not only the principal streets, but the shops, more particularly in the

[20] Ibid., p. 18.
[21] Anon., *Letters from Scotland by an English Commercial Traveller* (1817) p. 48.
[22] E. Mackenzie, *A Descriptive and Historical Account of...Newcastle upon Tyne* (1827) p. 162.
[23] Anon., *The Shropshire Gazetteer* (1824) p. 493.
[24] T. Hughes, *The Stranger's Handbook to Chester and its Environs* (1856) p. 46.

High-Street, which during the hours of business has much the appearance of the busy metropolis'.[25] Lincoln in the 1840s had 'several splendid shops, equal to anything of the kind to be found in far larger towns', but the prominence of ecclesiastical freehold in the town left 'unsightly masses of old buildings which disfigure the principal streets' and should 'be supplanted by erections unique with those which modern enterprize has produced'.[26] One suspects that the chronicler of Lincoln was something of a philistine, but it should be noted that many 'improvements' which were praised in the early decades of the century were under attack by mid-century. For example, a critic of the central area of Liverpool noted that 'improvement acts have done much to widen many of our thoroughfares, but little attention has been paid to the architectural character of the new structures which have been raised'. Lord, Castle and Dale streets had been the first to be improved, but 'Let any one compare the shop fronts of Castle-street, or of Lord-street, with the more modern fronts of Bold-street, and a few other places, and the improvement will be perceptible.'[27]

It is clear that a considerable volume of public and private capital was invested in the late eighteenth and early nineteenth centuries in reorganizing the central core of English towns and cities. Investment was needed in order to accommodate a growing volume of trade, and in addition, to satisfy the demands of a growing urban, provincial middle class for improved shopping facilities. The decision in 1833 to hold a Select Committee enquiry into 'the best means of securing open spaces in the vicinity of populous towns' suggests that by mid-century the major provincial cities at least had shaken themselves free from the countryside. We shall see that these urban changes had an impact on all participants in retail trading—on the market trader working in re-located and often radically re-designed markets; on the itinerant street trader whose activities might now be restricted by shopkeeper's complaints and bye-laws regulating street uses; and especially on the shopkeepers located in the central area. The civic pride and

[25] C. Andrews, *A Guide to Southampton* (1831) p. 5.
[26] Anon., *The Stranger's Guide to Lincoln* (1846) p. 95.
[27] S. Holme, *The Public Improvements of Liverpool* (1843) pp. 13–14.

inter-city competitiveness suggested by the nineteenth century guidebooks was related to a new competitiveness among high class retailers in the central area. A well designed shop front and attractive window display were increasingly important elements in a shopkeeper's entrepreneurial calculations. In addition, the high cost of central locations in the long run compelled retailers to calculate more carefully the allocation of space. Although the lock-up shop was still unusual in 1850, central area retailers had begun to move their dwelling units into the suburbs. Such a decision would radically affect the shopkeeper's labour inputs and his entire conception of profit calculation. Finally, with urban growth, central area shop-keepers found that custom derived from inter-personal links, such as through kinship or friendship, represented an increasingly less important element in sales. More and more, the shopkeeper's customers were social strangers, and to attract them into the shop, competitive skills shifted from those based on inter-personal relationships to those based on generalized service and price competitiveness. The introduction of price competition in its turn necessitated greater attention to consumer information services—attention to shop appearance and printed advertising and marked prices from which there would be 'no abatement'. In these and other ways, as we shall see, a change in the setting of retail distribution was associated with the introduction of new retailing techniques.

But the extent of change must not be exaggerated. As late as 1856 it was suggested that a virtue of the Rows in Chester was that they made shopping pleasant 'for old ladies of weak minds who quail at meeting cattle' in the streets.[28] An old resident of Epping recalled that in the 1870s it 'was a peaceful little country town....There were no footpaths or pavements, the High Street was rough and stony, and during hot weather it was watered to keep down the dust. The town was lighted by gas lamps, but these were few, and were only kept alight during the winter months. Hemnal street (then called the "Back Street") had no lamps at all. Some shop windows were illuminated with paraffin lamps or the old-fashioned tallow-candles. Practically all the buildings were centuries old, and quite a

[28] Hughes, *Chester*, p. 45.

number possessed typical Georgian bow windows'.[29] It is probably true that over much of rural England demographic changes in the country as a whole had little visible impact upon the appearance of towns until quite late into the nineteenth century. We must, then, give attention to what was static, or changing very slowly, as well as to what was new and dynamic.

2. *Transportation and Communications*

Division of labour (involving both horizontal and vertical specialization) is the most important source of higher productivity, and is directly related to the size of the market. The economic size of the market is determined by its physical extent and by the aggregate incomes of consumers.[30] In this section we will suggest how transport facilities can determine the physical extent of the market, and thereby have an impact on the distribution structure, while in the next section we will consider consumer's incomes, and their relationship to the distribution system.

The main function of a transportation system is to bridge the gap between producer and consumer, either by the movement of goods to consumers or, as is more commonly the case with consumption of services, by movement of the consumer. 'Whatever the distribution of the population, the greater the efficiency of transport services the greater will be the volume of demand brought within reach of producers. The market will be extended and a greater degree of specialization among productive resources will be possible.'[31]

The investment in transport facilities which is required to sustain a given degree of occupational specialization is directly related to the settlement of population. If the population is very scattered a larger investment will be required than if it is concentrated in dense clusters.

Demand for transport services in Britain grew with the expansion of commercial and industrial activity. But transport's call on the economic resources of the country was not as heavy

[29] E. A. Hills, *Recollections of an Epping Victorian* (Unpublished MSS, 1963, Essex Record Office, T/Z46).

[30] R. Nurske, *Capital Formation in Underdeveloped Countries* (1958) p. 18 tends to depreciate the significance of the physical size of the market.

[31] A. M. Milne and J. C. Laight, *The Economics of Inland Transport* (1963) p. 17.

as it might have been, since this activity, as we have seen, was associated with rapid urbanization and because Britain enjoyed some unique geographical advantages. No part of England was more than 70 miles from the sea, and the whole country was well endowed with rivers which could be rendered navigable at a low cost.[32] Moreover, most of the major urban centres were located on the coast or on a navigable river. But a great deal of inter-regional traffic could not be accommodated entirely or in part by coastal and inland water transport. Road transport, despite the improvements brought by turnpike trusts and the work of the early nineteenth century road engineers, remained slow and costly. Canal construction and the opening up of inland waterways had an important impact on the transport of grain and raw materials for industry from the 1760s, but their contribution to the movement of most food commodities and manufactured goods destined for domestic consumption was less important.[33] The most decisive aspect of the transport revolution was the development of railways in the 1830s and 1840s. All retail traders were affected by the resulting speeding up of goods transport and communication between producer and distributor. This will become more apparent in later chapters, but at this point we can profitably illustrate the point by examining how improved transport revolutionized the distribution and consumption of fresh fish.

Until the 1840s high land transport costs and perishability restricted regular fresh fish consumption to coastal areas of Britain and to the wealthy classes of inland centres. Even though London was the principal inland market, residents of St Pancras, Marylebone, St Giles and Bloomsbury complained in 1815 of an inadequate supply.[34] Liverpool residents complained that retailers maintained artificially high prices by destroying fish which could not be sold at those prices.[35] In the

[32] P. Deane, *The First Industrial Revolution* (1965) p. 73.

[33] Burnett, *Plenty and Want*, p. 6.

[34] Anon., *An Address to the Inhabitants of St. Pancras (etc) pointing out the means of obtaining a plentiful Supply of Fish* (1815). According to the *Second Report* of the Association for the Relief of the Manufacturing and Labouring Poor (1815) p. 27, retailers were reluctant to open shops in the London fringes because of porterage costs from Billingsgate.

[35] Anon., *A General and Descriptive History of the Ancient and Present State of Liverpool* (1795) pp. 182–3.

1790s, in order to secure a regular supply of fresh fish, prosperous Birmingham residents organized a cooperative society with a three guinea subscription cost.[36] A Midlands clergyman reported in 1815 that 'fish was as great a rarity with them, as in the interior of the Continent'.[37] In short, for most people in the country, fresh fish was a rare and expensive article of consumption.

Fears of food shortages during the Napoleonic Wars led the government to consider methods of increasing the volume of fish landed and to encourage its consumption among the urban working classes. But a Parliamentary Committee reported in 1801 that the most abundant supply would be of little value 'unless proper Means are empowered to regulate its Distribution...and to remove the Prejudices which at First usually oppose the Introduction of a new Article of Food'. The report recommended the establishment of local committees to organize supplies from central depots in port cities.[38] Subsidies to fishermen were introduced in the hope of extending the volume of fish which they would find profitable to market.[39]

Private associations were also active around this time in organizing the distribution of fresh fish and encouraging its consumption. Notable among them was the Association for the Relief and Benefit of the Manufacturing Poor. The committee contracted with fishermen to buy from ten to twenty thousand mackerel for the London market whenever the prices fell to 10s. 'the hundred of six score', which was the minimum price at which fishermen would market. On one day alone the committee bought 17 000 mackerel at £5 per thousand for distribution at cost price to Spitalfields weavers.[40]

Similar schemes were organized in the provinces. Around 1809 the Northumberland Fishery Society presented a scheme

[36] J. A. Langford, *A Century of Birmingham Life* (2nd. ed., 1870), i, 362 and 370 and ii, 19.

[37] Ibid., ii, 31.

[38] *B.P.P., Second Report from the Committee Appointed to Consider...the Present High Price of Provisions*; 1801 (174) ii, 7.

[39] 41 Geo. III, c. 99. The accounts, 1802-3 (7) vii, and 1803-4 (17) vii, and 1842 (394) xxvi suggest the subsidy did increase the volume of fish landed, as bounties paid out rose between 1809 and 1819.

[40] Sir Thomas Bernard, 'An Account of a Supply of Fish', *The Pamphleteer* (1813), i, no. 2, 433-4.

to supply Sheffield by shipping fish live in deep welled vessels to Hull, where they would be shifted into smaller boats for carriage to Selby and from there by land to Sheffield.[41] Apparently the scheme collapsed, because in 1812 or 1813 the London Association for the Relief of the Manufacturing Poor were organizing supplies of cod for Sheffield and Rotherham. In addition, the Association offered to supply fish to towns within one hundred miles of London by means of carriages with a 20 or 30 cwt. capacity, and towns within forty miles by light carts holding 7 cwt. of fish. The fish was to be sent as regularly as the cost price allowed, and a transport charge was included.[42] However, the Association was content to withdraw its services once private suppliers had entered the field. A few months after the first supplies had been sent to Birmingham it was found that 'private individuals began to embark in the measure' and 'dealers were bringing great quantities of fish from the Yorkshire coast, on such moderate terms as would render it necessary for the parties to close their engagements with the Association'.[43] In 1815 a firm employed the Association's methods to supply Buckingham, Oxford, Birmingham, and Berkshire.

It was a guiding assumption of the Association that an entrepreneurial *niche* existed which was not being exploited. The Association saw its task as that of demonstrating to private entrepreneurs that the *niche* existed and could be exploited for private and public profit. In fact, it was argued some years later that the Association had failed to develop a better distribution service than had already existed.[44] A development of the market for fresh fish was hampered by a fundamental transport bottleneck. This can be shown by a closer examination of the London situation in these years.

The supply of fish to the London market was very erratic since deliveries from the coast were frequently delayed or stopped by adverse winds on the Thames. An obvious first

[41] *The Tradesman* (1809) ii, 345–6. Hull and Leeds were also to be supplied.

[42] Second Report, op. cit., p. 32. Maidenhead took 15 tons of fish in six months in twice weekly shipments at a total cost of £501, about 3½d. per lb.

[43] Ibid., pp. 32–3.

[44] *On the Utility of Rail-Roads as a means of Increasing the British Fisheries* (1835) pp. 4–5.

solution to the problem was to organize land transport from the Thames mouth. Land carriage of fish to Billingsgate market had been in existence since at least the 1760s.[45] In 1765 a firm trading as Grant and Company operated 55 'fish machines' from ports in Devon, Dorset, Sussex and Kent with retail outlets in St James's, Shepherd's Market, Clare Market, Honey Lane and Leadenhall. The firm claimed that Billingsgate wholesale prices exceeded their retail prices by $2\frac{1}{4}$d. per pound, but the total volume supplied to London between June 1765 and December 1767 amounted only to some 152 tons.[46] Land carriage of fish to Billingsgate through the use of large vans and post-horses was an established technique until the coming of the railroads, although it was both slow and costly. A second method of improving the regularity of London's fish supply was introduced in the 1820s. River steam boats were introduced to tow fishing vessels up the Thames, though actual steam carriage from fishing ports was thought to be too costly.[47]

Apparently these modifications in traditional transport techniques made some improvement on the Billingsgate supply situation. According to one source, the London market was by the 1830s sufficiently well supplied that Devon fishermen, who had at one time marketed in London, were now concentrating on markets in Bath, Bristol, Exeter and Plymouth.[48] But the Clerk of Billingsgate Market testified that the London working classes remained deeply prejudiced against a fish diet: his explanation was that the supply of fish remained uneven and the price of quality fish too high.[49]

A wider and deeper market for fresh fish depended ultimately upon the development of railway transport. The role of rail-

[45] Grant and Company, *An Account of the Land-Carriage of Fish etc.* (1768). The account was a defence against a rival scheme.

[46] Loc. cit.

[47] A Hastings fishmonger believed that abolition of turnpike tolls would allow cheaper fish to be sent by land, *Select Committee on British Channel Fisheries*; Mins. of Ev., 1833 (676) xiv, Q. 1316, 1332 and 1333. But a salesman argued that the volume supplied would only be marginally affected by the dropping of tolls, Q. 1553–4. It was reported that 3 to 5 times as much fish came by water as by land, but that land transport had the advantage of speed and regularity, though not cost, Q. 1548 and 1552.

[48] Ibid., Q. 1464, 2178, 2182 and 2185.

[49] Ibid., Q. 1704.

roads in evening out supplies along a trunk line was foreseen very early,[50] but it was not until the 1840s that railroad companies began effectively to organize the fish carriage.[51] The Manchester market, for example, expanded rapidly in the 1840s when rail shipments from Hull began to arrive at a cost of 16s. to 20s. a ton, or about one-tenth of a penny per pound. The retail price on the Manchester market fell from a range of 6d. to 1s. per pound down to 1½d. to 2d. per pound. The volume consumed rose from 3 tons to 80 tons per week.[52] In Birmingham, where there had been 10 fish merchants in 1829, there were 40 by 1848. Fish consumption rose from less than 8 tons per week to over 77 tons per week in 1845.[53] In 1847 the Norfolk Railway was transporting anywhere from 20 to 40 thousand packages of fish (each package ranging from 20 to 168 lbs.) to London and provincial markets every month.[54] By the 1840s London was also being supplied with Irish fish and Scottish salmon by rail transport. In the 1850s Henry Mayhew remarked upon the regularity of London's fish supply and the substantial fall in prices. 'A fish diet', he suggested, 'seems almost as common among the ill-paid classes of London, as is a potato diet among the peasants of Ireland. Indeed, now, the fish season of the poor never, or rarely, knows an interruption.'[55]

Thus, in the early decades of the nineteenth century there were several English cities and towns which offered attractive mass markets for the fishing industry. But attempts to market fish in these towns, and thereby justify expansion of the fishing industry, were frustrated by the slow, high cost structure of transport. The development of railroads in the 1830s and 1840s broke down the main distribution bottleneck. In the 1860s and 1870s the steam trawler was introduced for deep sea fishing in the rich off-shore grounds, and the conjunction of an expanding fish catch with an adequate distribution system made

---

[50] *Utility of Rail-Roads* (see n. 44).
[51] At first fish was commonly thrust into the carriage with second and third class passengers, J. B. Williams, *J. Stat. Soc. London* ix (1846), 132.
[52] Loc. cit.
[53] S. Salt, *Facts and Figures Principally Relating to Railways and Commerce* (1848) p. 3.
[54] Ibid., p. 101.
[55] *London Labour and London Poor* (1851, i) pp. 23 and 62.

possible the heavy, fresh fish diet of the working classes in the last decades of the nineteenth century.

The transport system, then, is a key factor affecting the distribution and consumption of commodities. Major changes in the transport system may open up entrepreneurial opportunities in the distribution system where they did not exist before, and lead to significant changes in consumption patterns. We have illustrated this point with the extreme case of a commodity whose extended consumption was a function primarily of a radical change in transport technique. But retailers can be affected by less dramatic improvements, such as the growth of turnpike roads in England in the eighteenth and early nineteenth centuries. Any technical or organizational change which results in lower costs can alter the relationships among retailer, wholesaler, producer, and consumer. For example, a retailer may find that a new road, or an improved road, a passenger coach service, or a railway link has extended his sales market. This may offer him new opportunities for expansion or, alternatively, bring him into competition with larger, more efficient concerns. The retailer's range of wholesale suppliers may be extended, thus reducing dependence on local firms, such as the retail/wholesale shop. Greater confidence in the regularity and speed of goods transport may bring about higher rates of stock turn in provincial shops. The consumer should be the ultimate beneficiary of such changes in relationships in that there will be available to him a wider range of services and a retailing structure operating on lower costs.

3. *The Standard of Living*

The standard of living is another determinant of the structure of the distribution system. If average incomes are very low then, obviously, people will not be buying many goods and will require a distribution service which is low in cost and thereby spartan in service. Moreover, an economy with a low level of material comfort is usually one wherein occupational specialization is not advanced and subsistence production is common. Such an economy has little need for a large and sophisticated distribution system. But the system is not determined strictly in terms of that statistical figment 'average income'. Most societies are stratifieds in term of class, and class stratification is usually reflected in inequalities of income distribution. That aspect of the distribution structure which supported the material culture of the aristocracy in England necessarily differed markedly from that supporting the urban proletariat and rural farm labourer. But within these extremes were services orientated to consumers occupying intermediate positions on the continuum—shops which could not be neatly categorized as upper, middle, or lower class. From the entrepreneur's point of view, both total disposable income in the economy and its distribution determined the number and type of business opportunities available for exploitation, and exploitation of one kind of *niche* required the mobilization of skills and assets of a different kind from exploitation of another. Changes in these income variables would be reflected in the behaviour of entrepreneurs and thereby, through accumulation, in the overall structure of the distribution system. For example, the emergence of a mass consumer society in Britain has resulted in a narrowing of the range of distribution services available (such as the decline of itinerant services and rigidly upper-class orientated shops) and the definition of a set of skills which are broadly the same for all retail firms.

Since the problem first came under historical consideration in the late nineteenth century, discussion of changes in the standard of living during the Industrial Revolution has been a rich source of confusion. Interested readers have been treated alternatively to interpretations of unrelieved gloom, succeeded by those of cheery optimism, all of which have been punctuated by periodic academic battle. The most recent confrontation, between Dr Hobsbawm presenting a renewed and more sophisticated pessimists argument, and Dr Hartwell defending and adding to the optimistic interpretations of Professors Clapham and Ashton, has been useful in leading to more careful definition of the question.[56] It is recognized now that the problem has two sides: material living standards and quality of life. The first lends itself to quantitative measurement, the second does not. The confusion of earlier discussions of the problem derived from a failure to separate out the two problems,

[56] For the relevant works by these authors, see *Econ. Hist. Rev.*, x, xiii, and xvi.

or more fundamentally, a failure to appreciate that the two social aspects may run in opposite directions. It is a crude analysis which does not admit that rising material living standards can be associated with a deterioration in other aspects of social welfare. Although the subject has yet to be studied in depth, it is possible that the mass of individuals during the Industrial Revolution felt that the quality of their life had deteriorated.[57] Sociological studies of work, urbanization, the family, leisure, and changes in class relationships are needed. But to agree that material living standards improved on average during the early Industrial Revolution is not to deny the possibility that the early pessimists—Toynbee, the Hammonds, and the Webbs—were essentially right in characterizing this period as a savage experience for most of those who lived through it.

Recently J. E. Williams has attempted to measure the growth of private consumption per head between 1750 and 1850. Using normal social accounting procedures based on the historical statistics of Mitchel, Deane and Cole, Williams concludes that private consumption per head in Great Britain at constant 1791 prices, rose slowly from £8.7 in 1801 to £17.6 in 1841, leaping up in the next decade to £24.5 in 1851.[58] This supports the trend suggested by historians using more impressionistic techniques of analysis: that average incomes rose slowly from the end of the Napoleonic Wars to the early 1840s, but very rapidly after that.[59]

This first attempt at quantification does not, however, satisfy all criticism nor answer all relevant questions. Williams' conclusions can only be as good as the statistics upon which they are based. He admits that employing the Silberling price index renders suspect the absolute values of his consumption index, though not the trend. He also acknowledges that if Deane and Cole have seriously underestimated the value of

[57] See N. J. Smelser, *Social Change in the Industrial Revolution* (1959), E. Thompson, *The Making of the English Working Class* (1963) and P. N. Stearns, *European Society in Upheaval* (1967).

[58] J. E. Williams, 'The British Standard of Living, 1750–1850', *Econ. Hist. Rev.*, 19 (1966), table IV, 586.

[59] See A. J. Taylor, 'Progress and Poverty in Britain, 1780–1850: A Reappraisal', *History* xlv (1960), 28, and Deane, *First Industrial Revolution*.

Investment in National Income, then the trend itself might be different.[60] And finally, Williams' analysis does not include any hard evidence on the important question of income distribution. It is possible that private consumption per head was rising, but that the increase was monopolized by a small class, leaving the mass of the population no better off, or even worse off. National Income was very unevenly distributed in the nineteenth century as indeed it is today. It has been suggested, for example, that in 1860–69 some 49 per cent of the National Income in the U.K. was received by individuals in employment, whereas 14 per cent by receivers of rents and 38 per cent by receivers of profits, interest and mixed incomes—the latter two categories representing certainly a very small minority of the population. In fact, there is no satisfactory analysis of income distribution for the first half of the century, and other approaches to assessing the material welfare of the working classes have been inconclusive. 'The movement of real wages', wrote A. J. Taylor, 'can be determined within acceptable limits of error only in the case of certain restricted occupational groups: for the working class as a whole the margin of error is such as to preclude any dependable calculation.'[61] Similarly, an analysis of consumption patterns falls to the ground from the absence of proper household consumption surveys and other statistical series.[62] But given a degree of confidence in Williams' calculations, it would be necessary to posit that income distribution turned radically against the working classes after 1815 to suggest that they did not share to some degree in rising material prosperity. It would be difficult to find evidence of such a trend. Hence, the most sane conclusion to this contentious issue is that, (1) personal incomes per head were rising in England from 1815 at least; and (2) that the mass of the population enjoyed some of the benefits of rising material prosperity.

[60] One wonders why Deane and Cole did not undertake such an analysis themselves? Did they suspect that their National Income calculations were too crude for this kind of analysis?

[61] Taylor, 'Progress and Poverty', op. cit.

[62] Thus, Burnett, *Plenty and Want* and Taylor 'Progress and Poverty' while bringing forward much useful material are ultimately impressionistic on a problem which is fundamentally quantitative.

Although it is impossible to measure, there is much circumstantial evidence suggesting that rising disposable incomes in the first half of the nineteenth century were reflected in a buoyant retail trade. But retail trade also received a fillip from urbanization[63] and occupational redistribution of the labour force, both of which brought an enlargement of the cash-exchange economy.

Although too much weight should not be placed upon precise percentage figures, there are statistical estimates of the occupational distribution of the labour force. The percentage of the British labour force employed in agriculture, forestry and fishing fell from 35.9 per cent in 1801 to 21.7 per cent in 1851.[64] This represented a decline in the number of people receiving income through subsistence activities, and conversely, a rise in numbers relying upon professional distribution services. Cottage gardens remained an important source of foodstuffs for the shrinking rural population,[65] but the practice of employers housing and feeding rural labourers declined in the south, although less rapidly in the north. It is irrefutable that a large sector of the rural population was very poor, particularly in the southern and eastern counties; but in many parts of the country there was a class of small farmers and skilled labourers who provided an important market for the output of consumption goods industries. An itinerant retailer of hardware who worked in the southern and eastern counties in this period complained not of an insufficiency of demand, but the drawing-off of a growing demand by fixed shop retailers.[66]

Over the same period, the percentage distribution of the labour force employed in manufacture, mining and industry rose from 29.7 per cent to 42.9 per cent. Superficially, this represents a large growth in one of the cash wages sectors of

[63] See above, section 1.

[64] Statistics on the distribution of the labour force are from P. Deane and W. A. Cole, *British Economic Growth* (1964) table 30, p. 142.

[65] In the late 1830s the estimated yearly income of a labourer's family in rural Northumberland was £76 0s. 10d. Assuming that the wages of the wife and children were paid in cash, the family's cash income amounted to £32 18s. 0d., which is something over 50 per cent. A second family, with total earnings of 16s. per week received 12s. in cash, which is about 75 per cent. L. Hindmarsh, *J. Stat. Soc. London* i (1839), 397–409, and W. H. Charlton, ibid., 424.

[66] See chapter III.

the economy, but the real situation is more complex. Until the 1840s payment in truck was important in the textile industries, the Midland hardware trades, and in iron works and collieries.[67] Truck payments were a legitimate method of supplying necessities to workers in remote areas, but they were also a device for lowering the employer's labour costs. In areas with established distribution services, the spread of truck payment could cut into retail turnovers, particularly in small general shops. In 1845 a general shopkeeper at Hinckley argued that 'The evil was so great, I fully believe that it made a difference in my returns of from £10 to £20 a week.'[68] But in two towns where truck payments were said to be significant, Leicester and Merthyr Tydfil, the growth of shop outlets was not noticeably below that found in other areas of the country.[69] The impact of the truck system in distorting the growth of shopping facilities was probably not very significant over the period as a whole.

The trade and transport sector of the economy accounted for 11.2 per cent of the labour force in 1801 and 15.8 per cent in 1851. Those employed in domestic service accounted for 11.5 per cent and 13 per cent of the labour force at the same dates. In trade, domestic service and manufacturing as well, the labour force commonly 'lived-in' with the employer, receiving board and lodging and sometimes clothing. This reduced the cash element in earnings. The living-in system, however, had a mixed effect on the retail market. By reducing the number of independent households it led to a sharing of household furnishings, furniture and utensils, thus limiting the aggregate size of the market for these products. On the other hand, the cash earnings of shop assistants, journeymen and domestic servants were free for expenditure on clothing and other personal articles. 'Window-shopping' servant girls were a great trial to drapers and their assistants, but they were also recognized as an important group of customers. Shop assistants worked exceptionally long hours, but young men, especially in the city drapery shops, could earn as much as £100 a year in

[67] Hilton, *Truck System*, p. 10.
[68] *B.P.P.*, *Report of the Commissioners appointed to inquire into the Condition of the Framework Knitters*; Mins. of Ev., 1845 (609) xv, Q. 4158.
[69] See chapter IV.

wages and premiums in addition to their board and lodging. Ideally, these wages were saved to enable the young man to open his own shop, but a percentage was undoubtedly spent on clothing, watches, penknives, tobacco and other articles of personal consumption.

In the eighteenth century shopkeepers drew most of their custom from a small class of highly paid workers, tradesmen, farmers, gentry and aristocracy. The first half of the nineteenth century saw an expansion in the number of highly paid workers, such as spinners, engineers, boiler makers and some grades of mine and railway workers. In addition, skilled workers in the building trades, compositors, and workmen in the shops of ironmongers, braziers and tinmen might earn 20s. and more a week. On the other hand, at different times in this period, the standard of living of workers in the clothing and footwear trades, hand-loom weavers, silk and ribbon weavers, underwent a hard and prolonged decline. The towns were filled with masses of casual and unemployed labour which survived by hawking food, manufactured and re-manufactured goods. There was a small class of town and country hawkers who enjoyed a high and steady income, but it was an occupation filled largely by the unskilled and the defeated, the ranks swelling and contracting in sympathy with the trade cycle. But on balance, the growth of general shops in this period catering exclusively for working class custom would suggest some improvement in living standards.[70] Shop retailing was a more costly form of distribution, was associated with more expensive kinds of goods, and necessitated a more regular demand than its alternative—the market-itinerant distribution system.

Unquestionably, the first half of the nineteenth century saw some expansion of the middle class, including factory owners and managers, the professions serving industry, commerce and the growing towns, such as brokers, lawyers, surveyors, accountants and other clerks. This high consumption class was still a small segment of the population but it was probably getting richer and its modest growth is suggested by the rise in the number of domestic servants as a proportion of the occupied population. A second indicator is perhaps the spread of a

[70] See chapter IV.

rentier class into country towns. In the 1830s John Hancock of Hulse was asked:[71]

You would say that so far as the towns are concerned, comparing them with what they were some time ago, a person might think it was a flourishing country?—Yes.

Is there not a great appearance of wealth in the towns, but a great appearance of poverty in the country among the farmers?—Yes.

Who are the persons who spend this money in Taunton in improvements?—Persons that retire from London and other places.

Living upon fixed incomes?—Yes.

On the farms themselves there was apparently a decline in the role of women in dairy management and marketing:

...refinement in manners has gradually obtained an ascendancy; and learning has trampled upon industry: schools have multiplied, and accomplishments have become the reigning order of the day: so that a farmer's daughter...is now more agreeably engaged by the duties of the drawing, music, or dancing master.[72]

If this is a reliable insight into a social trend, then it would suggest that the more prosperous farmers were also beginning to move into the high consumption class.

One may conclude, with some assurance, that disposable incomes rose in the first half of the nineteenth century, and that the mass of the population enjoyed some of the fruits of economic growth. Growth of incomes was reflected in a buoyant retail trade over the long run, assisted by the economy's increased dependence upon distribution services through urbanization and the decline of occupations with a subsistence content.

4. Conclusions

In this chapter we have discussed some of the dynamic factors which can lead to extensive modifications in an existing distribution system. Implicit to the discussion is recognition of the growth of industrial enterprise—the growth in scale of production units, the separation of production and distribution

[71] B.P.P., Select Committee on Agriculture; Mins. of Ev., 1833 (612) v, Q.9417-33.
[72] 'On the Diet of Farm Labourers', The Agricultural Magazine, x (1812), 283. See also, I. Pinchbeck, Women Workers and the Industrial Revolution (1930) p. 34.

functions. Population growth, urbanization, the transport revolution and rising disposable incomes interacted with the revolution in production. The growth in size of manufacturing units obliged entrepreneurs to concentrate capital and skills on the production side and to call into being distribution specialists, wholesalers and retailers, to market this product and to communicate back to them changing consumer preferences. We have seen how population growth alone brings forth a greater absolute demand for distribution services, but added to this was the concentration of people in urban areas where subsistence activities decline in importance, and the shift of the labour force out of occupations with a self-sufficiency content. These massive social changes provided new opportunities for distributors, but also demanded the development of new skills. The retail market was growing in size, in terms of numbers involved, in *per capita* demand for services, and in terms of incomes available for expenditure. At the same time, soaring land values in central areas encouraged retailers to pay closer attention to location costs and opportunities, and hence to profit maximization. Together with the changes wrought by radically improved transport, retailers developed new skills in consumer information services, in more formalized customer service, in stock control and in price competitiveness. The following chapters are concerned with detailing the response of the distribution system to the manifold social changes of early nineteenth century England.

PART II
Retailing outside Shops

II

Fairs and Markets

COMMODITIES can be exchanged in a variety of ways. The simplest form is direct exchange between buyer and seller outside any formal institutional setting. Exchange can also take the form of itinerant distribution, where the seller seeks out the buyer at his home or on the streets. The reverse of this situation is where exchange is effected in fixed shops, where the seller makes his presence known in his market area and is approached by buyers at the shop. And finally, exchange can be carried on at markets, where at fixed times and in established locations, buyers and sellers meet.

Normally, a society organizes commodity exchange in several ways, although one form of exchange may predominate over all others, as is the case with the retail shop in modern industrial societies. The form of exchange which typifies the society depends upon many factors, especially the structure of employment, the spatial distribution of population, consumer incomes, and the relative scarcity of capital. For reasons which we will examine in a moment, market exchange usually correlates with predominantly agricultural economies. The market normally occupies a permanent site on a street, square or in a building. It may be completely or partially open and consist only of a few stalls and sheds, or it may be located in a covered building providing many facilities for both buyer and seller. The vendors in the market include the farmer and his dependants in their function as distributors of surplus farm product, the small professional traders with more or less fixed sites in the market place, local tradesmen retailing there as well as from shops, and travelling vendors who attend a number of markets on a regular circuit. The right to trade in the market is dependent upon conformity to rules, such as payment of tolls established by the market owners, who may be either private or public authorities.

The periodic market is designed to meet the normal needs of households in the market area, and the commodities exchanged consist largely of local output. But a rural market may also be the initial point from which agricultural produce makes its way up to regional and national markets and, in the other direction, the terminal point in the distribution of commodities imported into the area from regional and national centres for local consumption.

Markets in rural areas usually assemble regularly on one or more days in a week. For the farmer, periodicity economizes upon the time which must be spent marketing surplus product: it ensures that a maximum number of buyers will be assembled at one place for a minimum amount of time. Similarly, a tradesman can minimize production time lost if he bunches sales at the market. Periodicity also enables the itinerant trader to service several markets (where market schedules in a region are designed not to conflict) when the level of demand in any one market area is not sufficient to assure a sales volume warranting permanent presence. For the consumer, the periodic market reduces the time spent and distance travelled in order to obtain essential goods and services. The market may be held more frequently, and even daily, when the number of households it serves increases. But even in large urban centres where market trading is continuous, certain days are characterized by particularly heavy trading. These correspond to days on which wage payments are customarily made and most of the employed population has some leisure time.

For a relatively poor society, or poor classes in that society, market distribution has the important advantage of being low in cost. Capital expenditure on site and facilities need not be significant. The periodicity of the market and the resulting economies on time, travel and transport achieved by peasant distributors and local craftsman, mean that their distribution costs are low. In addition, the professional market trader may have few if any alternative means of spending his time, and since his opportunity costs will therefore be low, his profit margins will be small.

Distribution mainly through markets is characteristic of peasant economies. England was more than a peasant society, but markets were central to distribution in England at the beginning of the nineteenth century, though not at the end. Changes in demographic structure, in production, transport and consumer incomes, reduced their relative importance but did not eliminate them from the distribution system as the century progressed. In this chapter, then, we will examine the changing role of markets: their adaptation to new economic and social circumstances.[1]

1. *Fairs*

A fair is a market which is held infrequently but at regular intervals. In England, fairs coincided with times when stocks of consumer goods in country areas were at their lowest level (the spring) and when the agricultural community was anxious to dispose of surplus product (July to October). The agricultural fair was one means of shifting food from areas of surplus to areas of deficit, of marketing industrial crops, and of supplying farmers, agricultural labourers and even townsmen (whose liquidity frequently moved in sympathy with that of the countryside) with consumer goods.

It was argued by many people in the nineteenth century that fairs no longer made a significant contribution to internal trade. We shall see that in general they were right, though in particular respects they were not. But in general their value was diminishing 'because the communication between different parts of a country has become so easy that merchandise is much oftener ordered directly than formerly'.[2] McCulloch attributed their decline to urban growth and 'the opportunities afforded for the disposal and purchase of all sorts of produce at the weekly or monthly marts....'[3] Cobbett, who resented the collapse of older ways of life in this respect as much as in others, pointed to the growth of shopkeeping as weakening the position of both fairs and weekly markets.[4] But the strength of the early eighteenth century fair had been its wholesaling function, and

---

[1] In this chapter markets are examined primarily from an institutional point of view. In the following chapter the trading techniques of an important group of market traders, the itinerants, will be discussed in greater detail.

[2] *The British Cyclopaedia of the Arts and Sciences*, i (1835), 524.

[3] 'Fairs and Markets', *Dictionary of Commerce*, i, 574–8.

[4] *Rural Rides* (ed. G. D. H. and Margaret Cole, 1930), iii, 510.

it was this that was being rapidly undermined by improved transport and communications:[5]

If the trader waited, in former days, until the return of the Fair to lay in his yearly stock of goods, this is now superseded, as he has travelling-clerks from all sorts of *houses* connected with his business waiting upon him every month for his orders, and he sees them executed by canals, barges, fly-waggons, vans, stage-coaches, or steam packets....

This general analysis is valid in explaining the decline of Sturbridge fair, the most famous in England. When Defoe visited Sturbridge fair in the early eighteenth century, he found a large wholesale trade in hops, wool and all manufactured goods, especially cloth. An important aspect of the fair was that it provided a setting in which London merchants and their chapmen, resident and travelling in the provinces, could meet to discuss current business problems.[6] This wholesale activity was the heart of Sturbridge fair, but towards the end of the second week, when most of the wholesale transactions were complete, London and local gentry and Cambridgeshire residents generally participated in a rich retail fair.[7] But in the second half of the eighteenth century the wholesale trade at Sturbridge collapsed. Contemporaries suggested that trade was being deflected by the 'great increase of Land Carriages, the navigable Canals lately cut, and the Number of Riders from the Capital and other trading Places, who take orders for all Kinds of Merchandise all over the Kingdom. ... '[8] Significantly, the retail trade at Sturbridge was reduced to the hawking of 'toys' and other trifles.

The experience of Sturbridge fair was repeated elsewhere. In the eighteenth century Chester held the major Irish linen fairs in England, and in 1778 the principal linen merchants erected a hall for the trade. In 1809 Manchester and Yorkshire cotton dealers built a second hall to represent their trade, and as late as 1815 a third hall was built on speculation to accom-

[5] *Bristol Fair, but no Preaching!* (2nd ed., 1823), p. 3.
[6] *A Tour Thro' the Whole Island of Great Britain* (1927), p. 81.
[7] Ibid., p. 85.
[8] Anon., *An Historical Account of Sturbridge, Bury, and the Most Famous Fairs in Europe and America* (1773?), p. 38.

modate manufacturers from London, Nottingham, Birmingham and Sheffield. The Chester fairs were attended by manufacturers, wholesalers and shopkeepers from all parts of England, but the marketing needs of textile manufacturers were rapidly outstripping the functional capacity of such fairs, and in 1808 it was noted that they were 'not so well attended as formerly'.[9] On the other hand, at Wrexham in North Wales, the 'Yorkshire clothiers, the Lancashire and Sheffield manufacturers, bring their goods thither to supply the district, and a great part of South Wales, for the whole year';[10] but again, the rapid industrialization of South Wales in the decades after 1800 suggests that a periodic supply to shopkeepers in this fashion would be of decreasing relevance.

Rising levels of industrial output in textiles and metal goods called for professional marketing agencies, and the emergence of such marketing agents in London and the manufacturing centres, together with the diminishing importance of the small master, meant that wholesaling of industrial goods at fairs, even on a contract basis, was in decline. The fair for manufactured goods continued to be held only where it served the very different function of product demonstration and advertisement. In this sense the Great Exhibition of 1851 was an industrial fair, as was the Peterborough Market-fair, celebrated into the late nineteenth century for its display of farm equipment.[11]

In many ways the distribution functions of the *agricultural* fair were also in decline. With a rapidly growing population, it was essential that England mobilize its food resources in different ways if living standards were not to regress. The challenge was met in many ways, but one aspect of the response is to be seen in the wholesaling of foodstuffs and industrial crops. Increasingly, professional factors scoured the countryside, arranging for the purchase of crops before the harvest and entering into long range commitments with farmers. This meant that a decreasing proportion of farm product passed through

[9] H. Holland, *General View of the Agriculture of Cheshire* (Board of Agriculture Report, 1808), pp. 313–14. Henceforth titles in this series will be abbreviated.

[10] W. Davies, *General View of North Wales*, p. 386.

[11] R. H. Horne, 'Markets of Europe', *Saint Paul's Magazine*, xii (1873), 180.

the fairs, although even in the nineteenth century the more renowned fairs continued to attract wholesale buyers. For example, in 1827 Dorset and Somerset cheeses were bought at Lymington fair by factors from eastern Hampshire and Sussex.[12] In 1836 the Reading September fair attracted some 300 to 500 pounds of Gloucestershire and Wiltshire cheeses.[13] And as late as the 1850s the great October fair at Yarm in County Durham attracted up to 320 000 pounds of cheese.[14]

However, in the marketing of livestock the fair and market remained very important for most of the nineteenth century. In the towns and on the fringes of cities, weekly and bi-weekly markets were held for fat cattle, sheep and pigs. Nearly every provincial town of any importance held monthly cattle markets to supply local butchers, and surplus stock was drawn off by dealers for transfer to larger consumption centres.

Less frequent livestock fairs were held in country areas for the sale of lean cattle and sheep to buyers from the grazing districts. These were most commonly held in April and May and again from late September to early November.[15] Fairs were still the most efficient means of assembling buyers and sellers for the transfer of animals from scattered rearing grounds to the grazing areas near the towns and cities.

At one time, country fairs attracted itinerant retailers in large numbers, but by mid-century consumers looked to them for little more than novelties. For example, the small Ingatestone fair in Essex in December 1810 attracted some thirty traders, dealing in cloth, clothing, footwear, 'toys' and eatables. But in 1850 the fair was attended by only 17 traders, over half of whom were showmen and gingerbread sellers, while six more were toy dealers.[16]

Fairs in the cities and larger towns degenerated into pleasure haunts for the working classes with little or no serious trading function. Bartholomew fair in London had reached this state by the early eighteenth century, and by 1825 its retail trade com-

---

[12] Resident, *A New Guide to Lymington* (1827), p. 52.

[13] J. Doran, *The History and Antiquities of the Town...of Reading* (1836), p. 242.

[14] J. Haxton, 'Markets', *A Cyclopaedia of Agriculture* (Ed. J. C. Morton, 1855), pp. 357–70.

[15] For an exhaustive account of these fairs, see Haxton, (14).

[16] Essex Record Office, D/DP A. 82 and A. 186.

prised no more than eatables and toys.[17] Similarly, the July and November fairs in Liverpool by 1795 contained only 'a few standings for toys, and other small articles...', although the Richmond fair in Liverpool still attracted cloth and clothing dealers.[18] The Great Fair at Coventry in the 1850s was dominated overwhelmingly by showmen and drinking booths.

With the decline of significant trading at nineteenth century urban fairs, the 'respectable' elements in the community pressed for their total abolition. Some, like John Middleton might argue that they were 'a reasonable indulgence in favour of the labouring classes'[18] but others, like G. C. Smith, could see only vice, disorder and irreligion.[19] Bartholomew fair was threatened with closure in the late eighteenth century, and growing restrictions upon the activities of entertainers and traders brought it to a quiet end at mid-century.[20] At Coventry in May 1839 a deputation of householders from Warwick Green petitioned the Market Tolls Committee either to relocate or abolish the shows and drinking booths at the Great Fair. In this case, however, the Committee decided that regard to the 'General Interest of the Town' militated against such a move, but agreed to remove the drinking booths as far from houses as possible.[21] The decision no doubt owed a great deal to the happy congruence between the 'General Interest of the Town' and the particular interest of the Committee's market revenues: the 1855 Fair brought in over £100. But in some towns, where fairs contributed little or nothing to market revenues, attempts were made to accommodate both the pleasures of the common people and the need for public order. At Aldermaston, for example, the fair was removed in 1850 from Aldermaston Street by order of the Lord of the Manor, to Workhouse Meadow, but continued difficulties in shifting the fair to the new location led to its abolition in 1874.[22] The 1871 Fairs Act

---

[17] 'The Every-Day Book', in *Collections of Cuttings Relating to Bartholomew Fair* [British Museum, C.70 h. 6 (2)].

[18] *View of the Agriculture of Middlesex* (1807), p. 536.

[19] *Bristol Fair, but no Preaching!* (see n. 5).

[20] H. Morley, *Memoirs of Bartholomew Fair* (1859), pp. 489–92.

[21] Minutes of the meeting of 13 May, 1839, City of Coventry Record Office.

[22] Records relating to the abolition of Aldermaston fair are preserved in the Berkshire Records Office, D/EBb, L.2.

empowered authorities to abolish fairs which no longer performed a commercial function, and in its way this Act confirmed the elimination of the fair as a significant institution of retail, if not entirely wholesale, trade.

2. *Supplying Retail Markets*

Unlike fairs, weekly markets retained an important retailing function. The first problem we must discuss is how foodstuffs were transferred from the countryside and from abroad into the markets of villages, towns and cities.

Inhabitants of small towns in the early nineteenth century were still able to satisfy part of their requirements for vegetables and fruits from kitchen gardens,[23] and many kept fowl and even pigs. Milk, until the second half of the nineteenth century, was very largely a product of urban dairies. However, the lack of rapid transport in the new cities was reflected in high population density, and significant contributions to urban food supplies through household subsistence activities were impossible.

English towns had long been dependent upon the surplus production of the surrounding countryside. By the eighteenth century tradesmen from London and the larger provincial towns were travelling extensively into the countryside to buy livestock, cheese, butter and corn at fairs and markets and on the farms. Moreover, there had emerged a class of middlemen whose sole function was to buy on farms for resale to urban traders. Farmers and their families, however, continued to carry on distribution activities by carrying surplus product into the markets for both wholesale and retail sale. These producer/distributors included the professional market gardeners who ringed the large urban centres, the corn and livestock farmers, small cottagers, and the farm women and their servants who regularly marketed fruit, vegetables, poultry, eggs, butter and cheese in what was designated 'the women's market'. Their combined services resulted in what William Marshall described at Bideford in 1796 as 'a very respectable market'. He found a few fat and some store cattle, with three or four heifers and calves and a few sheep. The corn market was filled with long

[23] This was noticed by J. Carey, *General View of Derbyshire* (1811) ii, 208.

two-bushel bags, chiefly of wheat. The shambles was replete with good mutton, though little beef. There was 'salmon in considerable plenty; but no sea fish', and the women's market was 'well supplied'. He noted an unusual feature of Bideford market—the 'Cart loads of country bread, exposed in the market place, for sale.'[24]

Professional market gardeners produced usually for more than one urban market. For example, in the early nineteenth century gardeners near Cardiff supplied many towns in South Wales and Bristol.[25] In Cambridgeshire, gardeners produced 'to supply not only the neighbouring towns but counties', the produce being sent as far as King's Lynn by water and land transport.[26] Marshall noted that Norwich market was supplied by farmers from ten to twenty miles distant from the town.[27] But in some of the new factory towns production and distribution had to be organized in part by factory owners. A familiar example is Samuel Oldknow who kept a gardener on three acres of land at Mellor to grow and distribute all the common garden vegetables and fruits to the mill workers, and the Strutts for a time did the same at Belper.[28]

All the major cities were ringed by market gardens and grazing areas, and as late as 1850 consumers were still able to buy direct from the grower at the central market. But London by the late seventeenth century and the provincial cities towards the end of the eighteenth were increasingly dependent upon more distant sources of supply. Liverpool at the beginning of the nineteenth century drew eggs and poultry from areas as distant as Wales, the Isle of Man and Ireland.[29] Cattle, sheep and pigs came into the area from Scotland, Ireland and North Wales, as well as Lancashire and Derbyshire.[30] The Manchester market drew eggs and poultry from as far away as Lincolnshire and Nottinghamshire.[31] It also served as a wholesale market

[24] *Rural Economy of the West of England* (1796) ii, 61–2.
[25] W. Davies, *General View of South Wales* (1814) ii, 4.
[26] W. Gooch, *General View of Cambridge* (1813), p. 195.
[27] *Rural Economy of Norfolk* (1787) i, 195.
[28] Farey, *Derbyshire*, pp. 208–9.
[29] R. W. Dickson and W. Stevenson, *General View of Lancashire* (1815), pp. 603–4.
[30] *The Picture of Liverpool; or Stranger's Guide* (1805) p. 142, and *A General and Descriptive History of the Ancient and Present State of Liverpool* (1795) p. 182.
[31] Dickson and Stevenson, *Lancashire*, pp. 603–4.

for traders selling in the smaller industrial towns to the north.[32] Vegetables grown in Cheshire went via the Bridgewater Canal to Manchester, Bolton and other Lancashire towns.[33]

The Midland counties were also caught-up in the net flung out from the growing English cities. Farmers in the north Midlands marketed in Lancashire and the West Riding; those in the south supplied the London markets; while Birmingham and the Black Country towns drew upon both regions. It was said in 1813 that twenty to thirty horses were employed daily carrying butter, cheese and poultry from Worcester to Birmingham, and on a somewhat smaller scale from Droitwich and Bromsgrove.[34] The market gardens around Evesham grew vegetables and fruit for Birmingham and also, via the Severn, for Bath and Bristol.[35]

The small market towns were affected in obvious ways by the emergence of the great consumption centres. Marshall noted that they 'have no hucksters to supply them…and depend entirely upon the market day for their supply: and if, in times of scarcity, hucksters from large towns repair to a country market, they may, in a few minutes, clear the market; and leave the townspeople destitute of a week's provisions'.[36] Many towns, like Lymington, Lichfield and Preston, tried to protect the local consumer by prohibiting wholesale buying until the market had been open an hour or more; but very little could be done to prevent forestalling, and the knowledge that wholesalers were in the market would have an immediate effect on prices.

There was no national marketing system for foodstuffs until the second half of the nineteenth century, with a partial exception for corn and livestock. The Board of Agriculture Reports, however, support the impression that there were regional markets with price levels defined by the larger towns in those regions. For example, prices in Middlesex and Surrey were at London levels.[37] In Kent the ease of transport with

[32] Aston, *Manchester Guide*, p. 274.

[33] Holland, *Cheshire*, pp. 139–40, and *The Tradesman*, v (1810), 505.

[34] W. Pitt, *General View of Worcester* (1813), pp. 255–6.

[35] Ibid., p. 147.

[36] *Midland Counties*, i, 23.

[37] Middleton, *Middlesex*, p. 508, and W. Stevenson, *General View of Surrey* (1813), p. 545.

London rendered 'the markets of Smithfield and Mark-lane the regulating medium, by which the prices of all kinds of provisions that are sold in the country are governed'.[38] In the 1790s beef prices in Rutland were said to be only 1d. per pound lower than in London,[39] and in Lincolnshire meat prices were said to be at London levels less transport and wholesaling costs.[40] Leicestershire prices moved in sympathy with Birmingham's,[41] and for Warwickshire it was suggested that grain prices were more regular since canals had been cut and the *London Gazette* had regularly stated its prices.[42] The growth of manufacturing in the Midlands, it was said, had led to generally higher prices in the county of Worcester,[43] and the same was true for the West Riding and Durham.[44] It was said of upper Northumberland that transport bottlenecks kept grain prices the lowest in England, but livestock prices reflected those of national markets.[45] Manchester, Liverpool and the larger Lancashire towns were quoting provisions prices comparable to those in London,[46] and prices in the south of Westmoreland rose in sympathy.[47]

Urbanization offered improved market opportunities for farmers, and canal schemes and road improvements helped to extend the geographical area in which farmers could market profitably. But it is evident that the rapidly growing cities needed a much better transport link with the country and with each other. In 1856 George Dodd said that foodstuffs 'have never been brought to London to any great extent by canal; the road was the medium of transit until the modern days of railways and steamers. Even no longer back than 1843, the coaches from Norwich carried off, in the Christmas week, 3000 packages of turkeys, geese, fowls and game, of which

[38] J. Boys, *General View of Kent* (1805) p. 195.
[39] J. Crutchley, *General View of Rutland* (1794) p. 20.
[40] T. Stone, *General View of Lincoln* (1784) p. 25.
[41] J. Monk, *General View of Leicester* (1794) p. 49.
[42] J. Wedge, *General View of Warwick* (1794) p. 49.
[43] Pitt, *Worcester*, p. 255.
[44] Messrs. Rennie, Brown and Shireff, *General View of the West Riding of Yorkshire* (1794) p. 25, and J. Bailey, *General View of Durham* (1810) pp. 281-2.
[45] J. Bailey and G. Culley, *General View of Northumberland* (1794) p. 55.
[46] Dickson and Stevenson, *Lancashire*, p. 602.
[47] A. Pringle, *General View of Westmoreland* (1794) p. 37.

two-thirds were for London.'[48] In the early 1800s women had
carried fruit to London in panniers from the suburban market
gardens, and in the mid-1830s this system still prevailed,
although some of the growers had begun to use light carts hung
on pliable springs drawn by fast horses. But while these vehicles
carried twenty times the load of one woman, the fruit arrived
at market in damaged condition and could only be sold at
lower prices.[49]

It was steam transport, first on coastal waters and then on
land, which revolutionized the marketing of foodstuffs. We
have already noted its impact on the sale and consumption of
fresh fish,[50] and suggested that its impact was not unique to
this commodity. For example, the uncertain winds on the
Irish Sea had retarded the growth of Irish trade with England
in dairy produce and livestock. But by the 1820s fat cattle
were being brought over from Ireland in steam vessels for sale
in Kirkdale market in Liverpool, from where they were
channelled to Manchester, Birmingham, Leicester and London.[51] Egg, butter and poultry farmers around Liverpool and
Manchester complained in 1833 of the new Irish competition
which steam navigation and the Liverpool-Manchester railway had made possible.[52] Similarly, in 1839 Kent fruit growers
voiced their discontent over the marketing of European fruit
in England, which had been made possible by steam navigation
on the Channel.[53]

It took some time before railway companies built facilities
and developed techniques to exploit their potential in foodstuff
marketing. Many local markets in 1848 lacked sidings and other
facilities,[54] but the major cities felt the impact of the railways
very quickly. The Home Counties rapidly lost their strong

---

[48] *The Food of London* (1856) p. 105.
[49] Middleton, *Middlesex*, p. 98, and 'The Mode by which London is supplied
with Strawberries', *The Quarterly Journal of Agriculture*, vi (1835–6), 301–2.
[50] See chapter 1, section 2.
[51] 'The Cattle Trade in Liverpool', *The British Farmer's Magazine* iii (1829),
102–3.
[52] *B.P.P., Select Committee on Agriculture*; Mins. of Ev., 1833 (612) v, evidence of
W. Reed and J. Sanders.
[53] See *B.P.P., Select Committee on the Fresh Fruit Trade*; 1839 (398) viii.
[54] See S. Sidney, *Railways and Agriculture in North Lincolnshire* (1848).

position in the London provisions markets.[55] The Great
Western Railway undermined the bargaining power of graziers
in Middlesex at the Southall cattle market.[56] The herds of lean
cattle coming into East Anglia were much reduced, since they
were now being shipped directly by rail to the neighbourhoods
of the great cities.[57] Dodd noted in the 1850s that more than
half of London's grain arrived by ship and rail, and far more
livestock reached the Metropolis by steam transport than by
road.[58] Rail transport made it possible to multiply by several
times the volume of country-killed meat supplied to Newgate
market: in 1810 there were only a dozen salesmen at Newgate,
but by 1850 there were over two hundred.[59] Because railways
were now bringing up vegetables and fruit from distant counties
it was thought that London was 'perhaps destined to lose...
suburban market-gardens ere long'.[60] But railways also
facilitated a reverse flow of produce from the big London
wholesale markets. Dodd pointed out that when 'Covent Garden has a plethora of good things any one morning, she sends
off a telegraphic message to Birmingham or other large towns,
to ascertain the state of supplies there; if there be room for
more, waggon-loads of fruit are sent off by rail; and thus prices
become equalized and supplies diffused'.[61] Central markets in
provincial cities developed into wholesale markets for surrounding towns. Traders from these towns went into the city by rail
to buy for resale at their local markets.[62] Although some rural
isolation remained, English markets were a much more tightly

---

[55] J. Caird, *English Agriculture in 1850–1* (1852) pp. 15–16.

[56] H. Tremenheere, 'Agricultural and Educational Statistics of Several Parishes
in the County of Middlesex', *J. Stat. Soc. London*, vi. (1843), 122.

[57] Sidney, op. cit., pp. 8–10.

[58] Dodd, *Food*, pp. 169, 225 and statistics 242–3.

[59] Dodd, *Food*, p. 273. Carcase butchers had established themselves in northern
towns where they bought stock, slaughtered, cut and packed meat for shipment
by rail to London.

[60] Ibid., p. 367.

[61] Ibid., p. 394. The North-Western line to Birmingham was a principal means
of redistributing fish and fruit when gluts appeared on the London markets. The
South-Eastern carried grain out of London and the London and Brighton line took
cattle and dead meat down to Brighton. See the 'Commissariat of London', *The
Quarterly Review* no. 95 (1852), 306–7.

[62] See the *Royal Commission on Market Rights and Tolls*; Mins. of Ev., 1888, liii
(C-5550–1), especially ii, Q. 4786 and 4787.

integrated network in 1850 than they had been a half century before.

3. *Market Retailing*

Contemporaries were very impressed by the growth of shop-keeping in England, but nonetheless retail markets occupied a central position in distribution in the first half of the nineteenth century. Many upper class families, through their domestic servants, purchased provisions in markets rather than shops, while the low distribution costs of market retailing gave it a comparative advantage over shopkeeping in the supply of food, clothing and household goods to the working classes.

Although shops steadily increased their share of trade in several areas of consumer expenditure, retail markets could satisfy most of the normal needs of households. This is evident from the returns of a survey taken in 1851 by the Leicester Toll Committee on traders standing in the market. Table 2:1 indicates that about 79 per cent of the market traders dealt

TABLE 2:1. Traders Standing in Leicester Market in 1851

Trade		Numbers
A. Provisions		
Butchers		242
Fruiterers	(Variable)	50
Gardeners		20
Fishmongers		16
Toffee dealers		9
Cheesemongers		5
Bakers		1
Butter dealers	(Variable)	
Egg dealers	(Variable)	
Poultry dealers	(Variable)	
Carts		25
Casual carts	(Variable)	
B. Household Goods and Others		
Potters		15
Furniture brokers		7
Basket makers		6
Tinmen		6
Brushmakers		4

TABLE 2:1 *cont.*

Trade	Numbers
Old iron dealers	4
Twine spinners	3
Blacking makers	2
Coopers	2
Saddlers	2
Feltmongers, tanners	2
Doctors (Quacks)	2
Turners	1
c. Clothing Trades	
Shoemakers	30
Hosiers	8
Lace dealers	4

Source: Leicester Toll Committee Minutes, 6 May 1851 (Leicester Museum, Archives Office).

in foodstuffs, 12 per cent in household goods (utensils, pots, brushes, etc.) and 9 per cent in clothing and footwear.

Assuming that the survey was done on a 'normal' trading day,[63] it is evident that the market's principal function was to distribute foodstuffs. It is surprising, however, that butchers represented some 65 per cent of all foodstuff dealers. This suggests either that the meat trade supported larger numbers of marginal retailers or, what is more likely, that meat consumption was more general than historians normally assume.[64] Fruit and vegetable dealers were also prominent in the market, especially if we assume that most of the 'carts' and 'casual carts' belonged to country growers. The comparatively small numbers of cheesemongers and bakers indicate that sales of these commodities were dominated by shop retailers. Finally, the 'variable' quotation for butter, egg and poultry sellers suggests that casual attendance at market by country women was a major factor in the supply situation.

In the household trades group, pottery sellers were the most

[63] The assumption should be valid since the committee's object was to assess the demand on market facilities.

[64] The very large numbers of butchers found in the towns surveyed in chapter five suggests that the situation at Leicester was not peculiar.

numerous class of traders. The goods sold by many china and earthenware shops was of higher quality than the mass of consumers could afford, and their more prosaic needs were satisfied largely by general shopkeepers, and itinerant and market traders. The seven furniture brokers were probably journeymen who made up cheap furniture for sale to shops and for hawking in streets and markets. The six tinmen, two coopers, four brushmakers and one turner satisfied the remaining outstanding needs for kitchen and household goods.

In the clothing group of trades the shoemakers were predominant. It is possible that some of these dealers were connected with a shop as master or employee and attended the market only once or twice a week. The absence of dealers in drapery and clothing is remarkable. Although some of the hosiers may have dealt in drapery and smallwares, the situation at Leicester market supports the hypothesis that by 1850 shops dominated the retail trade in these goods.

A market day in Leicester at mid-century might find some 500 people attending as sellers and a few thousand as buyers. The very size of such an assembly and the tensions involved in the interaction between and among buyers and sellers called for some formal regulating institutions to minimize and to adjudicate conflicts. This was the function of the market owner and his agents. In return for the right to levy a toll on traders the market owner, who might be a private individual, such as the lord of the manor, a town corporation, or a group of individuals organized into a market commission, had a moral and legal obligation to provide trading facilities and to police market activity. In many of the smaller market towns the facilities and services provided by the owner were minimal or nonexistent. In this situation the market owner's right to levy tolls might be challenged.

For example, in Epping in 1831 the toll collector demanded 1d. from William Dennis who was hawking cakes in the street. Dennis refused to pay and the matter was placed in the hands of a London solicitor. The solicitor wrote to Dennis demanding payment and threatening legal costs, pointing out that the 'smallness of the amount will not protect you from prosecution', since it was 'the Rights of his Market that Mr. Conyers is determined to maintain...'. But a month later the solicitor wrote to Mr Harvey, the lessee of the tolls,

We have not been correct if Dennis was only hawking cakes in a basket without any stand or the like he is not liable. This if you recollect was the opinion of counsel on the former occasion. Pray let me know if there are others of whom you have taken the pennies, if so, we must consider what to do. It will be advisable however not to admit that we are wrong to Dennis. You had better see him and say that Mr. Conyers believing him to have acted in error will not this time make him pay the expenses and take the penny. You had better send the money.[65]

Conflicts of this nature were likely to arise wherever the market owner failed to provide a well serviced market site, since buyers and sellers regarded the toll as an unwarranted tax on trade.

In some towns population growth and the resulting expansion of trade moved market owners to make a considerable investment in facilities and to hire full-time employees to supervise the market. The Minute books of the meetings of the Leicester Toll Committee in the 1830s and 1840s illustrate the exercise of market rights and responsibilities at their best.[66] The markets at Leicester were municipally owned, and the market committee provided the stalls, determined their location and allocated them to traders on a yearly, quarterly and weekly basis.

Much of the committee's time was spent in considering applications for space in the market. For example, at the meeting of 22 February 1838, an application was made for stall No. 297, and it was resolved that Mr Tebbutt be granted it at a rent of 16s. a quarter. George Blankeley, a butcher, entered a request 'for John Sketchleys stall no. 171 when vacant'. An increasing number of such requests led the committee to establish a general policy on rentals at the meeting of 17 November 1841. This established the principle that stall-keepers renting on a yearly basis and paying in advance should have the first choice of stalls, and where multiple applications were received the applicants would draw lots. Second choice of

[65] Essex Record Office, D/DB, E. 79.
[66] The *Leicester Toll Committee Minutes* for 1837 to 1851 are held at the Leicester Museum, Archives Office.

stalls went to half-yearly renters, third choice to quarterly tenants, and the remainder were let weekly on a first-come-basis. This new policy was applied at the meeting of 22 January 1846 when Samuel Cheney, a shoemaker, applied for a stall occupied by a weekly tenant which Cheney sought to rent on a quarterly basis. The committee resolved that the stall should first be offered to the present weekly tenant on a quarterly basis, and if he refused the offer 'Cheney is to have a preference and is to apply again in a fortnight'. Competition among traders for optimum positions in the market was potentially explosive. The committee regulated this conflict by channeling it through a formal and apparently impartial institutional procedure: a space-rental system of allocation was substituted for its informal alternatives, such as customary occupancy, first-come possession, or coercion.

The committee was active in many other ways. It disciplined abuses of trade, maintained order in the market place, and restricted the proliferation of markets and street trading throughout the town. For example, at the meeting of 16 November 1837, the Assayer reported that William Rogers had been convicted a second time for selling bad meat. It was resolved that if he offended again the Committee would withdraw his right to a stall in the market. On 14 December 1837 it was resolved that the police be instructed that 'no person be allowed to have a Fish Stall outside the Fish Market unless all Stallage within is occupied and that no Stall be placed in front of the entrance to the Market or beyond the post opposite the corner'. Trucks and carts were not to stand in the market longer than was necessary for unloading. On 25 January 1838, it was resolved that 'Thomas Williamson be informed that in case he refused to extinguish his light at 11 o'clock he will not be allowed to occupy a stall'. At the meeting of 7 April 1842 the committee received a complaint from Mr Cripps, a shop-keeper, that Lewin's stall obstructed the view of his shop. A sub-committee was appointed to 'view the Market and see whether this ground of complaint can be removed without inconvenience', and on 21 April it reported 'that Lewin's stall has been removed and that all parties are satisfied'. Authority was also exercised over shopkeepers located on the market square. On 4 October 1838 it was resolved that the Town Clerk write to all the ironmongers having shops in the Market Place to inform them that 'they will not be allowed to place goods outside their doors'. The committee's policy on street trading outside the market was firm. In October 1850 a Memorial was received from inhabitants of Belgrave Gate, requesting the establishment there of a vegetable market. It was moved that the committee was of the opinion that it would be inexpedient to comply with the request 'inasmuch as the Town Council are now erecting a Market House which is intended to be appropriated on all the other days but Saturday for the Sale of Vegetables and other perishable Articles, and further that the Committee consider that Public Markets in the Streets of the Borough are highly objectionable'. There is little doubt that the inhabitants of Leicester and the market traders themselves benefited from the efficient work of their market committee.

The work of the Coventry Toll Committee provides a useful contrast.[67] The Coventry markets were also municipally owned, but unlike Leicester there was no consolidated market site and the buildings, stalls and other facilities were all inadequate. The market revenues at Leicester were derived mainly from the rental of stalls; but at Coventry, where stalls were in short supply and poor condition, the Committee's revenues were received in the form of commodity tolls. When market owners failed to provide adequate facilities, their authority over trading and power to maintain order was weakened. At Leicester, disciplinary action against a trader involved the simple but sharp sanction of removal from the market. This may be contrasted with the situation at Coventry in the same period. At a meeting of 6 May 1836 it was reported that Mrs Capewill's goods had been seized because she refused to pay 2d. toll on a bench of earthenware placed in the centre of Market Street, 'it being, she said, opposite her own door'. And on 7 May 1839 it reported that Mr Wilkins, who had a fish stall in Bread Street and had 'been in the habit of paying threepence every Friday and twopence every Saturday to the

[67] The *Coventry Toll Committee Minutes* are held at the City of Coventry Records Office.

Corporation, now refuses paying in consequence of his not being allowed to sell Mackerel on a Sunday'. In May 1836 Mr Taunton, the toll collector, reported that collection on Saturday morning should commence at 7 a.m. 'as many of the wholesale dealers come in with Carts loaded with Vegetables which they sell to the small dealers' and 'they drive off without making any payment'. A very serious incident arose in April 1836 when Taunton was reported to the committee for roughly handling a boy walking in the street with an empty basket. Taunton claimed the boy had avoided paying the toll the previous week and continued to refuse on this occasion:

...after entreating him many times not to compel me to seize he still persisted and I then took hold of his Basket he retaining hold of it and in that way he followed me to the Station House were [sic] it has been my custom to take all goods seized, according to your instructions he pertinaecously refused either to pay or relinquish his Basket. A Police Man of the name of Glaze was on duty and he Glaze took the Basket from him, according to my order; Goddard then sat down and declared he would not go without his Basket. I then asked him in whose employ he was, and he informed me. I took the Address and then told him I would see farther into it and as he was only a servant he might take the Basket, which he did, no effort was made to detain him, not more than Ten Minutes elapsed between him entering and leaving the Station House.

It is clear that Taunton lacked any really effective sanctions to back up his demand for tolls. At Leicester an offender was denied access to the market; but at Coventry the market place was very largely the city streets. Taunton often seized goods, but his right to impound property was not unquestioningly accepted by the traders, and appeals would be lodged with the Committee.

Is is possible that these problems entered into the Committee's decision in 1851 to write to Leicester, Nottingham and Northampton requesting information on the scale of tolls and stallage in these towns. But if the committee felt that market revenues were inadequate and tolls difficult to collect, the problem ultimately lay with the inadequate facilities and the lack of that disciplinary power which a complete reorganization would have brought. The situation was not overcome when in

1854 the committee decided to lease the tolls. In March 1855 the lessee wrote complaining of the very same difficulties of defining his rights and having those rights accepted by the traders. 'I have suffered', he wrote, 'to a considerable extent from a practice of many individuals who have purchased the use of the sheds in the Market by letting the ground in front of the same to another party of which I entertained an opinion I had a claim for Toll but which I have in no case been able to obtain.' In general, he complained that receipts from the tolls did not cover the costs of the lease.

As at Leicester, the committee was responsible for suppressing fraudulant trading, maintaining public order and adjudicating in disputes between market traders and shopkeepers. The minutes suggest none of that efficient despatch of business which characterized Leicester. On 5 March 1839 Taunton informed the committee that bad meat was frequently exposed for sale on Saturday nights. The committee wished to put a stop to this and directed the legal adviser to the corporation to inform them 'whether they or their Deputies properly appointed have Legal Authority to seize and destroy such Meat'. The problem remained serious during the following months, and in August it was decided to appoint 'a Person whose duty it will be to inspect the Condition of the Meat exposed for sale in our Market'. In October, policeman Charles Lord was appointed Saturday meat inspector at a salary of £5 a year.

Public disorder was a matter of constant concern. At the meeting of 14 December 1841 the committee asked Council to direct the police to keep better order in the market on a Saturday night 'and abate the Nuisance created by disorderly Boys and Girls'. At the meeting of 12 July 1852 the committee was confronted by a deputation of residents of Cross Cheaping 'complaining of great disorder and bad language used by Persons attending the Market on a Saturday Evening'. A response to this continuing problem was the decision in February 1854 to enforce market closure on Saturdays at 11.30 p.m., to be prefaced by the ringing of a bell at 10.30 p.m.

The Coventry committee also had to deal with disputes between shopkeepers and market traders. In October 1848 a complaint was received from a Cross Cheaping draper about a fish stall. A sub-committee was appointed 'to view the Obstruction and take such steps as they shall think expedient and also as to the Meat Stalls in Cross Cheaping. ... ' A reverse situation had occurred in 1840 when the committee had directed the removal of stalls from Cross Cheaping and Broad Gate on Mondays, Tuesdays and Thursdays, apparently because they impeded traffic. But the trade of the Cross Cheaping shopkeepers was thereby affected and they petitioned 'that the Market Gardeners may resume their standings in Cross Cheaping. ... '

The market committee periodically pressed the Council to improve market facilities. For example, on 19 February 1839, the attention of the Estates Committee was drawn to 'the dilapidated and dangerous State of the Womens Market Place' and the toll collector was ordered to 'cause Benches and Stalls belonging to the Corporation to be put into a proper state of Repair'. But by May the Estates Committee had not acted on the recommendation and the request was repeated. In 1840 the committee recommended the 'removal of the Horse and Beast Market from their present situations to Spon End'. But the committee did not, at least on an official level, put forward any more ambitious improvement schemes.

It seems that the Coventry market committee handled their responsibility less efficiently than the same body at Leicester. This was unfortunate both for Coventry residents and the market traders themselves. The Coventry body was at a comparative disadvantage in that the market facilities under its control lent themselves less well to efficient management; but there was much that might have been done in establishing and enforcing regulations and in pressing the Council for extensive improvements.

4. *Market Improvements*

Towards the end of the eighteenth century William Marshall wrote down a few thoughts on market improvement which the Coventry Council might have read with profit in 1850:

Market Places never struck me, as a subject entitled to particular attention, until I saw the good effect which had taken place, by a reform in the market places of this district.

In 1783, the markets of Gloucester, Tewkesbury and Cheltenham were kept on old-fashioned *crosses*, and under open market-houses, standing in the middle of the main streets; to the interruption of travellers, the disfigurement of the towns, and the inconveniency of the market people, whether sellers or buyers.

Now, these nuisances are cleared away, and the markets removed into well-situated recesses, conveniently filled up for their reception....

The old crosses and market houses are generally small, inconvenient, and now no longer adequate to the purposes for which they were originally erected. In winter they are chilling and dangerous to the health.... Besides, the corn market, the shambles and the women's market are frequently scattered, in different parts of a town: Whereas, in a square, inclosed with shops, shades and penthouses; with shambles in the center; and a corn market at the entrance—the whole are brought together; rendering the business of market commodious and comfortable; epithets which, at present, can seldom be well applied....[68]

Market improvement was an aspect of the whole nineteenth century urban revolution. Urbanization and rapid population growth placed heavy strains upon market facilities inherited from the past, especially when the market site was a central street of the town.

In the late eighteenth and in the nineteenth century a large number of bills were placed before Parliament which sought powers to improve the public markets in provincial towns and cities. Among the class of Local and Private Acts, there are over a hundred market improvement schemes for the period 1785 to 1850 affecting towns in England and Wales outside greater London. Before 1820 the majority of these improvement measures were part of general town improvement schemes, but after that date Acts concerned only with market improvement were common. In fact, in 1847 Parliament decided to pass a general measure entitled 'An Act for Consolidating in one Act certain Provisions usually contained in Acts for constructing or regulating Markets and Fairs'.[69]

It is very common for the preambles to these Acts to point to one or more of the typical urban problems as justifying an investment in new market facilities. For example at Bedford

[68] *Gloucestershire*, i, pp. 105–6.   [69] 10 & 11 Vict., c. 14.

the market carts and stalls were causing congestion in the streets, and a plan was put forward to demolish the Guildhall, the Butter House and several other buildings and to build a proper market square.[70] The growth of the pottery industry compelled the town of Hanley in Staffordshire to raise capital by public subscription for a new market house to be built on a site leased from the Lord of the Manor.[71] Bognor, which was 'greatly increased in Buildings and Population' and 'a great Resort for the Nobility, Gentry and others' asked Parliament to provide legal title to a new market built by a private citizen.[72] At Rochdale, Bilston, Maidstone, Canterbury, Stourbridge, Exeter, Bury and many other towns the principal grievance was that markets held on the streets brought traffic congestion and danger to the health and even the lives of buyers and sellers.

The means by which market improvement was promoted and financed varied with local circumstance. Where the market was privately owned interested townsmen might press the owner for improvements or attempt to buy from him the market rights. For example, at Sheffield in 1784 the Earl of Surrey, working with a body of local commissioners, was authorized by Parliament to borrow up to £11 000 for market improvement by mortgaging his lands.[73] Similarly, the Earl of Derby built a new market house at Bury in the 1830s, and the Lord of the Manor of Exmouth constructed new markets at his own expense.[74] At Hanley in the Potteries capital for the new market was raised by subscription under lease from the Lord of the Manor.[75] At Lewes the Lord of the Manor placed improvement powers in the hands of a body of commissioners.[76] A major reorganization of the Winchester markets was undertaken in 1835 by a private company.[77] Commissioners at Wolverhampton were empowered in 1814 to purchase the rights and tolls from the present owners and to carry out improvements on a new market site.[78] But agreement between the market owner and interested citizens was not always

[70] 43 Geo. III, c. 128.
[71] 53 Geo. III, c. 115.   [72] 3 Geo. IV, c. 57.
[73] 24 Geo. III, c. 5, s. 2.   [74] 2 & 3 Vict., c. 8 and 1 & 2 Vict., c. 5.
[75] 51 Geo. III, c. 115.   [76] 31 Geo. III, c. 86.
[77] 5 & 6 Will. IV, c. 50.   [78] 54 Geo. III, c. 106.

reached easily or quickly. A bitter quarrel developed in Manchester in the 1780s when the Lord of the Manor failed to respond to demands for improved facilities. With the support of the townspeople, Mr Chackwick and Mr Ackers purchased a site and arranged for it to be cleared and provided with drains, flagstones, stalls and a market house. The Lord of the Manor lodged a suit against the two men, but a settlement out of court was reached eventually.[79]

Where the markets were publicly owned, it was possible for town authorities to finance improvements on the backing of the rates. But town councils could sometimes be as unresponsive to demands for market improvements as the less enlightened of the private owners. The Durham markets, for example, were in a deplorable condition by 1850 and townspeople complained that market supply from the countryside was falling off. The corporation, however, refused to accept responsibility for improvement and townspeople therefore met to organize a joint-stock company. A bill was presented to Parliament proposing a capital subscription of £12 000 in 2400 shares at £5 each.[80] The bill was passed by Parliament in 1851.

A market improvement led usually to an increase in the level of tolls. An improvement at Maidstone, for instance, was felt to require 'an increase in present tolls and rents', and at Bridgwater tolls were raised and the inhabitants assessed. But raising tolls could have serious consequences for market supply. When tolls on butter were raised at Canterbury at the end of the eighteenth century in order to meet part of the cost of rebuilding the market house, it 'so offended the farmers in the neighbourhood that they entered into an agreement to bring no more to market, but to expose it for sale at a place without the liberties of the city; and instead of spending the money at the city shops…it was carried away to purchase goods at other places. The citizens finding that their interests lay in a free sale for provisions of every kind…took off the additional toll.'[81] Manchester was involved in a similar dilemma in the 1780s when citizens at a town meeting decided that the roads leading to the market place would require widening:

[79] *Description of Manchester* (1783) p. 65.
[80] Fordyce, *Durham*, i, 361 and p. 359 n.   [81] Boys, *Kent*, p. 202.

All agreed to the necessity of these alterations proposed, but some were for raising money by tolls, to be taken at the main entrances into the town: others foresaw that this method would exasperate the market people, and induce them to charge provisions higher; proposing, instead of tolls, to make a voluntary subscription.[82]

It was the latter proposal that was carried at the meeting, and it suggests how economically sensitive towns were at this time to good relationships with their surrounding countryside.

The whole question of market tolls was under review in these years. Both wisdom and necessity brought an end to many medieval survivals, such as town-end tolls. They were abolished in Darlington in the nineteenth century because it was found that they annoyed townsmen and, more important, were inducing country people to market in Stockton rather than Darlington.[83] Liverpool removed its town-end tolls in 1819, largely because the growth of the town made it impractical for them to be collected.[84] Another very important reform was the abolition of commodity toll schedules. At Chichester, for example, standage for meat and fish was levied at 1s. a day; for bacon, cheese and pickled meat 1s.; for every basket of butter (according to weight) from 1s. to 2s.; tolls on poultry operated on a sliding scale ranging from 3d. for under a half dozen to 1s. 3d. for under four dozen, rising by 3d. for each dozen over four.[85] Liverpool markets had operated on a similar commodity schedule but replaced it in 1819 with a system organized not 'in respect of the various articles exposed for sale, but in respect of the accommodation provided, and the space occupied by the same'. Hanley market, which introduced the same system a few years later, rented every covered shed, stall, trestle or standing at 1s. for 6 ft. or less; 1s. 3d. for 6 to 8 ft.; and 1s. 9d. for 8 ft. The same accommodation uncovered was rated at 6d., 9d. and 1s. A horse-drawn cart was assessed at 9d. a day and 1s. for two or more horses.[86] As we have seen, the bigger markets with a permanent body of retailers, quoted rents on a yearly and quarterly basis. The substitution of accommodation for commodity schedules could lead to a more

[82] *Description of Manchester* (1783) p. 65.
[83] Fordyce, *Durham*, i, p. 478.
[84] 59 Geo. III, c. 60.
[85] 49 Geo. III, c. 84, s. 2.
[86] 53 Geo. III, c. 115.

economic allocation of scarce market space and remove what was frequently an irrational tax on consumption of certain commodities. But the introduction of an accommodation schedule also indicated that the market proprietor was assuming responsibility for the provision of stalls, benches and other facilities, which was a sign in itself of improved market conditions.

The standard of facilities provided in markets varied very widely in these years. Table 2:2 shows that in 1890 some 162 of the 605 markets in England and Wales were held chiefly

TABLE 2:2. Retail Markets in England and Wales, 1890

Facilities	Ownership	
	Municipal	Other
Chiefly covered	81	81
Partly covered	114	98
Entirely open	92	139
	287	318

Source: *Final Report*, Royal Commission on Market Rights and Tolls; 1890–91 (C-6268) xxxvii, p. 54.

in covered buildings, and that 374 were either wholly or partly under cover. It is likely that before 1850 much less than half of the markets were wholly or partly covered and the number of markets 'chiefly in covered buildings' would have been much fewer. But covering was not the only index of good facilities. There were several markets held in open squares, such as at Nottingham, Leicester, Norwich and Northampton which were recognized as providing facilities of a high quality. By contrast many partly covered markets were very unsatisfactory. At Lincoln the roofed, but open-ended market hall was subject to 'the cutting winter blasts' and the population of the town had 'far outgrown the accommodation offered'.[87] Similarly, the hall built at Bishop Auckland failed to 'answer the purpose for which it was intended' as the open arches admitted 'such a strong current of wind as to render the interior platform uncomfortable to those standing on it'.[88]

[87] *The Stranger's Guide to Lincoln* (1846) pp. 96–7.
[88] Fordyce, *Durham*, i, p. 551.

It was usual for the industrial cities and towns of the Midlands and North to enjoy the most advanced market facilities. This is not surprising. The inherited social overhead capital was quickly made redundant in these centres of unprecedented growth and change. Moreover, as foci of national attention, much of it critical,[89] expenditure on public buildings was one way of directing that attention into favourable channels. Above all, there was a congruence of real needs and the possibility of satisfying those needs. That is, in the damp, filthy atmosphere of the industrial north, together with working hours which left most of the population only the night time for shopping, the need for a completely covered, gas-lit market hall was a more pressing priority than in the rural market town. Local government provided the means, if not always the impetus, for planning the market and mobilizing capital for its construction; and while the investment was often large in absolute terms, it was low in *per capita* cost for the community serviced and could be recovered rapidly through the market revenues.

In many ways Liverpool set the standard which other industrial towns followed. Liverpool's first partially covered market was built at the bottom of Islington in 1818. But the major development was the construction of St John's market, opened in 1822 at a cost to the Corporation of £35 296. St John's served as a model for covered markets throughout the country. It was situated in the centre of town, with the principal entrance of six on Great Charlotte Street. The market measured 183 yards by 45 yards and formed a covered space of 8235 square yards. It was gas-lit, substantially flagged and ventilated by over 135 windows. The market floor was divided into five avenues by four rows of cast iron pillars, with ranges of stalls and benches sectioned on a commodity basis. There were some 160 stalls for provisions dealers, 34 for green sellers, 18 for fruit dealers, 55 stone compartments for potato sellers, 36 fish standings, 201 table compartments for dealers in eggs, poultry and vegetables, and some 122 miscellaneous bench spaces. The market floor was ringed by 62 shops each measuring 16 square yards and occupied mainly by provisions dealers. Rents in the market were payable quarterly, shops being let at £18 per

[89] See Asa Briggs, *Victorian Cities* (Pelican Ed. 1968), especially on Manchester.

annum, cellars £5, butchers' stalls £8 (and £10 for corner locations), vegetable and fruit stalls £6, potato compartments £3, tables £1 12s. and benches at 12s.[90]

In the next few years the Liverpool Corporation constructed several smaller but otherwise comparable district market halls. St James' market on Great George Street was covered by a slate roof enclosing an area of 3000 square yards. It was begun in 1827 and cost £13 662 and was designed to service residents of south Liverpool. St Martin's market on Scotland Road was opened in 1830 at a cost of £13 000 and was built to service north Liverpool, Everton and Kirkdale.[91]

Birmingham did not enjoy comparable facilities until the 1830s. The Birmingham markets had been centralized at the Bull Ring in 1812, and the tolls were purchased from the Lord of the Manor at a cost of £12 500. An Act of Parliament in 1828 authorized the construction of a market hall, and construction began in 1833. The covered area was some 4356 square yards, rather smaller than St John's at Liverpool.[92] Birmingham did not build district markets (as was done at Liverpool) but the market commissioners were prepared to tolerate the growth of district street markets.

St John's market also served as a model for the smaller industrial towns. The covered market at Birkenhead measured some 6000 square yards and cost nearly £35 000. Its facilities were nearly identical to those provided at St John's market.[93] The Blackburn Improvement Commission constructed a hall covering some 2000 square yards in 1848 at a cost of £9000. The floor was flagged and the hall lit by gas. Much of the provisions market, however, was held outside, and a large number of the 34 shops surrounding the market floor were occupied by confectioners, booksellers, furniture dealers, smallware dealers, hatters, drapers, clothes dealers and hardware

[90] 'Description of the New Market, Liverpool', *The Economist and General Adviser* ii (1825) pp. 225–7, and *The Picture of Liverpool* (1832) pp. 153–5.
[91] H. Gawthrop, *Fraser's Guide to Liverpool and Birkenhead* (1855) p. 145, and *Picture of Liverpool* (1832) pp. 156–7.
[92] W. Hutton, *The History of Birmingham* (6th ed., 1835 with additions by J. Guest), pp. 62–5.
[93] *Strangers' Guide Through Birkenhead* (1848) p. 45.

men.[94] The Blackburn Market was much closer to a general shopping centre than a provisions market.

In London, covered market developments were not very successful. A private corporation spent over £200 000 in developing Hungerford Market in 1833. Its facilities were splendid, including a foot bridge over the Thames, but it was not a commercial success.[95] It has been suggested that its failure was attributable to the proximity of Covent Garden, but the latter, by this time, was primarily wholesale. The failure of Hungerford Market, as well as the attractive Fleet Market, is possibly attributable to the more settled character of central London compared with the new provincial cities, and to the fixed shopping habits of Londoners, who were already well served by shops, street markets and itinerant distribution services.

The volume of trade in the smaller market towns did not justify the development of facilities comparable to those in the new industrial cities. In the latter, as we have suggested, capital could be raised on the backing of the rates and the costs paid off from market revenues. For example, the revenues from the Birmingham Bull Ring in the mid-1830s were about £3000 a year with operating expenses running at about £700.[96] St John's market in Liverpool (capital cost £35 296) generated revenue of £6000 a year, and St James' market (capital cost £13 662) enjoyed annual revenues of £1500.[97]

It was argued in the Royal Commission on Markets and Fairs in the 1890s that markets controlled by local authorities usually were superior in facilities to those under private ownership.[98] Private owners predominated in the smaller towns, and in these places an elaborate market facility was not always an economic investment. But in Manchester, where local government was relatively slow in developing, the markets were owned by the Mosley family and the facilities were markedly inferior to those provided by public authorities at Liverpool, Birmingham and smaller industrial towns. Assuming that the family could mobilize the £30 000 or more necessary to provide the city with

[94] P. A. Whittle, *Blackburn As It Is* (1852) pp. 120–3.
[95] See *The Mirror* (Saturday, 6 July 1833). [96] Hutton, *Birmingham*, p. 63.
[97] Gawthrop, *Guide to Liverpool*, p. 145. [98] *Final Report*, p. 55.

equal facilities, it might not have been to their private economic interest given the high rate of return on some railway and industrial developments. But a moderately dynamic local government (Manchester did not have any until the mid-1830s) could overcome this conflict between private and community interests. At Birmingham, Durham and many other towns, as we have seen, the Council, or an improvement company, arranged to buy or lease the market rights and raised capital on the backing of the rates or through public subscription. Responsibility for market improvements might be obscured by private market ownership, but it did not amount to a hopeless constraint on development given sufficient community interest and organization.

5. *Conclusions*

How did England's markets and fairs, as institutions of exchange, interact with the country's rapidly changing economic and social structure?

It was the fair which revealed the weakest powers of adaptation. As an exchange mechanism it operated usefully in predominantly rural societies, characterized by slow communications and transport, a low level of material demand and a high degree of local and personal self-sufficiency. It could not play a crucial distribution role in an urban, industrial society. As an exchange mechanism, the fair in 1850 was of direct significance only to that segment of the agricultural community concerned with the marketing of livestock at the wholesale level. Fairs contiguous to, or surrounded by, mushrooming industrial towns lost their distribution functions, although where they were not abolished they did subsist with an entertainment role.

In rural areas which were still only marginally affected by social change, retail markets thrived, little changed, as exchange mechanisms for mainly local production. But throughout the century, the looming shadow of the industrial town, its products and exchange structure, was increasingly omnipresent in rural England. Unlike the fair, however, retail markets were successfully adapted, as exchange institutions, to urban conditions. We have noted that urban markets necessarily relied less upon proximate sources of supply, and therefore relied more upon a

permanent body of professional market traders, and that a network of exchange relationships among urban markets was
developed with the emergence of high speed transport. As urban
markets expanded in size far beyond the largest of the old
country markets, their location and design had to be more
carefully planned, facilities elaborated, and the activities of
buyers and sellers subjected to more formal institutions of
control.

III

Itinerant Retailing

PEDLARS 'were at one time very common', wrote J. R. McCulloch in the 1830s, 'but since shops, for the sale of almost every sort of produce, have been opened in every considerable village throughout Britain, their numbers have been greatly diminished'.[1] There was much contemporary comment of this kind, and it was usually misleading.

Several social and economic factors suggest why one would not expect itinerant distribution (defined here as all retail trading outside fixed shops) to disappear during England's early industrialization. Country people were accustomed to buying from market traders and pedlars, and when they moved into more urban environments they searched for known, or at least familiar, distribution services. The newly urbanized encountered enough bewildering experiences without adding such a vital function as shopping to the list. It has been shown that Puerto Ricans and Negroes from the rural South behave in a similar way in present day New York city. They rely much more upon pedlar services than does the white community of a comparable economic status. Moreover, pedlar involvement has not diminished appreciably with length of time in the city, as children have tended to inherit the pattern from their parents.[2]

In England, for reasons of bad planning and high entrepreneurial risk, a complete range of shop distribution services could not be found in the new working class suburbs and even in many of the middle class areas. The itinerant trader who worked these suburban areas, in effect, carried the facilities of centrally located markets and shops to the consumer. Itinerant services were a stop-gap between the development of housing suburbs and a comparable development of suburban shops

[1] *On Commerce* (1833) p. 6.
[2] D. Caplovitz, *The Poor Pay More* (1963) p. 75.

and a transport system which could get the consumer into the central area rapidly at low cost. Moreover, it represented an efficient use of the economy's real resources. It has been noted that economies with a large population relative to capital and natural resources are characterized by large supplies of unskilled labour and a low marginal productivity of labour in many sectors of activity. This situation is frequently manifest in over-population on the land and the presence of large numbers of people in the towns engaged in petty trading and other services. As the capitalist sector of the economy expands more capital becomes available for wage employment of labour, and workers are drawn out of agriculture and petty services until the labour surplus disappears.[3]

Certain features of this model seem relevant to England in this period. Population grew very rapidly and in the southern counties in particular there was a high level of rural under-employment. In addition, significant numbers of traditional craftsmen were made technologically redundant and many tended to drift into petty hawking, if not permanently at least temporarily. Down swings of the trade cycle forced unemployed workers from the factories and the rural and urban putting-out industries to seek a subsistence in service occupations. During this period, as we shall see, when the production system was striving to work near the technically efficient frontier, the distribution system acted, on the one hand, as a partial substitute for modern, state-organized welfare services, and on the other, for the welfare which had been buried in the now contracting peasant and craft production system. But in seeking subsistence in the distribution service, the 'unskilled' served the developing capitalist economy. If domestic mass markets for factory output were to be developed, it was important that distribution costs be kept low. Since capital was scarce relative to unskilled labour (including technologically redundant labour) distribution was characterized by mass employment of labour at a low supply price in terms of daily earnings.[4]

[3] W. A. Lewis, 'Economic Development with Unlimited Supplies of Labour', *The Manchester School* (May 1954).

[4] See P. T. Bauer and B. S. Yamey, 'Economic Progress and Occupational Distribution', *Economic Journal* (December 1951).

This was an economically efficient use of the economy's real resources.

1. *Employment in Itinerant Distribution*
The itinerant trading which McCulloch and others suggested was in decline was the old country peddling and not the numerically more important petty trading which grew with urbanization. Table 3:1 gives statistics for the number of

TABLE 3:1. Licensed Hawkers and Pedlars in England, 1820–1843

| Year | Rate Paid for Licence | | | | Total |
	£4	£8	£12	£16	
1820	5 369	912	36	2	6 319
1830	6 630	832	14	3	7 479
1840	6 020	1 005	30	2	7 057
1843	4 793	927	40	2	5 762

Source: *B.P.P.*, 'A Return of the Number of Hawkers Licensed in the Years 1800, 1810, 1820, 1830, and in 1843....' 1844 (123) XXXII. 377. Until 1820 only total receipts were recorded.

licensed pedlars in England at dates between 1820 and 1843. The basic pedlar's licence cost £4 and rose by £4 for every horse or mule employed. Dealers in foodstuffs or self-produced manufactures were exempt from licensing, and these licensed hawkers therefore represented only the body of itinerant traders buying manufactured goods for resale. Moreover, it was largely pedlars involved in the old country trade that troubled to take out a licence. Evasion of licensing laws was widespread among urban hawkers; as one observer noted it was not the 'hawkers who keep to one town and its environs, who take out a licence, but those who travel from town to town, from county to county. ... '[5] Table 3:1 certainly suggests that there was no growth in the number of licenced pedlars (whom we identify with the old country trade) but the statistics are too unreliable for us to infer any more.

The occupation abstracts of the census returns give the following returns for numbers engaged in itinerant trade:

[5] Felix Folio, *The Hawkers and Street Dealers of Manchester* (1858) p. 13.

TABLE 3:2. Number of Hawkers, Pedlars and Hucksters,
England and Wales

Date	Number
1831	9 459
1841	14 662
1851	25 747

According to these figures the number of itinerant traders rose by a multiple of just under three in these twenty years. While the ratio of *licensed* hawkers to population in England and Wales declined from 1:1725 in 1820 to 1:2835 in 1843, the ratio of itinerant traders to population enumerated in the census returns rose from 1:1470 in 1831 to 1:657 in 1851.[6]

Although these figures are of value in suggesting a trend, they are of little use as estimates of the total number of people employed either full or part-time in itinerant distribution. For various reasons, Henry Mayhew argued that the totals were a gross understatement of the numbers of itinerant traders.[7] Moreover, the census returns did not include among hawkers and pedlars the mass of country people selling in the markets, or the shoemakers, toy makers and other small manufacturers who hawked their output at markets and in the streets. They do not reflect, in a systematic way, the expansion and contraction of the ranks of itinerant traders in sympathy with swings of the trade cycle. At best, the census returns may give a rough indication of the size of the *permanent core* of *full-time* hawkers and pedlars between 1831 and 1851.

The 1841 census included a county distribution of itinerant traders. It indicates that itinerants were most numerous in heavily populated and urbanized counties. Lancashire, Middlesex and the West Riding, which contained just over 27 per cent of the population of England and Wales in 1841, included some 30 per cent of the enumerated itinerants. From the official statistics it can be calculated that Lancashire and Middlesex had ratios of itinerants to population in 1841 of 1:895 and 1:982 respectively, while the ratios for southern agricultural counties like Devon and Somerset were 1:2320 and 1:2169.

[6] Rounded calculations using population figures at mid-year in Mitchell and Deane, *Historical Statistics*, Ch. 1, table 3.

[7] Henry Mayhew, *London Labour*, i, 4.

It is probable, however, that these figures understate the actual concentration of itinerant trading in urban areas. In the early 1850s Henry Mayhew estimated that there were some 41 000 itinerants in London, or a ratio of roughly 1:63 people. Some 30 000 of these (75 per cent) were costermongers (fish, fruit and vegetable sellers) giving a ratio of 1:90 people; about 5000 dealers in manufactures, a ratio of 1:537, and the remainder dealers in greenstuffs, eatables and drinkables.[8] It is possible that Mayhew's estimates were too high, although he realistically included in his calculations women, children and part-time traders. When all factors are taken into account, his calculations are probably the best guide to the real ratios of itinerants to population in the big urban centres.

The available statistical data, then, suggests that while country peddling was probably in decline the number of people involved in itinerant trading was rising, at least between the 1830s and 1850s. This can be explained only by recognizing that the pedlar's trade developed into an urban rather than a rural occupation: in a sense, the pedlar followed his customers into the towns. And whether we accept the official statistics of the census returns or the upward revised estimates of informed observers, the very large numbers of people involved in itinerancy testifies to its importance in the distribution system, even though the 'typical' shopkeeper no doubt had a larger turnover than the 'typical' itinerant.

2. *Regulation of Itinerant Trading*

In 1840 the *Penny Cyclopaedia* suggested that 'it has been for more than a century the policy of English law to consider the conduct of trade by means of fixed establishments as more beneficial to the public than that of itinerant dealers....'[9] In fact, this was not true. In the reign of William III an Act was passed for licensing hawkers and pedlars, imposing a basic £4 fee with an additional charge of £4 for each animal employed in pulling a cart. The Act exempted from licensing hawkers of foodstuffs, craftsmen selling their output in markets and the streets, and travelling tinkers, coopers, glaziers and other

[8] Ibid., ii, 1. [9] 1840, xvii, 367.

repair men.[10] The Act was passed mainly for the purpose of raising revenue and not, it would seem, under pressure from shopkeepers. But in 1785 another Act was passed raising the tariff on the use of animals to £8 and forbidding pedlars to sell in towns where they were not residents, except on market days. As a concession, pedlars were allowed to settle in a town of their choice and open a shop for trade without satisfying any normal guild requirements of apprenticeship.[11] In this instance there was very considerable pressure by shopkeepers through Parliament to constrain the activities of pedlars with a view to their eventual elimination. An amending Act in 1789, while restoring the old licence fees, added an additional constraint, obliging the applicant for a pedlar's licence to present character statements from the officiating clergyman of his parish and two other 'respectable inhabitants'. Moreover, the licensed pedlar was obliged to display conspicuously on his cart, pack or rented shop, his name and licence number.[12] A second amending Act in 1795, however, marked a change of policy on the part of the government. The Act removed the 1785 restrictions on sales by pedlars in towns other than on market days since 'the said Restrictions have been found inconvenient to the Manufacturers in general, and also detrimental to the Revenue'.[13] In the nineteenth century there was no legislation fundamentally changing these provisions.

The eighteenth century legislation had been directed specifically at itinerant retailers of manufactured goods. The relationship between shopkeepers and itinerants was in some instances symbiotic and in others competitive. The area of acute sensitivity lay less in foodstuffs than in drapery and hardware, and it was the activities of travelling dealers in the latter that the legislation was designed to constrain. It was a common argument of shopkeepers in the eighteenth and nineteenth centuries that since shops had been 'open'd in *every* corner, and in the most *remote parts*' of the country and shopkeepers contributed to the maintenance of the community through rates, taxes and local government, they should be freed from the

---

[10] 8 & 9 W. III, c. 25.   [11] 25 Geo. III, c. 78.
[12] 29 Geo. III, c. 26.   [13] 35 Geo. III, c. 91.

competition of itinerants.[14] The government had imposed the severe restrictions of the 1785 Act on itinerant traders in return for the shopkeepers', no doubt sullen, agreement to a tax on shops.[15] It is clear from the Parliamentary Debates that the shopkeepers had pressed for a total abolition of itinerant trade. But Pitt replied that arguments in the House had convinced him that 'there were some parts of the kingdom that would be highly inconvenienced by this suppression, as from the distance from towns or cities, they depended on those people for a considerable part of their consumption'.[16] Significantly, when the shop tax was repealed in 1789,[17] the pedlar's licence rate was also reduced, and six years later the onerous restrictions of the 1785 Act were removed. Thereafter the government refused to consider appeals for the abolition of peddling, and shop-keepers' frustrations were confined to the correspondence pages of trade journals[18] and attempts at prosecution. For example, in 1834 shopkeepers in Great Dunmow in Essex wrote to John Bayley of the Middle Temple for an opinion on whether it was possible to expel a pedlar who had pitched a booth and 'is offering for sale a large Assortment of Fancy Articles to the great detriment of the Traders who inhabit the Town & pay to the Rates & Taxes and they conceive that the Hawker has no right to come into the Town to sell his Wares & Goods except on Market days and that in the Market Place'.[19]

None of this legislation applied to costermongers and peddling tradesmen. Control over unlicensed peddling was a local matter defined by town or market improvement Acts. Policy varied widely among towns. At Dover, for example, itinerant hawking was permitted only if market tolls were paid.[20] At Kings Lynn it was illegal to sell provisions outside the market place on market day, except in shops.[21] The

[14] A broadside preserved in the Goldsmith's Library, Senate House, 355 (1).

[15] 25 Geo. III, c. 30.

[16] *Hansard* (The Parliamentary History of England), xxv, 885.

[17] 29 Geo. III, c. 9.

[18] For the early nineteenth century, see *The Tradesman*, iv, no. 24, 529–32, v, no. 25, 45–51, ix, no. 50, 99–102.

[19] Essex Record Office, D/DU 152/56. Bayley gave an incorrect opinion on the basis of 25 Geo. III, c. 78, as he was unaware of the amending Act 29 Geo. III, c. 26.

[20] 7 Geo. IV, c. 5.   [21] 10 Geo. IV, c. 5.

Exmouth improvement Act gave the local authorities wide powers of discretion, for it stated that 'if any Person shall ... sell or expose to sale in the open streets or the Foot Pavements ... so as to obstruct or impede the said Thoroughfare' he would be liable to a 40s. fine.[22] At Bradford, Wolverhampton, Stalybridge and Ashton-under-Lyne the market proprietors were empowered to license hawkers. By the end of the century the assumption of licensing powers by market owners without legal right was very common and a source of bitter conflict with street traders.[23]

In the late nineteenth century, it was said that whether hawking should be restricted, prohibited or tolerated under licence was a burning question in a large number of market towns.[24] City authorities were generally more tolerant towards street traders than the market owners in smaller towns. The retail markets in the latter were faced with growing competition from shopkeepers and costermongers retailing in suburban districts and central areas, and if retailers by-passed the local market in order to buy wholesale in nearby city markets (as happened at Rochdale, for example) the market revenues would suffer.

Shopkeepers exercised considerable influence on the policy adopted by town authorities towards hawkers. Although the licensed pedlar was the shopkeeper's principal competitor, not the costermonger, shopkeepers periodically expressed real and imagined grievances against the latter. The hostility of shopkeepers derived from the fact that hawkers did not pay taxes and rates or face heavy overhead costs and they sometimes generated confusion in the streets. From the shopkeeper's material point of view, the presence of a body of street hawkers was beneficial in so far as it attracted consumers into the street. But social action is not always based on material rationality and shopkeepers, acting on the basis of their latent hostility to itinerant trading, would occasionally appeal to the authorities to remove the hawkers from the street. Very often, these

[22] 1 & 2 Vict., c. 46.

[23] Market owners' claims were often based falsely on the comprehensive market Act of 1847 (10 & 11 Vict., c. 14) which stated that in all *newly created* markets street trading on market days required payment of authorized tolls.

[24] *Final Report*; Royal Commission on Market Rights, op. cit., p. 60.

appeals would be soon followed by a counter-appeal, for as we have suggested, the relationship between shopkeeper and coster-monger (numerically the most important segment of urban hawking) was largely symbiotic. The working-class housewife purchased fish, fruit and vegetables from the market and street traders, and her bread, bacon, meat, cheese and groceries from the shopkeepers. Greengrocers, fishmongers and butchers retailing exclusively in shops (that is, not also in the markets and streets) catered to a higher class of trade. Moreover, while drapers might be in direct competition with contiguous street dealers trading in similar products, on another level the concen-tration of both shop and street services would attract a larger number of customers than if one or the other was lacking. Thus, London shopkeepers found that when the police suppressed a street market (usually at their request) trade in the shops fell sharply as women transferred their custom to other street markets and their contiguous shops. Shops alone could not hold the working class trade, for as Mayhew noted they 'will *not* be driven to buy at the shops. They can't be persuaded that they can buy as cheap at the shops; and besides they are apt to think shopkeepers are rich and the street-sellers poor, and that they may as well encourage the poor'.[25]

Whatever the attitudes held by shopkeepers and street traders towards each other, their outward behaviour was normally tolerant. Mr Anthony Rutt, a Metropolitan Police Superintendant, testified that he sometimes had the street traders removed from New Cut, but he recognized that 'the trades people generally all the time were in favour of their being there, and consequently they wished the police not to act so harshly towards them, but allow them to continue there'.[26] The normative practice in London was that where hawkers were in the habit of standing the police were not to disturb them unless there was a complaint from an adjacent shopkeeper or householder. In 1832 and 1837 respectively only 361 and 334 cases of obstruction were brought before the magistrates, and in only 145 and 112 cases were the traders punished by forfeiture

[25] Mayhew, *London Labour*, i, 60.
[26] *B.P.P.*, Select Committee on Sunday Trading (Metropolis); Mins. of Ev., 1847 (666) ix, Q. 1513.

of goods.[27] When it is considered that thousands of traders were on the streets of London each day, it is clear that this does not represent an oppressive level of prosecution.

3. *Capital, Credit, and Earnings*

Itinerant distribution was characterized by massive substitution of labour for capital. Typically, the hawker held very small stocks, enough for a day or a few days' trading; he went directly to the supplier at his market or shop to acquire his stocks; he broke bulk into very small units to accommodate the weak buying power of his customers; and he travelled, if not directly to the homes of all his customers, at least to a street or market which was near to the consumer's work or home.

The itinerant trader's investment in fixed capital ranged from papers in which goods were carried and displayed on the ground, to boxes, trays, baskets and carts powered by animals. The licensing figures in Table 3:1, however, suggest that few itinerants had animal powered carts: between 1820 and 1843 at most 1000 traders licensed a cart with one animal, and less than 50 employed two or more animals. The 'Cheap John', dealing in a wide range of hardware goods, and the quack medicine dealer were the principal users of animal-powered carts. A few prosperous costermongers in urban areas, and particularly those working suburban districts, employed animal-drawn carts, but the typical costermonger used a hand-barrow. The poorer hawkers dealing in oranges, nuts and other eatables sold from baskets and trays.

The wagons and barrows used by costermongers were very often rented from dealers. In London barrows could be hired in the 1850s at 3d. a day or 1s. a week in the six winter months, rising to 4d. a day and 1s. 6d. a week in the six summer months. The differential between summer and winter rates marked the movement of men into costermongering as summer produce came on the markets, and the higher earnings which characterized the summer season. Most hawkers could buy, or make, a basket or tray, but these too were rented at 1d. a day, mainly to casual entrepreneurs. No security or deposit was demanded by

---

[27] R. W. Rawson, *J. Stat. Soc. London*, i (1839) pp. 101–2.

the dealers on the rental of equipment,[28] and given the meagre capital resources of street hawkers, probably could not have been demanded.

The costermonger's weekly earnings were marked by severe seasonal fluctuations. Generalization is difficult, but in London in the 1850s earnings from January to April were as low as 4s. to 6s. a week, improving slowly with the summer fruit season to as much as 30s. to 35s. a week. After September earnings fell off, with the exception of the Christmas week.[29] A minority of costermongers with trades in prosperous areas could maintain relatively high earnings throughout the year. The earnings of itinerants selling oranges, nuts, brushes, toys and other small manufactures (commonly the wives and children of costermongers) were much lower than the 'aristocracy' of dealers in fruit, vegetables and fish.

The costermonger's low average earnings meant that his working capital was small and vulnerable to a short succession of days of short supply and high prices in the wholesale markets. Errors in buying, illness and other misadventures were a constant threat to the dealer's limited working capital. Capital could then be restored only by performing petty services for the wealthy classes, deploying any small capital remaining on oranges, nuts or other low-cost goods, or by securing a loan. Mayhew believed that no more than a quarter of the London itinerants traded on their own capital, and interest charges on loans constituted one of their heaviest trading expenses.[30] Loans were provided by a few of the prosperous costermongers, by shopkeepers and publicans. The rates quoted for London in the 1850s were 2d. a day for 2s. 6d. ($6\frac{3}{4}$ per cent), 3d. for 5s. (5 per cent), 6d. for 10s. (5 per cent) and 1s. for £1 (5 per cent). If interest payments were met regularly then rates might be reduced at the end of a month. Lenders did not necessarily demand repayment of the principal at some stipulated time, and a few were said to have up to £150 on loan. Publicans lent at the lowest rates but usually expected both the repayment of the principal and an outlay on beer. Shopkeepers lent to costermongers retailing near their shops whom they knew and

---

[28] Mayhew, *London Labour*, i, 30.
[29] Ibid., pp. 54–5.   [30] Ibid., p. 29.

trusted. A failure to repay loans and meet interest charges was said to be uncommon, since word of defaulting spread quickly and brought permanent exclusion from the loan market.[31]

Petty hawking was an unskilled occupation which involved little more than a large input of labour for very meagre returns. On the other hand, to secure the relatively high earnings of a costermonger or Cheap John involved considerable buying and selling skill. These skills were normally passed on to young people through the family, but outsiders entering the trade could gain the necessary experience by 'apprenticing' themselves to an established dealer requiring labour but lacking a kinship network from which to draw it. For example, prosperous costermongers purchased at the markets beyond their immediate needs in order to supply younger men who lacked the capital to buy stocks of their own. This was known as working 'on half profits'. A barrow of vegetables, fruit or fish would be handed over to the younger man with an estimate of the profits the barrow should earn. Thus, if the profit estimate was set at 2s. and proved to be accurate, the profits would be divided equally between the two men; but if the barrow failed to bring in 2s. profit the younger man was still indebted to the owner for 1s.[32] The half profits system could be abused, but it did give the inexperienced time in which to acquire selling skills before venturing into the wholesale markets on their own.

In addition to the half profits system, costermongers also employed young men as wage labourers. It was in this way that John Babbington, who left a diary of his experiences, became a London costermonger.[33] Babbington was born in Leeds in 1824 and went up to London around 1840. Unemployment and an attack of fever sent him to the Royal Free Hospital, but on discharge he wandered over to the New Cut and found himself 'gazing at a costermonger's barrow loaded with shrimp, but what was more important, I had attracted the attention and sympathy of the coster'. The coster offered him employment in exchange for food and shelter, but within six months other traders in the Cut had offered him wage employment.

[31] Ibid., pp. 29–31.   [32] Ibid., p. 33.
[33] John Babbington, *Autobiography* (Solly Collection, L.S.E. Coll. Misc., 154, section 10 (d)) Folios J. 346–461.

At this point his employer 'one Sunday at dinner ... gave me two shillings, saying he would give me the same every week, which he did'.[34] Babbington's apprenticeship lasted for two years at which time the necessity of supporting a younger brother forced him to begin trade on his own account.

4. *Wholesale Suppliers*

Some costermongers dealt exclusively in one product throughout the year, but most shifted their stock with the seasons and the supplies on the markets. It was noted that,

> they look in at Billingsgate, and if the supply runs short they are off again to Covent Garden, for they deal in everything, and the barrow that one morning you see filled with fresh herrings, the next is blooming with plums. If, on the contrary, a large cargo of sprats comes suddenly into London, or if soles should be unusually plentiful, it is known in an incredibly short space of time all over the town, and they flock to the markets in thousands....[35]

Greengrocers, fruiterers and fishmongers selling from shops dealt mainly in the best quality. The shopkeepers and a few of the costermongers who had middle class trades, were the first buyers in the day at the wholesale markets. When they had withdrawn prices for small lots fell and the ordinary costermongers began buying.

At Billingsgate fish market, the wholesale trade with costermongers was controlled by 'bommerees'. Bommerees were either salesmen specializing in the costermonger trade, or salesmen who had sold their consignments to shopkeepers and were buying and selling on speculation. More rarely, the bommeree was a speculating shopkeeper or costermonger.[36] We have seen that in the early nineteenth century fish supplies were irregular, and in these circumstances a major function of the bommeree was to hold stocks and even out market prices. But by the 1820s supply was more predictable and the bommeree's main task was to break bulk into volumes and qualities suitable for retailers serving the widely differing market areas of London.[37]

[34] Ibid., J. 350-4.
[35] 'Commissariat of London', op. cit., p. 276, and Dodd, *Food of London*, p. 364.
[36] Mayhew, *London Labour*, i, 21.
[37] 'Commissariat', p. 275, and Dodd, *Food*, p. 349.

Shipments of fish to Billingsgate were continuous throughout the day, but at the fruit and vegetable markets supply was bunched into the early morning hours. The salesmen, or higglers, evened out supplies through the day and held stocks for the 'bye days' when few growers attended market. Higglers received consignments from growers who were unable to attend market or doubted their selling skill on the market floor. The growers who attended the market preferred to sell their produce in bulk early in the morning in order to leave London promptly. Costermongers preferred to buy directly from these growers and would frequently club together for bulk purchases.[38] Those outside the clubs bought from growers who decided to remain longer in the market in order to sell in smaller volumes but at higher prices than could be had by bulk sales. Costermongers might also buy from regular salesmen and from costermongers outside the clubs who had enough working capital to make bulk purchases. Mayhew claimed to know one costermonger who bought enough fruit and vegetables each day to supply thirty street dealers.[39]

John Babbington's diary confirms and adds to many of the points made by Mayhew and others. On his first day as an independent costermonger, he rented a barrow for 1s. 6d. a week and,

went to Covent Garden market bought 3 bushels of pears which I sold the same day making a profit of 4s. 6d....The next morning again to the garden but being what is called a bye morning there were but few country growers present. I had therefore to purchase my first of one of the regular salesmen in the Market and only made a profit of 2s....[40]

Salesmen had a poor reputation among the costermongers. Their prices were higher than those of the growers, and they were generally believed to be dishonest. Babbington complained that they sold

baskets so closely resembling the honest bushel basket that it requires a sharp eye to tell the difference yet they hold from one to two gallons of fruit less than what we call the honest growers bushels

[38] Mayhew, *London Labour*, i, 68.
[39] Loc. cit.   [40] *Autobiography*, J. 356.

do and when a salesman receives a consignment of say 100 bushels of fruit he will take 50 to fill 40 of the short bushels...put a thick wad of straw at the bottom then fill them with fruit thus making 60 or 62 bushels of the 50...he will then mix them with the other 50 that has not been meddled with...[41]

One can sympathize with Babbington's distrust, for 'many a poor coster after getting up at 3 o'clock in the morning going to Market and dragging a heavy load about the streets all day often till 10 at night has not been able to earn a single farthing ... and sometimes be money out of pocket. ... '[42] On his own the costermonger was in a weak position as a buyer in wholesale markets, and awareness of this weakness led increasingly to bulk buying in clubs.[43]

The prices for most manufactured goods in this period were high relative to the incomes of the bulk of the population. This remained true until mass production prevailed in the consumer goods industries, and until increases in labour productivity raised the mass of working class incomes. It is not surprising, therefore, that much labour time was expended on maintaining the existing stock of consumer goods and arranging for the redistribution of cast-offs from higher to lower income groups. The urban and suburban areas of the country were scoured by men and women looking for discarded manufactured goods. If the collector did not refurbish and retail the goods himself, he sold them in used goods markets, (such as was held at the Islington horse and cattle market on Fridays or the Rag Fair near Tower Hill) or to second-hand shops.[44] Lewis Isaacs, the proprietor of the Houndsditch clothing market, explained that it was,

a receptacle for every article that is collected in London and its environs...they are brought there day by day, and sold to parties who are called 'forestallers'; and many of them are sent to Holland; many to America, and many are sent to Ireland; some are turned and manufactured; some of the old garments are made into caps

[41] Loc. cit.

[42] Ibid., J. 357. Mayhew also remarked upon the bitterness of feeling between salesmen and costermongers, *London Labour*, i, 67.

[43] For Manchester see Folio, *Hawkers*, p. 130.

[44] Whittock, *Complete Book of Trades* (1837) pp. 142–3.

and others boys' jackets. The old shoes are sold to Northampton manufactuers to work up again.... [45]

The Houndsditch market and others in London and the provinces were used by the street dealers as wholesale supply centres. [46]

Street hawkers did not, of course, deal only in used goods. Their stocks of new manufactures were bought in retail shops, 'swag shops' and 'slaughter houses'. Many shopkeepers would not deal with the street hawkers, but some did, if then rather surreptitiously. A Bristol draper in the 1830s found

> that when we showed whole pieces of fresh goods, we often attracted a new customer in the shape of a hawker, or a small shopkeeper, who would come in and ask if we would sell them goods at a lower rate than our usual retail price, for them to sell again. This we were quite willing to do.... [47]

By selling wholesale to hawkers, shopkeepers took a share in the trade to the poor without incurring the costs involved in the minute division of bulk which the poor required and demanded. As the Bristol draper remarked, with a note of amazement, 'Hawkers and those who served hawkers used to buy packages of sheet-pins, which an army of beggars hawked about the streets and the country. ... '[48] A major disincentive to trading with hawkers, however, was that they lowered the 'tone' of the shop and gave offence to the better class of customers. The Bristol draper 'laid down the rule that all this kind of trade was to be done before eleven o'clock in the morning'. But this proved inconvenient to hawkers living outside the town, and eventually he fitted up a back room with a separate entrance to handle all trade sales.

The 'swag shop' was a specialist wholesale house for hawkers and small shopkeepers, while the 'slaughter house' sold both wholesale and retail. The distinction between the two was not

[45] *B.P.P.*, Select Committee of the House of Lords Appointed to Consider the Bill Intitled 'An Act to prevent unnecessary Trading on Sunday in the Metropolis'; Mins. of Ev., 1850 (441) xiv, Q. 316.

[46] See J. Greenwood, 'The City Rag Shop', *Saint Paul's Magazine*, xii (1873) 655–61.

[47] Anon., *Reminiscences of an Old Draper* (1876) p. 144.

[48] Ibid., p. 146.

always clear, but the swag shop proprietor bought on regular order while the 'slaughterer' bought on speculation, mainly from local tradesmen.[49] In London around 1850 there were some 150 swag shops, mainly located in areas frequented by hawkers, especially in the East End and around New Cut. The largest London swag shop employed about two hundred salesmen, buyers, clerks, travellers, packers and porters, and its weekly receipts were reported to be £3000. But the typical swag shop did only about £500 business in a year.[50] The general swag shop stocked items like figurines, mugs, pincushions, gaming boards, necklaces, brooches, clocks and watches, musical boxes, shirt studs, tea trays, razors, shaving brushes and strops, knives, brushes, pens, pencils, tea pots, tableware and tools.[51] There were also swag shops which specialized in such things as Birmingham and Sheffield goods, crockery and haberdashery; but these specialist shops and the larger swag shops sold to shopkeepers and exporting merchants, and were hardly to be distinguished from general wholesale houses.

5. The Country Trade

The country itinerant trade can be classified into the suburban 'round', where both foodstuffs and manufactured goods were traded by city based hawkers, and secondly the long country excursion, where the itinerants dealt only in manufactured goods.

Costermongers based in the cities made regular suburban rounds extending from two to thirty or more miles from the central markets. Around London, the most frequented, to the south, included Wandsworth, Richmond, Kingston, Guildford and Farnham. A popular round to the north included Kilburn, Edgware, Watford and Barnet. London costermongers went into Kent as far as Maidstone. Similarly, in the North, 'Dollopers' travelled around the suburbs of Manchester and Liverpool and out to the surrounding Lancashire and Derbyshire towns and villages.[52] Contrary to what might be expected, railway development facilitated the suburban hawkers by

[49] Mayhew, London Labour, i, 333.
[51] Ibid., p. 334.
[50] Mayhew, London Labour, i, 336.
[52] Folio, Hawkers, p. 131

extending the geographical range within which they could sell perishable goods. Frequently, they walked into the country and had their loaded carts sent down by rail. Country coster-mongers also travelled into the cities for supplies. Mrs Hills of Epping recalled that as late as the 1870s James Hills, a fish seller, 'walked to Billingsgate market for his supply, returning with the boxes of fish on his head'.[53] In the same period, Lancashire costermongers travelled into the city markets for supplies and returned by rail with their loaded carts.[54]

The long country excursions were made by Cheap Johns and numerous petty hawkers working the markets and fairs in the spring to autumn months. The Cheap John was by far the most important of the licensed hawkers, and was generally recognized as the 'prince' of the itinerant traders. A man who worked as a Cheap John in this period recalled that 'A Man that travels as a Cheap John is thought nothing of as a master unless he has at least £100 worth of goods ... a good horse, and a good carriage'.[55] He was the son of a Portsmouth butcher, and went to work as a 'journeyman Cheap John' in the 1830s. After three years as an apprentice he began on his own at Birmingham 'by buying a few goods and standing in Birming-ham fair selling from off a pot-crate. ... ' In London, shortly after, he bought a pony and cart from a costermonger and began travelling to markets in the south east:

I used to go out with a lot of goods on the Wednesday to Romford Market, on Thursday to Bishop Stortford, Friday to Chelmsford, Saturday to Colchester, Monday to Hadleigh, Wednesday to Bury St. Edmunds, Thursday to Diss, and on the Saturday to Norwich.[56]

Within about eighteen months he was able to buy a big, covered cart and a strong horse. This enabled him to undertake longer trips, particularly to the circuit of fairs held in the spring and autumn.

There were few itinerant traders who prospered as quickly and substantially as this anonymous Cheap John, and there is

[53] *Recollections of an Epping Victorian*, p. 30.
[54] *Royal Commission on Market Rights*; Mins. of Ev., Q. 4788.
[55] Charles Hindley, ed., *The Life and Adventures of a Cheap Jack* (1876) p. 2.
[56] Ibid., p. 33.

little reason to doubt the accuracy of his high regard for himself. The secret of his success he believed to be cash buying:

I can state, as a positive fact, that I have sold thousands upon thousands of pounds sterling of goods to shopkeepers in Brighton and its immediate neighbourhood cheaper than they could buy the same class of goods, and of the same manufacturer, my experience and ready money, or short payments, being the talisman.[57]

He also revealed his considerable skill in selling. In or near the big cities he sold mainly 'sixpennies', such as pocket knives, spoons and other small items which could be conveniently carried away. But 'at country fairs everything sells—bridles, saddles, whips, guns, padlocks, saws, etc. ... '[58] He suggested that his profits were never less than 20 per cent or never more than 40 per cent, and generally around 30 per cent. Since he sold by auction from the cart, larger profits were occasionally made by persons 'snapping before we got down to the lowest price we meant to take. ... '[59]

In the winter months earnings were low in country areas and the roads very bad. Cheap Johns commonly moved into the towns in the winter and set up shops. In January and February 1839, for example, the Coventry Market Tolls committee rented the 'Mayors Parlour' to Mr James Withy, a licensed hawker, at 30s. a week. The Cheap John would stock the shop with the lighter Birmingham and Sheffield goods and 'by the aid of a few paper flags and silken bannerets, and a large musical box or two' make the shop as attractive as possible. The 'bazaar' trade, as these winter 'pitches' were known, was steadily weakened, however, by the growth of fancy goods shops and the fact that,

there no longer remains the chance or opportunity...of getting a closed-up shop in a good position, which I reckon as a sure indication that business...is much better and at all events more firmly fixed than it was twenty to five-and-twenty years ago.[60]

Moreover, this Cheap John foresaw that railroad development was enabling wholesalers 'to despatch their representatives to all the principal towns for the purpose of supplying the shops

[57] Ibid., p. 312.   [58] Ibid., p. 26.
[59] Ibid., pp. 28-9.   [60] Ibid., p. 209.

with the very description of goods that Cheap Johns had almost
a monopoly in. ... '[61] He noted that,

> there are now shops in most large cities and towns where the same
> description of goods can be obtained by the working and lower
> middle classes, that even in my time could only be had at the annual
> fair of a small town or village, and on market days in cities and
> boroughs. All this I could see must inevitably happen, and was the
> reason of my relinquishing the travelling part of a Cheap John's
> life, and determined me...for the then future to serve the same goods
> over a counter instead of from the cart....[62]

There were probably less than a thousand substantial Cheap
Johns in England in any year in the first half of the century.
The more typical figure in the country trade was the petty
hawker, wandering from town to town selling light hardware,
toys and any other goods he could buy and thought he could
sell. John Babbington was forced into country hawking by the
cholera epidemic of the late 1840s. The fruit trade fell off sharply
and in June he decided to leave London for the country. It was
a wet summer, and 'Fair after Fair, Market after Market did I
stand in the drenching rain ... without taking a single penny
and in ... dread of the tollman coming for his toll for they must
be paid no Matter where or how you get it. ... '[63] He arrived
in Birmingham with only 1½d. and slept rough that night. The
following morning he earned 6d. by holding a farmer's horse
and went into a swag shop to buy a 'lot' of tin cups and saucers
which he had seen in the market. The cups were 9d. a dozen
and since he had only 7½d. the proprietor agreed, with reluctance, to break the dozen on Babbington's assurance that he
would return for the remainder. He then went into the fair,

> and taking the paper my little stock was wrapped in spreading it
> on the ground laying out my goods to the best advantage began to
> shout about a wonderful Chinese ship having been wrecked off the
> coast of Cornwall. I had received a large supply of silver-plated
> cups and saucers that had been fished up from the bottom of the
> sea but as they were liable to be seized by the excise ... I was there-
> fore compelled to keep the bulk in hiding and bring out a few at a
> time which I was offering to the intelligent public of Birmingham at

[61] Ibid., p. 315.
[62] Ibid., pp. 329–30.   [63] *Autobiography*, I. 377.

the enormous sacrifice of one penny a cup & saucer just to ensure a quick sale to save them from the clutches of the excise-men etc.[64]

No one would believe such a tale: it was part of the hawker's 'patter' which everyone expected. But by eleven in the evening Babbington had turned his 7½d. into 6s. 9d. On the following day he found a number of hawkers at the swag shop buying the same cups and so switched his stock to a lot containing a £5 Bank of Elegance Note, a sheet of songs, two rings, a scarf, a thimble and four other items:

I purchased half a gross of these then went to a herring shop bought a penny hearing [sic] box fastened a piece of string to it placed the string over my shoulder so as to carry the box in front of me I then got a sheet of blue paper to cover the box & then set out my goods and entered the fair and was even more successful because I started with a better stock and on the close of the fair on Saturday night was master of a sovereign. ...[65]

Babbington travelled through England until December when he returned to London 'a richer man by many pounds than I left it'. But whether one gives attention to the articulate rationality of the anonymous Cheap John, or observes the behaviour of a Babbington (the goods he sold and how he sold them) it is clear that the itinerant country dealer was being pushed into an increasingly marginal role. It is significant that Babbington, as an older man in the 1860s or 1870s was again reduced to hawking at country markets and fairs, but on this occasion was unsuccessful and returned to London to live off the charity of middle class philanthropists.

6. *The Itinerant Tally-Trade*

The typical itinerant trader turned-over stock quickly and sold for cash. Since most hawking was characterized by the distribution of low-cost goods and the breaking of bulk into small units—packets of pins and matches, for example, were broken open and their contents sold in units—retail credit facilities were not necessary. But there were goods which it was impossible to retail in small units without destroying their use value, and other commodities with unit prices which were higher than

---

[64] Ibid., J. 379.   [65] Ibid., J. 379.

most of those sold by itinerants. This was true of cloth and clothing, for which there was a larger working class demand than for any other manufactured commodity. Petty hawkers did carry on a cash trade in used clothing, where unit prices were low, and in haberdashery, where bulk could be effectively broken down into small units. But new cloth for making-up into dresses, shirts and other clothing articles had to be sold in larger units, and cash sales for these were difficult to arrange.

An itinerant trade in new cloth and clothing became possible only when the principle of small unit sales was abandoned for that of small instalment payments. This required that the hawker had a command over a larger capital than was typical in the itinerant trade, and that the hawker's itinerancy be restricted to a small area with a stable population, or at least one where debtors' movements could be observed.

The 'tally trade', where goods were delivered upon agreement that small, regular payments would be made, dated back at least to the eighteenth century,[66] and was most common in sales of cloth and clothing. The tallyman concentrated his trade in a comparatively small area in order to minimize the travelling time lost between houses where sales were made, goods delivered and instalments collected. He had a regular round which he visited at least once in a fortnight. He sold by pattern and delivered the goods on the next round, a procedure which freed him from taking out a pedlar's licence.

Tallymen were the subject of much debate in this period. McCulloch argued that they were mainly thieves preying on the ignorance of housewives; drapers argued along much the same lines; and the courts would not prosecute tally debtors with the same savagery that was accorded to other debtors.[67]

It is no doubt true that tallymen persuaded women to buy goods they could not afford; that 'earnings, which ought to be expended in the purchase of useful and durable garments' was 'thrown into the bags of these panderers to vanity';[68] and that

[66] See W. Owen, *The Tradesman's Director, or the London and Country Shopkeeper's Useful Companion* (1756) p. 61.

[67] See J. R. McCulloch, 'The Tally Trade', *Dictionary of Commerce*, ii, pp. 1110–1, and the letters from 'Leeds Draper' and 'Diss Draper' in *The Clothier and Draper*, i (1859) pp. 10–11 and 42–3.   [68] 'Leeds Draper', ibid.

many, if not all, sold indifferent goods at high prices. The system of weekly payments, while on the one hand making it possible to reduce bad debts, also provided the tallyman with the opportunity of selling other items to the customer and keeping him in perpetual indebtedness. By working a neighbourhood and knowing it intimately, the tallyman used the existing network of social relations (kinship and friendship links) both to sell goods and control debts. Because of the hostility of the courts, the tallyman depended upon personal rather than legal controls over his customers.

If consumer's were exploited by tallymen, how did the trade survive? To some extent, the tallyman exploited a niche which exists in some poor communities to this day.[69] The poor consumer could not buy on credit at the better shops, and poverty makes it impossible to save over long periods for cash purchases. The poor were left choosing between the credit shops and the tallyman, and frequently the choice was not a real one as tallymen worked directly or in association with shops. Shops sometimes employed or worked with tallymen because, as Mayhew noted, it was difficult to get the poor into the shop. By employing tallymen the shop, in a sense, was taken weekly or fortnightly to the consumer, where the tallyman could see what goods the customer might be persuaded to buy, could develop and exploit a more personal relationship, and could capitalize on those subject to impulse buying.

The tally trade had its defenders.[70] Some, it was argued, never dealt in lucklow checks, ribbons, expensive accessories and steam prints, but limited their stocks to useful prints, dresses, stuffs, calicoes, linens, flannels, blankets, carpets and ready-made clothing. The same relationships which some tallymen exploited could work to protect the consumer. Since the tallyman worked a regular area, he was known in the area and his sales, to some extent, depended upon local confidence in the goods he sold and the prices he charged. However closely he watched his customers he ran a real risk that customers would default and that the courts would not back his claims.

[69] See Caplovitz, *The Poor Pay More.*
[70] J. Foster, 'The Tally System v. the Drapery System', *Clothier and Draper,* ;(1859), 42-3.

Moreover, by insisting upon regular, small payments the tally-men introduced a discipline into credit trading which was too often absent in shops.

7. Conclusions

Before the late eighteenth century, the itinerant retail trade was predominantly a rural trade. The itinerant carried manufactured goods from centres of production and wholesale distribution into rural areas and satisfied requirements for manufactures which were not locally produced. Country areas were, however, much better provided with shops and transport and communications facilities in the early nineteenth century, and by 1850 the country itinerant trade was visibly in decline. Its decline, however, was parallelled by the growth of urban itinerant trading as London and provincial towns and their surrounding areas began to grow rapidly. This was most marked in food retailing, as residential areas became increasingly distant from central markets. With female employment and long working hours, costermongers provided, at low cost, an essential service by extending the distribution functions of the retail markets into the factory and residential streets.

The costermonger was more flexible than the shopkeeper in switching from one commodity to another with seasonal and daily changes in market supplies. A fruit salesman at Spitalfields market commented that,

there are many of our customers who deal in fish and other things, and if they can retail fish and other things with more profit to themselves, they will not buy apples, and the consumer goes without them; so that we do not sell sometimes when they are very cheap so many as we do when they are a better price. ...[71]

But cheap fruit was neglected only when fish or some other foodstuff was cheaper still. As James Briggs, the solicitor for Spitalfields market, explained some years later,

the greengrocer carries on an entirely different business from the costermonger. A greengrocer buys a limited quantity; he only buys what he can sell, whether the price is high or ... low, and then he will buy any amount. So that it is the interest of the greengrocer to

[71] *Select Committee on the Fresh Fruit Trade*, Q. 719.

sell a few goods at a high price, but it is the interest of the costermonger to sell a great quantity of goods at a low price.[72]

Until the end of the century, when imported foodstuffs began
to modify sharp seasonal fluctuations in market supplies, the
flexible itinerant distribution was the most efficient means of
clearing supplies on the markets. In shops, adjustments to
market supplies were slower, if only because it was necessary
to provide some stocks for consumers who were indifferent to
price relatives. Moreover, high fixed costs in shop retailing
required that turnover and revenue did not fluctuate too
radically in different seasons of the year. Shops for fruit,
vegetables and fish were few in London and elsewhere (outside
retail markets) before 1850, and then they catered mainly for
the wealthier classes.

The itinerant trader's place in the distribution of manufactured goods to the working class was less secure than with
foodstuffs. Few itinerants had enough capital to stock and
distribute the more expensive manufactured goods, and among
the working classes the demand for them was weak in any case.
Apart from matches, blacking, brushes, the lighter Birmingham
and Sheffield goods, used clothing, and haberdashery, unit
prices were high relative to working class spending power, and
it was difficult to break bulk into small units for cash sales. The
tally trade was a partial adaptation to this situation, but for the
most part it is probably incorrect to represent the tallyman as an
alternative, with respect to price and cost, to the working class
shops. In contrast to much food retailing, the level of supply
and demand for manufactures was more regular throughout
the year and shop distribution was therefore more viable.
Shopkeepers held larger stocks with wider choice than the
itinerant could offer, and shop stocks were better protected
from deterioration. While the shop-tally trade connection tried
to modify this, consumer purchases of manufactures were
occasional rather than daily, and as consumer suspicion and
fear of shops diminished with familiarity, the convenience of
street and door distribution became less important than the
choice and prices available to the consumer moving from shop

[72] *Royal Commission on Market Rights*, Q. 1508.

to shop. When working class demand for manufactured goods expanded in the second half of the century, it was the shop-keeper rather than the itinerant who profited most, whereas the erosion of the itinerant's place in food distribution was much longer in coming. At no time in the early nineteenth century did the itinerant retailer have a truly secure hold on working class demands for simple manufactures, since the general shop, as well as the specialist shop, was an important distributing point for candles, blacking, household chemicals, hardware, crockery and cloth and clothing.

PART III

Shop Retailing

IV

The Growth of Shop Retailing

IT WAS accepted by political economists of the early nineteenth century that retailing from fixed shops was becoming, if it had not yet become, the dominant form of distribution. There were two assumptions which were never, in fact, tested: (1) that the absolute number of shops was growing; and (2) that the share of the fixed shop in the total volume of retail sales was increasing at the expense of other forms of retail distribution. In this chapter we will attempt some quantitative tests of these assumptions. The first is relatively easy to test; the second is impossible to test directly as it requires statistical data relating to total retail trade volumes and shop sales volumes over time, and this data is impossible to compile.

The most obvious, but unfortunately not the most satisfactory, source of statistical data on shop growth is the occupation abstracts of the decennial census returns. The 1841 occupation abstract provided data for calculating the numbers of people employed in shops, but it underestimated the numbers employed in itinerant distribution. Moreover, in many key trades, such as ironmongery and tailoring to name only two, the shop was a manufacturing centre as well as a distribution point, and hence the census cannot tell us how many man hours were devoted to distribution activities alone. The 1851 census marked an improvement from our point of view in that a distinction was made between 'masters' and 'men', which makes it possible, at least roughly, to calculate the number of shops in existence at that date, although it does nothing to disentangle production, processing and distribution activities in those shops, and does not allow comparison with earlier decades.

The least unsatisfactory approach to the problem is through the trade directories. The best continuous series of national directories was issued by James Pigot and his successor Isaac

Slater.[1] Pigot completed his first national survey in 1823 and fresh surveys were made in 1828–31, 1831–40, 1841–7 and 1848–51. Unfortunately, the London series was abandoned in the 1830s and the firm gradually restricted its activities to northern England, Wales and Scotland.

An attempt to test the first hypothesis—that the number of shops was growing—was made by selecting eleven cities and towns in England and Wales and, at roughly decennial intervals, counting the numbers of tradesmen listed in the major consumer goods trades. The cities and towns selected include four of the largest population centres—London, Liverpool, Manchester and Leeds—five towns which contained around 50 000 people by 1851—Norwich, Bolton, Leicester, Nottingham and Merthyr Tydfil—and two cathedral cities, York and Carlisle, which contained less than 35 000 inhabitants in 1851. If the hypothesis is true, then a growth in the number of shops should be reflected in these towns.

The results of this count are recorded in Tables A:1 to A:11 in Appendix I. Their interpretation is made difficult by several factors, involving the firm's accuracy and problems of classification. The Pigot directories were renowned for their accuracy and consistency, but it is likely that techniques of enumeration had been improved in the 1850s over techniques used in the 1820s. If this is true, then the tables in Appendix I would have an upward bias. Secondly, there is some evidence that the quality of the surveys lapsed in the 1840s. The 1846 survey of Liverpool (A:2) is not reliable, and the quality of the 1841 surveys of Manchester (A:3), Leeds (A:4), Leicester (A:7) and Nottingham (A:8) are perhaps also open to question. Thirdly, it is probable that the city surveys were less comprehensive than the town surveys where accuracy would be easier to obtain. Fourthly, there are a number of problems concerning classification. The imperfect degree of trade specialization made classification very difficult, particularly in smaller towns. The census commissioners encountered the same problem and reported in 1841 that the 'hatter would figure in the list as

[1] J. E. Norton, *Guide to the National and Provincial Directories of England and Wales* (1950) wrote that Pigot's 'great series of country directories has no rival during the early part of the 19th century', p. 43.

draper, grocer, bookseller, or shopkeeper, according as he might prefer one name to the other'.[2] Similarly, in Pigot's directories, tradesmen listed as grocers in one survey might be listed as shopkeepers or provisions dealers in the next, and this could lead to fluctuations in category totals which bore no relation to real changes in the town's trading structure. But Pigot did attempt to come to terms with this problem in a rational way. In the early directories he introduced multiple categories, such as 'Haberdashers and Glovers'; and in addition he listed tradesmen by their principal line of business with their subsidiary trades noted in brackets. In later surveys these two approaches were abandoned in favour of multiple listings. It was impossible, as a result of this later method, to eliminate double counting from Tables A:1 to A:11, but random checks suggest that the upward bias is not serious. For reasons of economy, Pigot limited the number of multiple listings, and in the early 1830s he introduced the category 'Shopkeepers and Dealers in Groceries and Sundries' to group all shops where trade specialization was not very developed.

Tables A:1 to A:11 list, at roughly decennial intervals, the principal consumer goods trades in eleven towns and the total number of tradesmen producing and/or distributing in those trades. These totals suggest that contemporaries were correct in stating that there was a rapid growth in the number of fixed shops.

Table 4:1 is a *first* approach to isolating the *retail* trades (as defined at the bottom of the table) and calculating the per cent increase in the total number of shops in nine of the towns (London and Carlisle excluded) between 1822 and 1848–51. These calculations indicate a per cent increase in shops ranging from a high of 855 per cent at Merthyr Tydfil to a 'low' of 100 per cent at York. As we have suggested, the calculations in Table 4:1 may be subject to an upward bias, since enumeration techniques in 1848–51 may have been better than in 1822, and double counting errors are also possible. In 1822, moreover, the directories did not have the category 'Shopkeepers and Dealers in Groceries and Sundries', and while many general shopkeepers were probably listed under other categories, it is

[2] *B.P.P.*, *Occupation Abstract*, p. 8.

possible that the smallest were not entered in the directories. The rates of growth suggested by Table 4:1, however, are too large to be attributed simply to bias in the data.

TABLE 4:1. Per cent Increase in Number of
Retail Shops,[1] 1822 to 1848–51 (to nearest 5%)

Town	% Increase Shops	% Increase[2] Population
Merthyr Tydfil	855	165
Manchester	645	140
Bolton	425	90
Leeds	370	104
Nottingham	350	42
Liverpool	345	100
Leicester	300	135
Norwich	150	36
York	100	60

[1] The calculations exclude all tradesmen listed in the directories as manufacturers or wholesalers, and all provisions merchants, leather workers (except saddlers), cigar merchants and dealers and working jewellers. Since we are concerned with *shop* trades, it has been necessary to exclude also butchers, fishmongers, fruiterers and greengrocers, many of whom no doubt were retailing from markets rather than from shops.

[2] Population estimates are from Mitchell and Deane, *Historical Statistics*. Estimates of population at inter censual years is calculated on the assumption that decennial increases were evenly distributed within the decade.

Table 4:1 suggests that the percentage increase in the number of shops in these towns was much larger than the per cent increase in population. Table 4:2 presents a calculation of the population per retail shop in 1822 and in 1848–51 for the same nine towns, employing the definition of 'shop' used in Table 4:1. In 1822 the ratios range from 1 shop to every 340 people at Merthyr Tydfil to 1:55 at York. In 1848–51 the ratios were more favourable[3] in every case. At Merthyr the ratio had improved, or 'risen', from 1 shop for every 95 persons to 1:35 at York and 1:30 at Nottingham, while deviations from the mean for all towns were much smaller at the later date.

The definition of 'retail shop' used in the calculations for Tables 4:1 and 4:2 can be questioned, and at a later point the

[3] The use of the word 'favourable' and its negative does not, of course, imply a value judgement with respect to shop retailing and other forms of distribution.

tables will be recalculated on a narrower definition. They do suggest, however, that the rate of growth of shops, and the ratio of shops to population, was not the same in all the nine towns, although the data used in the calculations certainly distorts real differences in growth rates, since the enumeration of tradesmen in the 1822 directories was probably less satisfactory than in the 1848–51 series. But there is no reason to believe that the size of the distortion is the same in each town. For example, we can assume that the enumeration of bakers, butchers, shoemakers, tailors and milliners at Merthyr in 1822 (Table A:9) is seriously in error, while the enumeration of the same trades at York (Table A:10) is more satisfactory. At least some of the enormous difference in the calculated growth rates of shops in the two towns must be attributed to these relative errors. The calculation of the population per shop (Table 4:2) might be distorted in another way. The population figures used

TABLE 4:2. Population per Retail Shop[1] 1822 and 1848–51 (to nearest 5)

Town	1822	1848–51
Merthyr Tydfil	340	95
Liverpool	135	80
Bolton	200	70
Leeds	180	70
Manchester	175	55
Norwich	100	55
Leicester	80	45
York	55	35
Nottingham	95	30

[1] Population is calculated as in Table 4:1; and retail shop is defined as in Table 4:1.

in calculating this table were drawn from census data, but the trade directories surveyed a trading area which did not necessarily correspond to this administrative district. Again, there is no reason to assume that the resulting distortion would be the same in each town. For example, it is possible that tradesmen at Leicester, York and Nottingham did a large business with residents of surrounding villages, and that the real ratios of shops to population were closer to those calculated for Liverpool, Bolton and Leeds.

However, there are no valid reasons for assuming that shop growth rates and ratios of shops to population would be the same for all towns. With respect to the former, rates of population growth differed among the towns and one might therefore expect rates of shop growth to vary accordingly: in fact, the coefficient of rank correlation in Table 4:1 (0.66) is acceptable at a 95 per cent significance test in demonstrating a strong relationship between percentage increases in shops and population. With respect to the latter, in old and established towns an increase in population might result in larger average turnovers in existing shops, with only a small net increase of new shops. In an emerging industrial town, based on a village nucleus, a similar rate of population growth might require a larger net increase of new shops to provide services for which there was an insufficient demand in the old village. The ratio of shops to population might be lower in a big city than in a medium sized town because the former was better serviced by itinerant traders. It is also possible that there were significant differences among towns in the average size of shops, measured by turnover. Only the cities, for example, had the mass markets which encouraged experiments in large scale retailing. It is very likely, moreover, that there were different levels of *per capita* consumption among towns, and therefore differing patterns of demand for high cost (shop) distribution services. These are variables which it is impossible to measure, but their possible effect can be illustrated through a contrast of Merthyr Tydfil and York.

Table 4:1 indicates that the highest percentage increase in shops between 1822 and 1848–51 was at Merthyr (855 per cent); but table 4:2 indicates that in both 1822 and 1848–51 the town had the least favourable ratio of shops to population (1:340 and 1:95). Merthyr grew rapidly from an obscure village in the late eighteenth century into a town and a surrounding population of some 17 000 in 1822. Between 1822 and 1848–51 the rate of population growth at Merthyr was higher than in any of the other nine towns, and in 1850 Merthyr and its surrounding area contained some 45 000 people. In 1822 (Table A:9) the town had few shops and these were only partially specialized. As late as 1850 the directories did not distinguish between grocers, tea dealers and general shop-keepers. There were few tradesmen in 1850 dealing in jewellery and toys, luxury foodstuffs and clothing.

By contrast, York experienced the lowest percentage in-crease in shops (100 per cent) among the nine towns, and its rate of population growth (60 per cent) was also comparatively low. But Table 4:2 suggests that in both 1822 and 1848 it enjoyed the most favourable ratio of shops to population (1:55 and 1:35) of all towns except Nottingham. York, unlike Merthyr, was an old and established cathedral city. There was little industry in the area, and the compilers of the 1848 directory noted that 'the principle trade ... is retail, which is generally pretty brisk, supported by many genteel and opulent families resident in York and its respectable vicinage'. Table A:10 shows that York shops were numerous and highly specialized in both 1822 and 1848. There were large numbers of booksellers and stationers, the drapery shops were distinguished between woollen and linen cloth, and there were specialist lace dealers, hosiers, hatters, poulterers, game dealers, silversmiths, jewellers and toy dealers.

In 1851, then, Merthyr and York were towns roughly equal in size; but the number, range and quality of retail shop facili-ties was very different. These differences can be attributed in part to the relative sizes of the towns fifty years earlier, their rates of population growth, and the small middle and upper class consuming groups at Merthyr. The contrast between the two towns suggests that we should not expect the distribution of shops in particular towns to conform closely in all cases to some calculated mean for the country as a whole.

Although it is now clear that contemporaries were correct in assuming considerable growth of retail shops, the second hypothesis (that shops were increasing their share in total retail sales) cannot be confirmed directly. But the improved ratios of shops to population indicated in Table 4:2 does provide some support for the hypothesis, although it is possible that average shop turnovers fell drastically with their growth in numbers.[4] But at this point it is essential to reconsider our

[4] Given the growth of neighbourhood and back-street shops, such a possibility cannot be dismissed out of hand. But at the other end of the scale, the period also

definition of 'retail shop' in order to give more assurance that what we are counting is an expansion of retail shop outlets and not shopcraft production. In Tables 4:1 and 4:2 butchers, greengrocers and fishmongers, among others, were excluded from the calculations on the assumption that many of those listed were probably market retailers. But there are reasons for excluding other trades in a search for a more 'pure' quantification of retail traders. Thus, the master tailor's business often comprised a retail woollen drapery trade, a retail trade in made-up clothing, and a bespoke tailoring trade. But it is probable that many of the tailors listed in the directories (especially in the cities) were outworkers for tailoring and clothing shops with, at most, a small bespoke trade. Much the same argument applies to the millinery trade, and the boot and shoe makers. Each of these trades was strongly represented in Tables A:1 to A:11, and while they all had retail distribution elements, they were not purely retail trades and their exclusion would give more heuristic power to the calculations.

With these trades excluded the growth indicators are recalculated in Tables 4:3 and 4:4, which should now have a

TABLE 4:3. Per cent Increase in Number of Retail Shops,[1]
1822 to 1848–51—Recalculated (to nearest 5%)

Town	% Increase Shops	% Increase Population
Merthyr Tydfil	584	165
Manchester	500	140
Leeds	315	104
Liverpool	305	100
Bolton	305	90
Nottingham	270	42
Leicester	240	135
Norwich	130	36
York	75	60

[1] The calculations exclude all trades excluded in Table 4:1 and tailors, milliners, dressmakers and shoemakers.

saw the emergence of department stores and small multiple shop concerns. These matters are discussed at a later point in the chapter.

TABLE 4:4. Population per Retail Shop,[1] 1822 and 1848–51
—Recalculated (to nearest 5)

Town	1822	1848–51
Merthyr Tydfil	400	145
Liverpool	170	110
Leeds	225	100
Bolton	210	95
Norwich	135	80
Manchester	195	75
Leicester	115	75
York	70	60
Nottingham	130	50

[1] Retail shops are defined as in Table 4:3.

downward rather than upward bias. Table 4:3 continues to show a significant percentage increase in retail shops in all towns between 1822 and 1848–51.[5] It is only at York that other errors and biases could upset the hypothesis that shop outlets grew faster than population. Table 4:4 indicates that the improvement in the ratio of shops to population remained significant in all towns except York, where the ratio was already low in 1822. It would seem very likely, therefore, that there were shop retail trades which underwent significant growth in this period, and an important task is to isolate which trades these were.

The category 'Shopkeepers and Dealers in Groceries and Sundries' was the largest single category in all towns (London excluded for lack of data) in 1851. In Table 4:5(A) column 1, shopkeepers are calculated as a percentage of all shops, including shoemakers, tailors and milliners.[6] At Bolton, the general shop in 1851 accounted for as much as 34 per cent of all shops thus defined, and a mean in all towns of about 24 per cent. The specialist tea dealer, the grocer and tea dealer, and the provisions dealer were high class specialists in almost the same market. In column 2 these trades are combined with general shopkeepers. As a group these shops accounted for as much as 44 per cent of all shops at Bolton and as little as 24 per cent

[5] The rank correlation coefficient for the two variables in Table 4:3 rises to 0.77.
[6] In other words, as we initially defined retail shops in Table 4:1.

at Leicester. In 4:5(B) the same calculations are made excluding shoemakers, tailors and milliners.[7] On this basis the general

TABLE 4:5. General Shopkeepers, Grocers and Provisions Dealers[1] as a
per cent of all Retail Shops, 1848–51

(A) Excluding trades as defined in Table 4:1			(B) Excluding trades as defined in Table 4:3		
	(1)	(2)		(3)	(4)
Town	General Shops	Grocers, Provisions, and Shopkeepers	Town	General Shops	Grocers, Provisions, and Shopkeepers
	%	%		%	%
Bolton	34	44	Merthyr	—	62
Merthyr	—	40	Bolton	46	59
Manchester	26	40	Carlisle	42	52
Carlisle	29	36	York	40	50
Leeds	27	33	Leeds	38	47
York	25	31	Manchester	37	46
Liverpool	15	28	Nottingham	37	46
Nottingham	22	27	Leicester	31	41
Norwich	18	27	Liverpool	22	39
Leicester	19	24	Norwich	27	38

[1] The combined category (columns 2 and 4) is comprised of grocers and tea
dealers, tea and coffee dealers, provisions dealers and shopkeepers.

shop (column 3) accounted for 46 per cent of all shops at Bolton
and some 22 per cent at Liverpool, and for the combined
grocery and provisions trades (column 4) the range went from
62 per cent at Merthyr to 38 per cent at Norwich.

In the general shopkeeper category the evidence for growth
of retail shops is very strong. Tables B:1 to B:10 in Appendix II
indicate that the ratio of general shops to population improved
between the early 1830s and the 1850s in all towns except
Liverpool, Manchester and Nottingham.[8] In these towns,
however, the problem is one of classification rather than
differing development, as the deterioration in the ratio was small
and the tables indicate an improvement in the ratio of grocery

[7] In other words, as re-defined in Table 4:3.
[8] There are no figures for London in the 1840s and 1850s, and thus Table B:1
is excluded from the analysis.

shops to population at Manchester and provisions shops at Nottingham and Liverpool. Excluding Liverpool, the ratios ranged from a high of one general shop to 300 people at Norwich to a low of 1:130 at Nottingham. The mean ratio in the eight towns was about 1 general shop for 210 people.

The 'Grocers and Tea Dealers' were the larger and better class shops retailing only a limited range of sundries in addition to grocery stocks. Interpretation of the growth trend is difficult since, to some extent, it was arbitrary whether a tradesman was listed as grocer, provisions dealer or shopkeeper. But in six of the eight towns the ratio of grocery shops to population deteriorated between the early 1830s and 1850s. At Carlisle, York, Leicester and Nottingham the ratio ranged from 1 grocery shop to 450 people to 1:620 in the early 1830s, and from 1:765 to 1:850 in the 1850s. The specialist tea dealers, retailing mainly to the middle and upper classes, were comparatively few in most towns. In 1848–51, on average, there was about 1 tea dealer's shop to 4000 people, except at York (1:1880) and Liverpool (1:8775).

Evidence of a growth in the better class shop trade in groceries is not, then, very strong. Growth in this trade seems to have been concentrated among the class of small, general shops serving the working class with provisions, household sundries, cloth and clothing. In all towns in 1851 the ratio of these general shops to population was more favourable than any other category.

Among the shopkeeping food trades, bakers were only marginally less numerous than general shopkeepers. In all towns there was an improvement in the ratio of bakery shops to population between the early 1830s and 1850s, except at York (where there was a significant growth in confectionery shops) Leicester (where there was no significant change) and Bolton. In the smaller towns the ratio was low in 1851, ranging from 1:345 at Nottingham to 1:850 at York. At Liverpool, Manchester, Leeds and Bolton the ratios were over 1 shop for 1000 people; and it is possible that these higher ratios in industrial cities reflect larger production units and retailing through general shops.

The cloth and clothing trades were second in importance

only to the food trades. Tables A:1 to A:11 show that the manufacturing tradesman was the most important figure in the clothing trades; but the enumeration of shoemakers, tailors and milliners in the early surveys was too erratic to sustain useful inter-decennial analysis. In 1851 the range in the ratio of boot and shoemakers to population was as low as 1:160 people at Nottingham, and only as high as 1:770 at Bolton. But the output of footwear in a town was not consumed exclusively by its inhabitants. Bootmakers hawked their products at markets in surrounding towns and villages, or exported to shops and warehouses in larger cities. It is probable, moreover, that a large number of bootmakers listed in the directories were outworkers with only small retail or bespoke trades; and repairs to old footwear were prominent in the production time of the typical shop.

In 1851 the ratio of tailors to population was slightly less favourable than the same ratio in the footwear trade. Ratios ranged from a low of 1:335 people at York to a high of 1:925 at Liverpool. Man hours devoted to producing a unit of clothing were probably less than for a unit of footwear. The conceptual problems involved in defining the footwear trade as a retail trade applies equally to tailoring and millinery.

The most distinctly retail shopkeepers in the clothing trades were the slopsellers and clothes dealers. There were few shop traders in ready-made new and used clothing in this period. At Manchester the ratio of clothes shops to population is calculated to have declined from 1:5980 in 1822 to 1:8190 in 1851; at Leeds, a future centre of the clothing industry, from 1:7325 to 1:9555. At Bolton, however, the ratio showed an improvement from 1:8250 to 1:6780; at Liverpool from 1:4813 to 1:2646; at Norwich from 1:4645 to 1:2345; at Leicester from 1:9165 to 1:3170. At Carlisle, Nottingham and York, the ratios in 1848–50 were 1:2770, 1:2690 and 1:1995 respectively. The calculations indicate some improvement in most towns in the ratios. New and used clothing was also retailed from general shops, drapery and tailoring shops. It is possible that there was a trend towards acceptance of ready-made in this period, which accelerated after 1850 when it became technically possible to organize a mass production clothing industry.

The drapery shop was one of several trades involved in the retail distribution of textiles. Heavy cloth for outer-wear was also retailed from tailoring shops; millinery shops dealt in a range of drapery and smallwares; and general shops sold all kinds of cheap drapery and haberdashery. At Liverpool the ratio of drapery shops to population in 1822 was 1:1375, but by 1851 this had deteriorated to 1:2440. There was, however, a marked improvement in the smallware group, the ratio changing from 1:8000 to 1:2410. There was a similar trend at Norwich, Bolton and Nottingham. At Leicester the drapery shop ratio deteriorated from 1:1250 in 1822 to 1:1770 in 1850; and at York from an improbably low ratio of 1:475 to 1:970. At Leeds the ratio of textile outlets to population was more favourable than the figures for drapery shops alone would suggest; but in general the figures do not indicate any growth in the ratio of drapery shops, strictly defined, to population in this period.

The food, clothing and textile shops dominated the shopping streets in these days. The demand for retail shop services in other trades was reduced by the generally low level of consumption. In all towns except Leicester and Carlisle there was a small improvement in the ratios of stationery and book shops to population, though at Leeds, Norwich and York the improvement was not significant. The mean ratio for such shops in 1848–51 in the nine towns was about 1:2600 people.

All towns recorded an improvement in the ratio of chemist shops to population, apart from York where the change was marginally unfavourable. Excluding the suspiciously low figure for Nottingham in 1850, the mean ratio in the eight towns was about 1 shop for 1720 people.

The calculations for the glass and pottery trades are very erratic. At Liverpool, Norwich and York the ratio was less favourable in 1848–51 than in 1822, while a significant improvement was calculated for Leeds and Bolton. At Leeds, however, the ratio was still very high in 1851 (1:7165) and also at Liverpool (1:5770). Excluding Leeds, the mean ratio for the eight towns in 1848–51 was about 1 shop to 3600 people.

Specialist cutlery shops were very rare in provincial towns, and the comparatively low ratios calculated for Norwich and

Leicester in 1850 and 1851 probably include more general hardware shops. Outside the larger cities little distinction was made between hardware and ironmongery shops; but at Liverpool, Manchester, Leeds, Norwich and Bolton in 1848–51 the mean ratio of hardware shops to population was well over 1:10 000 people. Ironmongery was a more important trade, but with the exception of Nottingham there is no evidence that the ratio of shops to population underwent significant improvement in this period. In 1848–51 the ratio was as low as 1 shop to 3100 people at Carlisle and as high as 1:7165 at Leeds. In the nine towns in 1848–51 the mean ratio was about 1 shop to 4300 people, but deviations from this mean were significant.

Retained imports of tobacco in the U.K. showed an actual *per capita* decline between the late eighteenth century and the mid-nineteenth century;[9] but in several towns the tables indicate a significant improvement in the ratio of tobacco shops to population. This improvement probably reflects the growth of neighbourhood shops styling themselves tobacconists but retailing a wide range of food and household goods.[10]

The retail trade in candles and soap was concentrated in grocery and general shops. The tallow chandler's shop was primarily a production centre and this is reflected in the high ratios of shops to population in most towns. Toy dealers, jewellers and silversmiths served higher income classes, and the number of these shops in any town was very small.

Tables A:1 to 11 and B:1 to 10 indicate there was a significant growth in the number of general shops, measured both in absolute terms and by ratio to population; but the evidence of growth in terms of population is not strong in other retail trades. Since the general shop dealt in the whole range of normal consumer needs this growth is important in two ways. We have noted the cultural factors which oriented working class people towards the market and itinerant traders, and away from shops. The general neighbourhood shop, however, acted as a socializing institution by breaking down these prejudices and educating the recently urbanized consumers in

[9] See Mitchell and Deane, *Historical Statistics*, Ch. xii, table 6.

[10] See the testimony of Edward Peacock of Islington in, *B.P.P.*, *Select Committee on Sunday Trading* (*Metropolis*); Mins. of Ev., (666) ix, Q. 1952.

the techniques and style of shop trading. In other words, the social gap between the market and itinerant traders and the neighbourhood shopkeeper was less wide than between those institutions and the established High Street shopkeeper. In addition to performing a useful economic function, the general shop acted as an educative bridge for working class people into the more formal, bureaucratic High Street shops. Secondly, the growth of the general shop suggests that a larger percentage of the total volume of retail sales was being effected in fixed shops. It is probable that this was true, although the possibility cannot be ignored that the emergence of many small shops served only to reduce the average turnover in all shops. Conversely, the evidence is not strong of significant growth in terms of population in the better class and more specialized shops, but the possibility cannot be ignored that the average turnover in all shops increased in this period.

It is impossible to prove, one way or the other, whether average shop turnovers rose or fell. There is evidence, however, of the emergence of multiple shop retailing and large-scale single shop retailing in the cities.

The share of the multiple shop in the total volume of retail trade in this period was insignificant. The success of multiple shop trading depended upon a spacial separation of production and distribution functions, an advanced systems of communications and transport, and a supervisory staff upon whom trust could be placed on grounds other than kinship.[11] None of these factors was sufficiently developed in 1850 to support a large multiple system. But tradesmen with shops in big towns very often extended their operations to neighbouring towns and villages, if only temporarily and from a market stall or the back of a wagon.[12] The most common multiple shop concern in this period consisted of a main shop in a market town or large village with satellite shops in surrounding villages. The satellite shops were staffed by relatives, partners and trusted shopmen, and were supplied from the central shop in order that the system might be under the direct control of the tradesman. For example, in 1822 and 1823 William Holmden operated two

[11] This was especially important in a situation of unlimited liability.
[12] See the *Reminiscences of an Old Draper*.

small general shops, one at Milton and the other at Leeds in
the county of Kent.[13] In the same decade James Bowles, with
his principal shop at Balsham, operated a second grocery shop
in a neighbouring village, which was under the immediate
control of his sister.[14] Partnership agreements might also lead to
the establishment of multiple shop concerns. For example,
Aaron and William Penley in the 1820s divided the responsibility of managing two stationery shops at Portsea and
Portsmouth.[15] It is probable that the firm of Poole and Alderton, furnishing ironmongers, divided the management of their
Dover and Folkestone shops in 1848 between the two partners.[16]

In Tables 4:6 and 4:7 multiple addresses in the Liverpool
and Manchester trade directories have been interpreted as
indicating multiple shop retailing. On this assumption the
number of multiple shop firms rose from 16 in 1822 to 127 in
1851 at Liverpool, and from 15 to 88 at Manchester. In both
towns multiple shops were most common among grocers,
bakers and chemists. A large majority of these tradesmen,
however, listed only two addresses, and it is possible that we are
counting lock-up shops and residences rather than multiple
outlets, or a storage warehouse and a retail shop. But there were
tradesmen listing three and more addresses, and we can be
more certain that these were genuine multiple shop concerns.
For example, at Liverpool in 1846 a firm of bootmakers was
listed as having four outlets; in 1846 and 1851 a firm of grocers
was listed as having five outlets.

Multiple shop concerns which operated in several distant
towns were rare. The fashionable London shops operated
branches in spa towns,[17] but they were, in effect, merely
following their London customers. In the 1850s George
Summers, a boot and shoemaker enjoying royal patronage,
operated two shops, one in Bold Street, Liverpool and the second
at Eastgate Row, Chester.[18] In 1822 a firm of chemists operated
a shop in Liverpool and a second shop on High Street in
Birmingham; and in 1841 a firm of Liverpool drysalters

[13] Public Record Office, Court of Bankruptcy, B.3. 2330.   [14] Ibid., B.3. 649.
[15] Ibid., B.3. 4112.
[16] Advertisement in *Hand-book to Folkestone*.
[17] See A. Adburgham, *Shops and Shopkeeping* (1964).   [18] Hughes, *Chester*.

TABLE 4:6. Firms with two or more Shop Outlets—Liverpool

Trade	1822	1834	1846	1851	Note Refer.
Booksellers, Stationers	0	1	2	3	1
Chemists, Druggists	1	5	4	11	
Boot & Shoe makers	2	3	12	5	2
Clothes Dealers	0	0	4	3	
Haberdashers, Smallwares	0	1	2	2	
Hatters	0	0	3	4	3
Hosiers & Glovers	0	2	3	1	
Drapers	1	3	2	0	
Tailors	1	1	2	2	4
Bakers	0	9	12	20	5
Confectioners	0	1	3	9	6
Butchers	0	5	0	6	
Cheesemongers	0	1	0	0	
Fruiterers & Greengrocers	0	0	0	1	
Grocers & Tea Dealers	3	6	21	29	7
Tea Dealers	0	2	7	8	8
Shopkeepers	0	0	0	3	
Provisions Dealers	1	5	5	11	
China & Earthenware Dlrs.	1	2	2	0	9
Ironmongers	2	3	3	1	10
Drysalters	2	0	0	1	
Pawnbrokers	2	0	3	4	
Tobacconists	0	2	1	2	11
Toy Dealers	0	1	1	1	12
Totals	16	53	92	127	

[1] One of the 1846 firms had 3 outlets.

[2] One of the 1846 firms listed 4 outlets.

[3] One of the 1846 firms listed 3 outlets.

[4] One of the 1834 firms listed 3 outlets.

[5] One of the 1846 firms listed 3 outlets; a second 4 outlets. In 1851 3 firms listed 3 outlets and 3 listed 4 outlets.

[6] In 1851 one firm listed 3 outlets.

[7] In 1846 3 firms listed 3 outlets, 1 firm 5 outlets, also in 1851.

[8] In 1846 one firm listed 5 outlets; in 1851 2 firms listed 3 outlets and 1 firm 5 outlets.

[9] A third firm was listed as Thomas and John Carey, Manufactories at Land End and Lane Delph, Staffs.

[10] One firm listed 3 outlets in 1846.

[11] In 1839 one firm listed 3 outlets.

[12] The 1834 firm was Kendall & Son discussed in the text. The firm is not listed in the 1846 directory. In 1851 one firm had 3 outlets.

TABLE 4:7. Firms with two or more Shop Outlets—Manchester

Trades	1822	1834	1841	1851	Note Refer.
Booksellers, Stationers	1	1	2	1	
Chemists, Druggists	2	1	8	5	1
Boot & Shoe Makers	0	0	4	6	
Clothes Dealers	0	0	0	1	
Haberdashers, Smallwares	0	1	0	1	
Hatters	1	1	2	1	
Hosiers & Glovers	0	1	1	5	2
Milliners & Dress Makers	0	0	0	2	
Tailors & Drapers	0	1	2	5	
Bakers	2	7	8	21	3
Cheesemongers	0	0	0	1	
Confectioners	0	1	1	4	4
Grocers & Tea Dealers	5	5	12	19	5
Tea & Coffee Dealers	1	1	3	4	6
Provisions Dealers	0	3	0	0	
Shopkeepers	0	0	5	2	
China & Earthenware Dlrs.	1	0	2	1	
Ironmongers	0	2	1	2	
Drysalters	1	3	2	0	7
Pawnbrokers	0	0	1	0	
Silversmiths & Jewellers	1	1	1	2	
Tobacconists	0	0	3	4	
Toy Dealers	0	0	2	1	
Total	15	29	60	88	

[1] One firm in 1822 was also on High Street, Birmingham.

[2] Two firms listed 3 outlets in 1851.

[3] In 1834 one firm listed 3 outlets; in 1841 2 firms listed 3 outlets; and in 1851 2 firms listed 3 outlets.

[4] In 1851 one firm listed 3 outlets.

[5] In 1841 one firm listed 3 outlets; in 1851 one firm listed 3 outlets.

[6] In 1841 1 firm listed 3 outlets; in 1851 3 firms listed 3 outlets.

[7] In 1841 one firm listed a Liverpool address, a second firm listed a Glasgow address.

operated a second shop in Glasgow.[19] In 1834 Kendal and Sons, a firm of toy dealers and cabinet makers, operated shops on Lord Street in Liverpool, Market Street in Manchester, Foregate Street in Worcester, in New Street and Lombard Street in Birmingham, and on the Strand in London.[20] In the early 1850s a firm of clothiers advertised that they had

[19] See Table 4:6.   [20] Loc. cit.

'numerous establishments' in 'some of the principal towns in the country' and stressed the advantages to customers of the firm's central buying policies.[21]

The small multiple shop concern, operating in a city or a town and its surrounding area, was fairly common in the third and fourth decades of the century. But the few concerns which for a time secured representation in the principal towns did not have lasting success.

The large-scale shop, unlike the small multiple shop concerns, did have a significant impact on retail trade in the cities. There were gradations in the size of retail units in every trade, but the 'monster shop', as it was then known, was confined to drapery and related trades.[22] As early as 1821 it was noted that some of the London drapers 'transact daily, so much business, as almost to exceed belief ... we have known persons in this line, whose receipts have averaged five hundred pounds per day, for a long time. In such a shop twenty or thirty persons, or more, are constantly employed. ... '[23] In 1833 Thomas James, an important City wholesaler, said that 'some very large establishments (have) grown up in the last few years, and business perhaps is more concentrated in large establishments than it was some eight or 10 years ago'.[24]

It is possible to identify some of these big drapery shops. In Glasgow, James and William Campbell opened a drapery business in the Saltmarket in 1817, moving to larger premises on Candleriggs Street in 1825. They introduced there a system of fixed prices and cash sales, and built-up one of 'the first of those monster retail houses that are now to be found in nearly all the towns of any note in the kingdom'. By 1850 Messrs Campbell was the largest wholesale/retail firm in Scotland, with annual turnovers of over £1M a year and employing around 300 people.[25]

[21] Advertisement for Harrall & Co. in P. Whittle, *Blackburn*.

[22] Drapery goods, compared with the situation in most other trades, were received almost ready for sale, requiring little processing from the retailer.

[23] Anon., *The Book of English Trades and Library of the Useful Arts* (New Ed., 1821) p. 193.

[24] *B.P.P.*, *Select Committee on Manufactures, Commerce and Shipping*; Mins. of Ev., Q. 1414.

[25] (J. D. Burn?), *Commercial Enterprise and Social Progress* (1858) pp. 105–7.

At mid-century, Shoolbred and Co. of Tottenham Court Road in London was the largest retail drapery firm in the country. The firm boarded and lodged 500 employees and its annual turnover ran into the millions of pounds. In the emerging ready-made clothing trade, Hyam Brothers and Moses and Sons of London were the pioneer firms.[26] Lewis Isaacs, himself a clothier and draper on a big scale, said that the working class purchased from these shops 'a pair of shoes for 8d., or 1s., purchase a shirt for the same sum, or a coat for 2s.', that 'they will buy a handkerchief for 1d. or 1½d.' and 'there is something like £400 000 or £500 000 turned over in a year in the very articles I have spoken of'.[27] In Manchester in 1839, it was claimed, several retail firms enjoyed sales over £1M per annum,[28] and in Dublin in 1850 there were four big drapery firms dating back to the founding of Harvey & Co. in 1827.[29] It is not true that urban mass markets were unexploited until the last decades of the nineteenth century: this widespread assumption is based largely on the failure of these early giants to survive into the twentieth century.

In all these big drapery and clothing shops, goods were arranged in departments. Usually, sales assistants had sales books in which they entered the number and amount of the sale. The sales slip and the cash was then taken by a porter to a central desk in each department where the transaction was posted and the discharge returned to the customer.[30] Basically, the system was not unlike that used in many big stores today. In the big Dublin shops, and no doubt elsewhere in Britain, each department had a manager; the daily receipts of the department were recorded and banked in the central office at the end of the trading day. Each department had travellers making monthly trips to Britain and the Continent.[31]

In Dublin 'the principal supporters of the large shops are servants, workpeople, and ladies; or in other words, the class in the community who have the least money to spend, the class who attach the greatest importance to small differences of

[26] Ibid., p. 56. [27] *Lord's Committee on Sunday Trade*, Q. 356.
[28] *Manchester As It Is*, p. 200. [29] Burn, *Commercial Enterprise*, p. 105.
[30] (R. Kemp?), *The Shopkeeper's Guide* (1853) p. 7.
[31] Burn, *Commercial Enterprise*, p. 188.

price'.[32] The big shops bought on cash or short term credit and sold in volume on small margins. W. N. Hancock estimated that the big shops turned their stock about four times in a year as opposed to about three times among smaller tradesmen. Fixed prices in the big shops raised labour productivity (measured by sales volume) by four to ten times that of smaller shops.

The impact of the big shops on retail distribution in Dublin is suggested by the protest meetings organized by small shop-keepers in the 1850s.[33] Whether similar protests were organized in England is not known, but Hancock claimed that the smaller English shops had met the competition by introducing fixed prices, cash sales, and achieving better stock control. The small shop, he argued, could successfully compete with the large establishment by offering a wider choice in a narrower range of goods, and by providing warm, personal service.[34] It is interesting and important to note that the question of the survival of the small, independent shop had already been raised by the mid-nineteenth century.

[32] W. N. Hancock, *Is The Competition Between Large and Small Shops Injurious to the Community?* (1851) p. 23.
[33] Burn, *Commercial Enterprise*, p. 187.   [34] Hancock, *Competition*, pp. 15–16.

V

Shop Tradesmen and their Craft Skills

IN THIS chapter we will examine some of the key shop trades within the food, cloth and clothing and durable goods groups, detailing the range of stocks which were held, sources of supply, the development of specializations and the importance of production and processing in the retail shop. In the following chapter we will examine in a more analytic fashion the social and economic organization of work and trade in shops.

A. THE FOOD AND HOUSEHOLD STORES TRADES

Food and household stores accounted for the major share of weekly family expenditure, but probably less than half of the national expenditure on these products was channelled through shops. Industrial and agricultural labourers bought most of their meat, vegetables and household stores in markets and from itinerant dealers. Fruit, vegetable and fish shops were comparatively rare, outside big cities, and the grocer-shopkeeper and the baker were the main shop retailers in the food trades. The High Street grocer served mainly the middle classes, the tradesmen and skilled workmen, and what the poorer classes did not buy in the streets and markets, they bought from the back-street shopkeepers and general dealers.

The food trades can be distinguished for analytical purposes between the more purely retail and the producer/retail types. Butchers and confectioners may be defined as producer/retailers on the grounds that the materials they purchased underwent a radical transformation for retail sale. But even in the more purely retail food trades, such as grocery and household stores, the tradesman's processing responsibilities were very heavy. Moreover, in many shops it was impossible to distinguish them as being mainly retail or producer/retail in structure. For example, a general shop in Epping in the 1870s was still heavily involved in production of stock for retail sale. Bread was made in a bakehouse in the yard and delivered to customers in Epping and surrounding villages. Hanging in the shop were

joints and sides of pork, hams, bacon etc., and mixed between them were slabs of 'flare' (pig fat). Under the counter were brick pans filled with pork in salted water and sold as 'salt pork'. Our people kept their own pigs at the back of the premises and killed them there, and so it was home-fed pork which was sold....

The shop produced its own sausages, blood puddings, saveloys, brawn, cooker pork, pigs' trotters, and sweet puddings. The latter

was made of stale, soaked bread, with plenty of raisins and 'foot' sugar and sold in penny and ha' penny pieces; quartem bread tins of cake, made of sugar and lard rubbed in dough, with plenty of currants, and sold in penny and ha' penny pieces.

The shop window contained baskets of home-grown straw-berries and baked pears:

My grandfather had large gardens hence plenty of pears. These were cut in lengths and put into brick pans, covered with cold water with plenty of 'foot' or moist sugar, and cloves, and sold over the counter, in saucers, for one halfpenny or even a farthings-worth.

Confectionery was made for sale in the shop: 'A marble slab was fitted on one of the kitchen tables, with a long bar overhead to throw the sweet conglomeration over. This was pulled down and cut into different kinds of sweets.'[1] In addition to these production activities, the shop also retailed groceries, crockery and household stores. As in this shop, production functions in association with retailing were very common in the smaller towns and villages. The size of the market made small scale production and compound trading desirable; but in the larger centres there was a trend in this period towards the separation of production and distribution activities.

[1] Hills, *Epping Victorian*, pp. 2–4.

1. *The Grocer and Shopkeeper*

In the grocery trade, initial processing was done by the whole-saler. A visitor to a Bristol wholesale grocery warehouse noted:

Here they are breaking up tierces of sugar, and mixing the different kinds. There, they are weighing flour. In this corner, you find a man before a solid heap of currants, which stubbornly retains the form of the cask, belabouring it with an instrument. ... Here, they are with an order-book, making up the items of an order. There, they are weighing and packing. In a central position, an inspector is placed in a counting house glazed on all sides, from which he can look out on the whole stream of business. ... In another place, you find a monster coffee-roaster in full play. Again, you are in a room where some half dozen kinds of tea are ready to be tasted by one of the principals.[2]

But in this period the wholesaler's principal function was to break bulk, and the retailer was responsible for the ultimate blending, sorting, cleaning and packaging for retail sale. This meant that the quality of goods sold could vary widely between two grocers buying from the same wholesaler. To fulfill these processing functions, the grocer was obliged to equip his shop with a wide range of weights and scales, shovels, scrapes, scoops, sieves, breakers, mills and wrapping materials.[3] The processed goods would be held in bulk in drawers, bowls, jars and canisters, and normally all packaging was done at the time of sale.

A survey of the major items of stock will provide a clearer understanding of the specific trade skills demanded of grocers. Tea was certainly one of the major commodities in which they dealt. While classification was subject to frequent redefinition, in our period green teas were normally classified into Imperial, or Bloom, Hyson and Singlo and black teas into Souchong, Cambo, Congou, Pekoe and Bohea. Within each category there were further classifications with respect to quality. For example, a Colchester grocer in the 1840s issued a sale catalogue which

---

[2] W. Arthur, *The Successful Merchant: Sketches of the Life of Mr Samuel Budgett* (2nd ed., 1852) pp. 11–12.

[3] See the inventory of equipment held in the Coventry shop of Joseph Ward in the 1830s, at Public Record Office, B.3. 5366. (Hereafter all references to the P.R.O. bankruptcy files will be shortened to read, B.3. 123...).

offered Congou, good Congou, fine Congou and finest Congou, with similar gradings for other black and green varieties.[4] The range of teas stocked by a grocer would vary, of course, with the incomes and tastes of his customers. Although teas were sorted into their respective classifications long before they reached the retailer's shop, at the very least the grocer needed some understanding of the various grades in order to buy wisely from the wholesaler. But in the better class of grocery shop customers expected knowledgeable advice and many grocers developed their own blends.[5]

Coffee was also subject to complex classification. Mocha, or Turkey coffee, imported from the Red Sea area, enjoyed the highest reputation; East Indian the next best, and West Indian and Brazilian were regarded as very inferior. The Colchester grocer's stock was further divided into fine, finest and very old Mocha, Plantation fine and finest, Ceylon fine and fine raw.[6] Retailers could buy already roasted beans from wholesalers and coffee roasters, but the high class tradesmen usually assumed roasting responsibilities himself. It was a highly skilled function, for if the bean was overheated it lost much of its potential flavour. By the 1840s grocers were offering their customers a type of 'instant' coffee sold in bottles as 'essence of coffee' and advertised as 'a convenient preparation for making Coffee instantly, by the addition of boiling water'.[7]

Much of the retail market for sugar was for sweetening tea and coffee. Sugar was sometimes sold by grocers as a 'leading item' to attract custom for complementary products, and they might refuse to sell sugar without a purchase of one of the beverages, especially if they suspected the customer was buying his teas from itinerant dealers.[8] As with the beverages, grocers faced processing and packaging responsibilities with sugar. In the West Indies sugar was boiled down into a moist brown substance which was retailed in Britain as raw or muscovado sugar. Raw sugar was further refined in Britain into loaves and lumps, the quality of each being determined by the number of

[4] Essex Record Office, T/P 160/2–4.
[5] Blending, of course, was too often synonymous with adulteration.
[6] Catalogue of stock, Essex Record Office, T/P 160/2–4.
[7] Loc. cit.   [8] Mayhew, *London Labour*, i, 455–6.

times which the raw sugar underwent refining. For example, a grocer's sugar stocks might be classified into good and finest loaf, and good, fine and finest lump. The refuse from the refining process was collected and formed into large loaves of cheap sugars known as 'bastards'. The syrup scraped from the refiner's moulds was sold as golden syrup and treacle, and these presented the retailer with many handling problems. For example, an entry in the diary of a Kent grocer for September 1809 read,

I was removing my Treacle Puncheon with my Iron Crew and in my hurry I set it most too Proud. It fell down and broke a $\frac{1}{2}$ Bushel Crock of Treacle and a fine Mess I had. But I got it up with a very little lost, say 3 or 4 lbs. The best way to draw Treacle off is to Tap it in the Bunghole, and draw as much out as you can, and then you can take out the Head without injury.

The moist raw sugar was wrapped in paper packets on sale, while loaf sugar had to be cut and pounded into granuals and finally packaged in sugar paper.

Cocoa imports in 1822 amounted to only 523 000 lbs., but consumption grew steadily throughout the century, mainly in the form of the cocoa beverage.[9] Brand names dominated the retailer's shelves before 1850: the Colchester grocer advertised stocks of 'Sir Hans Sloane's chocolate—the original and only genuine Article, manufactured by Messrs. Chambers and Lumby' and many products from Fry's, including soluble cake chocolate, soluble cocoa, dietetic cocoa, soluble chocolates in $\frac{1}{2}$lb. canisters, cocoa paste in $\frac{1}{2}$lb. jars and Fry's & White's Patent cocoas.

The high class grocer stocked many spices, such as mace, cinnamon, nutmeg, cloves, ginger, several grades of pepper, allspice, mustard, chilies, curry powder and arrow-root. They were purchased from the wholesaler in an unprocessed form and, where appropriate, they were ground, mixed and wrapped by the retailer. At this time, however, grocers were also stocking these spices in essence form, pre-packed in bottles for immediate sale.

The grocer's stocks of dried, foreign fruits and nuts might

[9] Burnett, *Plenty and Want*, p. 98.

include several types of plums, figs, dates, raisins, currants, oranges, lemons, pears and apples, almonds, chestnuts and Brazil nuts. By 1850 fruit merchants undertook some pre-packaging, especially in gift package form. But typically the retailer was responsible for final cleaning, sorting and packaging: as the Kent grocer wrote in his diary on 29 August 1809, 'I picked 2 Baskets Raisins of 112 lbs in 2 Hours and a half.'

Grocers dealing in 'Italian goods' stocked vermicelli, macaroni, tapioca, sago, gelatines and most carried groats, barley, flour and boiling and split peas. By the 1840s Italian warehousemen and grocers sold many pre-packaged sauces, some of which were nationally distributed and a few which are still available today, such as Lea & Perrin's Worcester sauce.

The household stores market was shared among grocers, tallow chandlers, oil and colourmen, chemists, ironmongers and hardwaremen. Soap was retailed in three basic varieties: white soap, which was sometimes perfumed and was prepared from olive oil and soda; yellow soap, a common household variety made from soda, tallow and resin; and soft soap, manufactured from fish oil and potash. Starch could be had from manufacturers in stove-dried packets, which might then be broken down for retail sale. The white and yellow soaps were sold in moulded bars or in cuttings from the bar, but the soft soap involved the retailer in many handling problems. Soft soap had an unpleasant lard-like consistency and was stored in bins to be scooped into a customer's container. Shrinkage in the volume of soft soap after sale was a common source of friction between tradesmen and their customers, for in the shop the soap would be kept in the darkest part of the cellar to reduce weight loss.

Grocers would normally stock oil for lamps, cleaning and polishing oils, linseed oil, currier's oil and many others. Candles of the moulded and dipped varieties were sold in many varieties. There were a few manufacturer-branded candles by mid-century, such as Clarke's & Field's and Price's Patent Belmont, but most were undistinguished as to origin.

Among the many sundry articles which the grocer might stock were alum, blacklead, blacking (with a few brand names, such as Day & Martin) brimstone, emery cloth, lamp black, lamp cottons, lucifers, sulphur, colour and paints, corks, carriage grease. There would also usually be a large stock of brushes for in-door and out-door use, brooms, cloths and mops.

Grocers' stock assortments varied with the market situation. A High Street grocer in a market town would stock in depth in the grocery and household lines; but where the market was small or the shopkeeper's trade was oriented towards the working class, his stocks would be horizontally rather than vertically distributed. Compound trading took two general forms. In the first, the grocer added a second major line to his grocery trade, most commonly drapery or drugs, which might be stocked in a depth comparable to the grocery lines. In the second case, he stocked groceries and very lightly over the fast moving items of several other trades. The Epping shop cited earlier is an example of compound trading in this sense, although the incorporated trades were mainly in the food line. But a Daventry grocer in the 1840s dealt in medicines, cutlery and crockery;[10] and a grocer at Eastchurch in the 1830s added ironmongery, crockery, medicines, stationery and clothing.[11]

Retail grocers drew their stocks from three sources: (1) specialist wholesale grocers, tea dealers and merchants, (2) manufacturer's and manufacturing tradesmen, and (3) wholesale/retail grocers.[12]

The largest wholesale grocery firms were located in London, Bristol and Liverpool, the major entry ports for groceries and provisions. These firms assembled stocks from importing merchants, sugar refiners, commission brokers and from other wholesale grocers. If they supplied general country shops the wholesale grocer would also hold stocks of medicine, household stores and even drapery and clothing. Bristol wholesalers tended to dominate the trade in the West Country, West Midlands and South Wales; Liverpool firms the North Midlands, North Wales and the North; but the biggest London firms supplied shops in most parts of the country. To give only one example, Denis, Lambert & Co., a City firm capitalized

[10] Northamptonshire Record Office, D. 2992.

[11] Records of Richard Sinden, Kent County Record Office, Q/Ci 147/1–4.

[12] It is possible to trace the channels of distribution by examining claim sheets filed in bankruptcy cases.

at over £30 000 trading between 1815 and 1829, sold to shop-keepers in Bath, Exeter, Birmingham, Leicester, Nottingham, Derby, Sheffield, York, Newcastle, and many other towns in the same regions.[13] Normally, the country retail grocer would minimize his transport costs by buying in the nearest wholesale centre, but services offered by wholesalers in more distant import centres might prove sufficiently attractive to overcome the transport factor.[14] For example, Thomas Dunlap, a grocer in Pontefract, bought mainly from wholesale grocers in Liver-pool but he also maintained accounts with London wholesale firms.[15]

The import merchant and specialist in fruit, cheese, tea, wines and provisions, organized supplies for the city wholesale grocers. They did not usually maintain staffs of commercial travellers, but the smaller import specialists would fill orders from retailers which were sent to them by post, although the bigger firms would only handle bulk orders. Retailers would usually have several accounts with import specialists in addition to their connexions with general wholesale grocers. For example, Edmund Bumpstead of Halesworth had accounts with several London oil, wine and orange merchants and an Ipswich cheese factor.[16]

Although many wholesale grocers stocked a wide range of sundry items, retailers placed many direct orders with local or regional craftsmen and manufacturers rather than pay middleman and transport costs from London, Liverpool or Bristol. For example, William Alcock of Fazeley in Stafford-shire bought his tobacco in Derby and his soap in Shrewsbury; Richard Rose of Sutton Valence in Kent bought his drugs from two Maidstone chemists; and William Towers of Nottingham purchased his soap in West Bromwich and his candles from a local chandler.[17] Other household stores were commonly bought from local colourmen, drysalters, ironmongers, and brush manufacturers. Grocers also went directly to the farms for stocks of eggs, butter, cheese, vegetables and fruit.

---

[13] B.3. 1454.
[14] 'Services' is used here to include frequent calls by travellers, price, discounts and credit terms, quality and choice.
[15] B.3. 1437.   [16] B.3. 791.   [17] B.3. 63, B.3. 4403, B.3. 5055.

It is possible that grocers' purchases from the city whole-salers were subject to seasonal fluctuations. Tea and grocery stocks in the country as a whole were lowest in the late summer before the arrival of the clipper ships, and heavy stock ordering might, therefore, have followed in the autumn. But the London dealers appear to have been at the centre of tea stock-holding at least, not the retail grocer: by the late eighteenth century the London dealers, who controlled most of the trade to the provinces, kept in their shops only enough tea to meet current demand, and the remainder of stocks purchased at the sales were left in the East India Company warehouses.[18] Evidence from remaining stock order invoices suggest that retail grocers did not order in large volumes at infrequent intervals but every fortnight or as their stock levels demanded. For example in 1813 Thomas Chapman's orders for his Lewis shop, placed with Toms & Hicks of Southwark, assumed the following pattern:[19]

Aug.	4	£138.	17.	4.
	18	19.	10.	2.
Sept.	15	64.	1.	2.
	20	162.	1.	2.
Oct.	16	31.	12.	0.
Nov.	17	84.	19.	9.
Dec.	20	175.	9.	6.

John Smith of Faversham who also dealt with Toms & Hicks placed orders more frequently than fortnightly, sometimes for very small amounts:[20]

Apr.	5	£18.	15.	10.
	21	78.	6.	0.
	28	17.	15.	0.
May	18	7.	18.	8.
	25	9.	11.	4.
June	10	99.	14.	1.
	24	5.	18.	7.
	29	86.	14.	3.

[18] H. C. and L. H. Mui, 'The Commutation Act and the Tea Trade in Britain', *Econ. Hist. Rev.*, 2nd ser., xvi, no. 2 (1963) p. 245.
[19] B.3. 898.   [20] B.3. 4541.

July 14	64.	14.	3.
28	42.	5.	0.
Aug. 18	51.	4.	0.

The frequency with which stock orders were placed no doubt varied with the distance of the shop from a major wholesale centre, but improvements in transportation and the development of commercial travelling was tending to equalize the situation for shopkeepers throughout England by mid-century.[21]

Stock orders might be placed by letter or through the wholesaler's commercial traveller. The growth of railways in the 1830s and 1840s allowed wholesalers' travellers to effect a more intensive and extensive penetration of the market; but throughout this period they strove to concentrate sales and economize on travelling time by largely ignoring the small shopkeepers. The latter depended upon the wholesale/retail grocer to fill small orders at frequent intervals. The account books of Jonathan Pedlar, a St Austell grocer, show that he had several accounts with small shopkeepers in the area in the early 1840s. One of these, a Mr Wakeauer, usually placed a weekly stock order with Pedlar ranging in value from £2 to £6; slightly bigger orders, ranging over lard, flour, bran, meal, tobacco and other goods, were placed at similar intervals by a Mr Elliot.[22] Similarly, Hannah and Thomas Biven of Mortlake bought groceries and household stores from tradesmen at Twickenham, Richmond and Brentford, and little or none from London wholesalers.[23] James Bowles, a shopkeeper at Balsham in Cambridgeshire in the late 1820s, drew all his grocery stocks from three Saffron Walden grocers.[24] While the major High Street grocers dealt mainly with the city wholesalers, they too might buy from regional wholesalers and, when confronted by time gaps between stock orders and deliveries from the city, place emergency orders with local tradesmen. Jonathan Pedlar's Inventory Account for the summer of 1840 indicates that he made purchases of this kind for £8 or less at a time. William

---

[21] The available information on rates of stock turn will be discussed in the next chapter.

[22] P.R.O., Chancery Master's Exhibits, C. 103, no. 82, 'Geach v. Pedlar', Account Book 'A'.

[23] B.3. 372.   [24] B.3. 649.

Alcock of Fazeley in Stafford spread his grocery orders among London firms and a Birmingham wholesaler, but he also maintained a small account with Hannah Boyes, another Fazeley grocer.[25] Thomas Bumpus was a substantial Northampton grocer in the 1840s: he drew the bulk of his stocks from London wholesale firms; but he also maintained small buying accounts with three other Northampton grocers.[26] The net effect of these widespread country wholesale/retail activities was to spread stock holding costs and to facilitate rapid movement of goods, locally and regionally, in response to unpredictable demand situations and delays in stock order deliveries from the cities.

A great deal of this country wholesaling, but not all of it, was *passive*, in the sense that the wholesaler was approached by the shopkeeper rather than the reverse, while sporadic *active* wholesaling might result from over-buying in job-lots. Job-lot buying, however, could lead to the development of a permanent wholesale trade of an active kind. For example, a draper at Bristol in the 1820s on one occasion bought an enormous job-lot of merinoes at a low price. There was no hope that he could sell even a substantial portion of them by retail and hence was forced into active wholesaling. He sold some to drapers he knew at Chatham and Merthyr, and then hired a horse and cart and instructed his shopman to call on small country drapers to encourage 'a fresh connexion for all kinds of general drapery goods that we sold' but 'to especially push this lot of merinoes'.[27] In the grocery trade, over-buying in tea, sugar, butter and cheese also developed into permanent, active wholesaling. For example, Samuel Budgett, who founded a wholesale grocery firm at Bristol with annual turnovers approaching £1M, was introduced to wholesaling when he over-bought sugar for his retail shop at Kingwood. He followed up his success in disposing of the sugar by making,

a modest sort of commercial journey; and among tradesmen to whom he would not venture to offer the higher articles of grocery, raised a considerable trade in such description of goods as he might supply without seeming to push into too important a sphere.

[25] B.3. 63.   [26] B.3. 741.
[27] *Reminiscences of An Old Draper*, pp. 150–4.

Budgett found his best customers to be 'the smaller dealers, who were overlooked by the wholesale houses and obtained supplies from their neighbours, who, though retail dealers, were so on an extensive scale'. By establishing a reputation among the small tradesmen, Budgett's business grew and by 1850 the firm's travellers sold throughout the West Country and as far north as Birmingham.[28] The more typical figures in country wholesaling, however, were men like the Bristol draper: they remained principally retail traders with a local wholesale connexion. By mid-century, however, the wholesale/retail dealer usually advertised himself as such, and the decline of job-lot buying meant that sporadic wholesaling by retailers declined—an indicator of a developing specialization of function.

2. *Butchers*

The retail trade in meat was dominated by the skilled, independent butcher who bought animals on the hoof, killed and dressed the meat, sold all cuts and disposed of wastes through industrial buyers. The country butcher bought his animals on the farm and at the cattle markets: for example, Joseph Collins a Brighton butcher in the 1830s dealt with several Sussex farmers, and William Blizzard, a Petersham butcher, dealt with farmers and salesmen at Southwell.[29] Butchers also bought and sold among themselves both live animals and dressed meat: Blizzard bought dressed meat from a Wandsworth butcher and Collins purchased calves from a Washington butcher. The city butchers also bought live animals on the farm as well as buying at cattle markets. Samuel Chappel, a London butcher in the 1820s and 1830s, purchased animals from salesmen at Islington, and it seems very probable that he dealt with at least one farmer.[30] The urban retail butcher could also purchase whole or quarter carcases from the specialist cutting butcher. The cutting butcher's function was to buy live animals, slaughter and dress the meat for wholesale sale to the retailers. Animal buying was a highly skilled task, since

---

[28] Arthur, *Successful Merchant*, pp. 145–55.   [29] B.3. 1228 and B.3. 505.

[30] Chappel bought animals at country cattle markets, but he also received loans from a country gentleman who possibly supplied him with animals.

mistakes in estimating the animal's weight and quality would result in serious losses. The functional specialization between the cutting and the retail butcher simplified entry into this growing trade in two ways: it narrowed the range of skills required of any one entrepreneur, and secondly, it reduced the capital required to enter the retail side of the trade.[31] City butchers who dealt in the whole animal and chose to dress the meat themselves rather than buy wholly- or partially-dressed meat from the cutting butcher, could also arrange to have the animal killed by specialists at the abattoir. Killing in itself was a highly skilled function as errors could spoil the meat, but this area of specialization also meant that the retailer could eliminate the cost of maintaining a killing shed. Samuel Chappel, the London butcher, utilized all of these specialized trades: he bought carcasses from several cutting butchers in Whitechapel and Newgate markets and spent about £45 a year to have animals killed for him at the abattoir.

The critical distribution problem was to dispose of cuts before the meat putrefied.[32] Market authorities were obliged to maintain a constant vigil over butchers' stalls since retailers had developed techniques for disguising signs of putrification. In the country trade, wastage was reduced to the extent that butchers shared animals by buying and selling cuts among themselves, and by extending their distribution range through regular attendance at markets in nearby towns and villages. In the cities, shop location introduced an income-demand factor which could make it difficult for the butcher to dispose of either the most expensive or the cheapest cuts from one shop. This problem was reduced by buying select cuts from carcass butchers; by selling cuts to butchers retailing for a different demand pattern; and by selling outside the shop through retail markets and street trading. For example, Samuel Chappell of London disposed of cuts to other butchers, to City and East End taverns and cook shops, and employed hawkers to sell in the streets and the street markets.

[31] Whittock, *Book of Trades*, p. 82.
[32] The importance of refrigeration in the meat trade is illustrated by the rise in the average number of weeks' stock held by butchers from 0.33 in 1932 to 0.61 in 1961. McClelland, *Costs and Competition*, Table VI/1, p. 126.

The butcher who killed his own animals had to find markets for the waste products. Normally, hides would be sold to tanners and leather dressers, and fats and other wastes to soap boilers and tallow chandlers. Joseph Collins of Brighton, for example, had an agreement to send all wastage to a Newhaven tallow chandler; but the problem could also be solved by moving into compound trading: in the 1850s a Staffordshire butcher hired skilled workmen and organized his own tallow chandlery business.[33]

The pork and the butcher's meat trades in the cities were usually distinct occupations. Samuel Chappel had a pork trade for some two years, but he carried it on in a separate shop from his butcher's trade. The city pork butcher bought killed animals from market salesmen and processed it into hams, salt-pork, bacon and sausage. It was said that in London in the 1830s 'so great is the sale of sausages by the porkmen, that many of them have a steam-engine erected to work the machinery used in cutting the sausage meat'.[34] In the country, pig-ownership was fairly common. Many households raised, slaughtered and processed their own pork meat, and it was not uncommon for general shopkeepers to carry on a trade in pork products.

3. *Provisions Dealers and Cheesemongers*

The emphasis of the provisions trade was on processed meats, dairy products and imported non-tropical foodstuffs. Provisions encompassed articles such as hams, tongues, hung beef, salt-pork, bacon, lard, butter, cheese and Italian warehouse goods. Until the 1870s the trade in imported meat and dairy products was small (apart from cheese) and in the first half of the century distribution of domestic processed foods was carried out mainly by market traders from the countryside, butchers, cheese-mongers and grocers. The retail provisions dealer emerged at mid-century in competition with grocers and superseding the old-established cheesemongers. It was not so much a new trade as a re-definition of the grocery trade or a formal recognition

---

[33] Staffordshire County Record Office, A. Hall, Butcher's Ledger, D688.
[34] Whittock, *Book of Trades*, p. 182.

of the compound trading in foodstuffs which many grocer-shopkeepers had pursued for decades. Thus, the tradesman defining himself as a 'grocer and provisions dealer'—a style which became increasingly more common—assumed responsibility for assembling a wide range of foodstuffs for regular stocks—items which the more traditional grocer might sell casually as an additional service. Consumer appeal for this broadened service led, in the second half of the century, to the eclipse of the better class but rigidly specialized grocer's shop.

The retail cheesemonger dealt principally in cheese, butter and bacon. It was one of the old-established food trades, but Tables A:1 to A:11 indicate that while it remained a specialist trade of some importance in London (which may account for the recognition given to it in various 'books of trades') it was rarely accorded separate classification in the provinces, outside Liverpool and Manchester.

The retail cheesemonger had to be knowledgeable with respect to the many varieties of cheeses and a sound judge of quality; but his processing functions were limited to cutting, weighing and packaging. These were functions which the broadened grocery and provisions trade easily absorbed in the second half of the century, relying upon the provisions merchant and wholesale grocer to break bulk and distinguish qualities by price.

4. *Bakers and Confectioners*

For many families bread was the most important article of food consumption, but home baking began to decline in the eighteenth century—sooner in the South than the North. In the South there was a fuel shortage, while in the Midlands and North rapid urbanization and factory employment led to greater reliance upon professional baking. Overcrowding of houses left many working class families without adequate baking facilities, while factory work militated against baking in the few leisure hours available to the working class family.

There were a few large bakery production units by 1850. At Birmingham and Carlisle (and earlier at Hinckley in Leicester) steam driven machinery was used to grind, sift and dress the flour and prepare the dough. The bread and biscuits produced by these firms were wholesaled to small shopkeepers in the working class districts.[35] There were also a few bakery shop chains, operated by millers and employing journeymen as their agents,[36] but production techniques were not affected by the capitalist ownership.

The bakery trade was dominated by the independent master baker, living, producing and distributing through the typical shop and house combination. The baker assembled fuel from coal merchants, flour from flour factors and millers, oil, salt, yeast and other ingredients from oilmen, drysalters and grocers. The turnover of the shop was measured in sacks of flour consumed and gross profits were calculated at so many shillings per sack. For example, James White, a Fleet Street baker, calculated that in 1827: 'From January to October last I consumed about 583 sacks of Flour and do consider the profit upon each sack to be about 8/0.'[37] Retail sales were concentrated mainly at the baker's shop, although some bakers sold from market stalls, wholesaled to small shopkeepers,[38] and employed hawkers to sell through the streets. In the country, grocer-shopkeepers often baked bread for sale. In 1838–40 Henry Stokes operated a bakehouse behind his grocery shop at Lympne in Kent.[39] In some bakery shops sales of pastry and other confectionery made substantial contributions to profits. James White's total gross profits for ten months in 1827 at his Fleet Street shop amounted to £400, of which profits on 'Pastry and small Goods' accounted for about 40 per cent. The bakery trade also involved cooking dinners (particularly baking joints of meat) for working class families who lacked baking facilities. This aspect of the trade was resented by both the bakers and their employees, since demand for the service was particularly heavy on Sundays.[40]

The term 'confectionery' included boiled sweets, such as

---

[35] Dodd, *Food of London*, p. 197–8.

[36] Burnett, *Plenty and Want*, p. 83.   [37] B.3. 5745.

[38] See the testimony of James Clay and Benjamin Holloway in, *B.P.P.*, *Report of the Commissioners Appointed to Inquire into the Condition of the Framework Knitters*; Mins. of Ev., 1845 (609) xv.

[39] Kent County Archives, Q/Cl/297.

[40] See testimony by Peter McEwen and Joseph Manton in, *B.P.P.*, *Select Committee on the Observances of the Sabbath Day*; Mins. of Ev., 1831–32 (697) vii.

barley sugar, fruit drops and lozenges, fruit jams and preserves, and pastry. Eating chocolate was relatively unimportant before the 1870s. In 1850 there were a few comparatively large production units, such as James Wotherspoon of Glasgow, with steam powered factories producing packaged and branded products.[41] Grocers and general shopkeepers retailed boiled sweets, jams and preserves which they either made-up themselves or bought from wholesalers and confectioners.[42] Among the middle classes home production of boiled sweets and preserves was very popular at this time.[43]

In smaller towns the aggregate demand for confectionery rarely justified a specialist production and distribution unit, and the pastry side of the trade was usually associated with bread baking. For example, John Mitchell a Tonbridge baker in the 1830s and 1840s made and sold rolls and cakes as well as bread.[44] The specialized concern producing and retailing boiled sweets, jams, preserves and pastry was restricted to the larger towns and cities, and here the trade was oriented towards the wealthier classes. Prices in these shops reflected much more the shop location, rich decorations and furnishings, skilled labour costs, and the expensive pewter, glass and china on which goods were sold and displayed, than the materials which went into the product. Accordingly, surviving records suggest that confectioners in the city were markedly indifferent to searching out cheap sources of supply: they tended to assemble their supplies of eggs, milk, cheese, fruit, sugar and meat from nearby retail tradesmen. Competition among high class confectioners was based on quality rather than price. The importance of trade skills is reflected in the high apprenticeship fees which a skilled confectioner might demand: William Jarrin, a Bond street confectioner, charged £100 per annum in apprenticeship fees in addition to board and lodging, and he was able to sell a copyright for a confectionery recipe for £400.[45]

---

[41] Burn, *Commercial Enterprise*, pp. 129–31.

[42] Grocers catalogue in Essex Record Office, T/P 160/2–4, and the inventory of Denis, Lambert & Co., wholesale grocers, B.3. 1454.

[43] Burn, *Commercial Enterprise*, pp. 131–32.

[44] Kent County Archives, Q/Cl/331/1–5.   [45] B.3. 2739.

5. *Conclusions*

The distribution of real resources in the economy and technical factors determined which foodstuffs were distributed through shops, markets and itinerant tradesmen. Market and itinerant distribution was most important where the unit value of a mass consumption article was low, and where producers and consumers were in close proximity, and where perishability reduced the available time for distribution. This was generally the case with fish, fruit, vegetables and most dairy produce. In small market towns direct exchange in the market place was advantageous for both producers and consumers since middlemen's costs were eliminated. Where the supplying area was too extensive to permit direct exchange, or where the physical size of the market place was too small to accommodate all buyers and sellers, the costermonger gave the market place a greater spatial range by carrying foodstuffs into residential areas, at a lower cost than the only alternative—the fixed shop. The retail markets also overcame the perishability problem by concentrating exchange at places and times formally recognized by sellers and consumers. Both low unit values and perishability lowered the minimum amount of capital required to enter distribution activities to levels which permitted a massive substitution of unskilled labour for capital.

Foodstuffs distributed mainly in fixed shops were characteristically those which required stockholding, manufacturing and processing. Groceries involved heavy stock holding since production was widely separated in time and space from consumption; the stock was extremely variegated (by types and qualities) over a range of complementary goods (such as tea and sugar) which favoured 'basket purchases' and thus severely limited the mobility of the stock in terms of market and itinerant distribution. Where it was essential to invest capital in manufacturing equipment (such as a bakehouse) or in warehousing facilities and processing equipment (as in the grocery trade and the butcher's trade) distribution costs would only be increased by shifting the selling function into a retail market or by carrying goods into residential streets, although perishability made this essential in the butcher's trade. Grocery items, moreover, were subject to rapid deterioration when removed from the protection of the shop.

The interaction of these factors meant that the relationship between shop and market and itinerant distribution was broadly complementary rather than competitive. It is true that few products were distributed exclusively by one channel or the other. Butchers, as we have seen, were obliged by the factor of perishability to make use of the consumer-seeking services of the markets and itinerant trade in addition to the shop. Tea was sold on an itinerant basis in the cities, and bread was sometimes sold in markets and on the streets, but these were instances of the extension of distribution from the shop rather than competition between distribution systems. There was a shop distribution structure for fish, fruit and vegetables, but this service was organized mainly for the upper income classes who were indifferent to marginally higher prices in return for the convenience and comfort of the fixed shop outlet. It seems clear that with the prevailing low *per capita* incomes and an abundance of unskilled labour relative to capital, itinerant and market distribution of foodstuffs prevailed where it was a technical possibility.

B. THE CLOTH AND CLOTHING TRADES

The cloth and clothing trades were functionally divided between the cloth retailers (drapers, haberdashers and mercers) and the clothing producer/retailers (tailors, dressmakers, bootmakers and hatters). Drapers enjoyed a small trade in ready-made clothing, but their main function was to provide materials for the home production of clothing, for the clothing and footwear trades, and for household furnishings. Technical developments in the textile industries (notably cotton) provided a basis for an expanding mass market for cloth, and by the 1820s there were drapery shops in the cities of a size equalled in no previous century and found in no other trade. Tailors and dressmakers often had a complementary trade in cloth retailing, but their main function was to produce new clothing and to repair old. The technical basis for mass produced, ready-made clothing and footwear was lacking before the invention and application of the sewing machine in the second half of the century, and the small producer/retailer remained the typical figure in these trades before then. But this period did see the growth of clothing and footwear workshops, employing large numbers of journeymen tailors and shoemakers for the production of finished and semi-finished goods for retailing and finishing in shops.

1. Drapery and Haberdashery

In the eighteenth century the woollen draper specialized in heavy cloth for men's clothing; the mercer dealt with the lighter fabrics used in women's apparel; and the haberdasher sold threads, tapes, binding, ribbons and other trimmings.[46] In the nineteenth century the term 'mercer' began to fall into disuse, except among some high quality silk dealers, and the term 'linen draper' was more usually employed for tradesmen dealing in linen, cotton and silk piece goods. Drapers usually maintained a haberdashery department, and haberdashers commonly sold printed muslins and scotch cambrics.[47] Woollen cloth outlets were normally tied to tailoring shops, although there were woollen drapers who were not involved in tailoring. In smaller towns, but even in the cities, piece goods, haberdashery, hosiery, hats and small stocks of ready-made clothing were retailed from general drapery shops.

The three most important 'departments' in a drapery shop were the piece goods section, stocking an enormous range of textiles in different qualities and colours; the haberdashery section, with its irritating and in many shops uncontrollable collection of pins, ribbons, threads etc.; and the 'fancy goods' section, which stocked handkerchiefs, neckerchiefs, lace, womens' 'caps', gloves and hosiery. Most drapery shops at this time stocked little or no ready-made clothing, although one draper argued that,

The first approach to made-up goods was advanced by the drapers themselves, who made up women's cloaks, with circular capes; they were merely a straight garment, without any pretensions to style, that reached down nearly to the feet ... and were generally of coloured merinos. ...[48]

---

[46] R. Campbell, *The London Tradesman* (1747), see the appropriate trade entries.
[47] Whittock, *Book of Trades*, see the appropriate trade entries.
[48] *Reminiscences of an Old Draper*, p. 54.

In country areas with less highly stratified trading structures, however, drapers very commonly moved farther towards integrating the cloth and clothing sectors: William Doubleday, an Essex draper, dealt in cloaks, hosiery, gloves, caps, shirts, shoes and sandals.[49] A draper trained in London noted that when he went into a drapery business at Chatham he found it,

wholly different to anything I had seen done before. A good many men's goods were kept—sailor's tarpaulin hats, and a few ready made clothes. Sailors frequently came to the shop for complete suits, which we, being unable to provide ourselves in all cases, would sometimes fetch from across the road from a neighbouring Jew clothes-dealer and pawnbroker with whom Reece had an understanding to halve the profit.[50]

In small country towns the complete range of cloth and clothing trades might be subsumed in one shop. For example, Thomas Gibbon of Wrotham in the 1820s was a tailor, milliner, draper, haberdasher, hatter, hosier and shoeseller.[51]

In the drapery trade the retailer was responsible for little in the way of processing. An exception was thread, which was received in pound packets of mixed colours and which had to be untangled and re-wrapped in open-ended paper packets containing uniform colours. But if there was little processing work, the labour input in selling drapery was very high. In the food trades customers bought weekly and developed fairly standardized patterns of consumption, and if they were uncertain whether to buy Congou or Bohea tea, the decision could be made quickly from the sample bowls on the shop counter. But in the drapery trade purchases were more occasional and customers were therefore less certain as to what was available and what they wanted, and there was little in the way of customer self-service. While some rolls of linen and cotton goods were on open display and bundles of goods for 'pushing' displayed in the windows and inside the shop, most of the stock was kept in drawers and boxes and wrapped in paper packets. The customer expected a demonstration of the stock range,

[49] Essex Record Office, D/DQ 27/1–5.
[50] *Reminiscences of an Old Draper*, p. 94.
[51] Kent County Archives, Q/Cl 399/1–3.

which the shopman had to fetch from storage and replace when the customer left the shop. Shopkeepers paid their assistants premiums for 'introducing' slow moving items to customers, and there was thus an incentive to demonstrate as much stock as possible. Accordingly, the idle rich and the servant girls who visited drapery shops to see but not necessarily to buy were bitterly resented by the drapery assistants.

The retail draper and haberdasher drew his supplies from warehousemen, manufacturers and retail/wholesale tradesmen. London was the centre of the wholesale cloth trade, although warehousing firms were located in the manufacturing areas, including declining areas like the West Country and Norwich. London dominated the inland trade by virtue of the size of the metropolitan market and the advantages of location in the financial centre of the kingdom enjoying the most developed transport and communications facilities. It was pointed out in 1821 that,

The truth, perhaps, is that the greatest quantity of floating capital is always to be found in the metropolis, and, therefore, the manufacturer will send his goods to that market, where they will be sure to obtain a ready sale, and that too, generally, for prompt payment. ... Hence it in general happens, that no wholesale Linen-Draper, residing in any other part of the empire, can effectually compete with the London houses. ...[52]

Some of the great London houses had backward linkages into production. For example, J. B. and W. Nevill & Co. in the 1850s had hosiery factories at Nottingham and Godalming, and shirt factories in Ireland and London.[53] Pelly, Hurst & Co., founded as a hosiery manufacturing firm in 1785, employed up to 3000 in 1850 at the production end in Nottingham, and had an export and inland trade wholesale depot in Gresham Street London.[54] John and Nathaneil Philips & Co. were smallware manufacturers and wholesalers. The firm was founded in 1747 and by 1822 owned mills in Staffordshire; in 1830 it amalgamated with James Chadwick Brothers of Bolton and London.

[52] *The Book of English Trades* (new ed., 1821), p. 192.
[53] D. Puseley, *The Commercial Companion* (1858) p. 162.
[54] Ibid., p. 167.

The haberdashery and general warehousing branch in London exported to America and Australia and served the inland trade.[55] The London warehouse with factories in the country did not necessarily deal exclusively, however, in the output of those factories. For example in 1816 the warehousing firm Earle and Lyon of Old Change in the City (the wholesaling arm of Lyon and Earle, Wigan cotton manufacturers) bought stock on its own account from manufacturers, merchants and warehousemen in London, Bolton, Wigan, Manchester and elsewhere.[56]

Warehousing firms tended to specialize in certain lines, such as cottons and linens, silks, woollens or tapes and threads. The big firms were usually involved in overseas trading, but even comparatively small firms had connexions abroad. There was some feeling in the trade, however, that overseas merchanting was best left to the specialist exporter and the big wholesale houses. When a 'silent' partner in the firm of Rowlandson, Isaac & Co., a comparatively small firm, heard that the active partners were shipping abroad, he immediately took steps to terminate the partnership.[57]

In 1833 Thomas James of Moore, James & Co. explained that the function of the London warehouseman was 'to purchase from the manufacturer, to hold stocks, and to supply country dealers and the shopkeepers in town with these goods'.[58] He noted that it was 'the practice of our house, and I believe all houses of our class, to pay certainly four-fifths of our business cash at the end of the month'.[59] Obviously, it was to the advantage of the manufacturer to market with these firms in bulk on short credit, and in this and other ways the wholesalers enjoyed considerable coercive power over the manufacturers. In fact, the warehousing firms of this period enjoyed something of the same relationship with manufacturers that the giant retail chain does today. In the 1860s J. S. Wright, a Birmingham button manufacturer, explained that he would not market his buttons with his name for fear of encouraging direct orders from retailers: 'that would be a very unhappy

[55] Ibid., p. 174.   [56] B.3. 1556, 7 and 8.
[57] B.3. 4181 and 2, testimony of William Brien, February, 1812.
[58] *Select Committee on Manufactures*, Q. 1348.   [59] Ibid., Q. 1398.

thing for me, for it would destroy my trade with the wholesale people'.[60]

The wholesaler maintained contact with the country retailers through letter, by retailers' periodic journeys to London, and through the wholesaler's staff of commercial travellers. Morrison, Dillon & Co., one of London's largest warehousing firms, was exceptional in maintaining no travelling staff at this time, for firms of an equal size employed as many as twenty or thirty travellers at an annual cost of from £300 to £600 for each man.[61] Commercial travelling underwent a very rapid development in the first half of the century, as is suggested by the establishment in that period of a travellers' association, school and magazine.[62] The eighteenth century 'Rider' had travelled by horse and spent up to six months on the road, sending back orders by post every week or fortnight and working a district until he had written enough orders to stock it for a year.[63] In the early decades of the nineteenth century the traveller worked a district by gig and used the coaches for movements between major centres,[64] and the development of a railway network completed the transportation revolution which enabled the London wholesale firms to achieve a more intensive and extensive penetration of the inland market.

In London 'the usual manner of replenishing ... stock is for the Draper to walk round, on Saturdays, to the wholesale house, and agents of the country manufacturers; that being the implied market-day, when those houses prepare to make exhibitions of their new arrivals. ... '[65] But some London shopkeepers went to the wholesale houses as much as three times in a week, and the wholesalers themselves had travelling staffs working the London shops.[66]

The wholesaler relieved the manufacturers of stock holding

[60] B.P.P., Select Committee on Trade Marks, and Merchandize Marks Bill; Mins. of Ev., 1862 (212) xii, Q. 1066.

[61] Burn, Commercial Enterprise, p. 55.

[62] Allen, Ambassadors of Commerce, and The Commercial Travellers' Magazine, first published in 1856.

[63] Allen, Ambassadors, p. 102, and 'The Commercial Traveller as he was and Is', The Early Closing Advocate and Commercial Reformer (1854) p. 116.

[64] See the Letters from Scotland by an English Commercial Traveller (1817).

[65] Whittock, Book of Trades, p. 312.

[66] See Reminiscences of an Old Draper, p. 27.

and marketing costs, thereby releasing capital for increased production. For the retailers, he broke bulk in order to satisfy stock mix requirements and provided invaluable trade and stock information.[67] But retailers did not buy exclusively from the warehouseman. To offer only two of many possible examples, in 1830 Robert Bishop, a Birmingham draper and tailor, dealt with several London warehousemen, but his large accounts with West Country clothiers were equally prominent; and he also bought from merchants at Leeds, Huddersfield and Halifax, from manufacturers in Yorkshire and Lancashire, two London drapers, a Stourbridge draper and Birmingham drapers and button manufacturers.[68] In the early 1820s a Manchester draper, Isaac Worthington, bought stock from London warehousemen, from calico, flannel and ribbon manufacturers in Manchester, from Manchester and Glasgow merchants, a Macclesfield silk manufacturer, several Manchester drapers and tailors, and from Nottingham and Leicester hosiers.[69] London retailers, by contrast, seem to have relied more exclusively upon the City warehousing firms: at bankruptcy in the 1820s, for example, the big Holborn drapers W. & H. Hart, were indebted to London warehousemen, merchants, silk and ribbon manufacturers, glovers, lacemen, drapers and haberdashers, and their only account payable to a firm outside London was with a Taunton draper.[70]

Although the warehousemen occupied a powerful position *vis-à-vis* manufacturer and retailer, it is clear from these examples that neither manufacturer nor retailer relied upon them exclusively. A Colchester draper testified in 1821 that he ordered directly from Yorkshire and Wiltshire manufacturers;[71] Thomas James, himself a warehouseman, admitted that 'some of the large retail dealers do buy directly from the manufacturers';[72] but he was no doubt right in believing that 'much the larger proportion of purchases in London are from the wholesale houses'.[73] A London draper who made a trip up to the North in the 1830s to buy stock for his newly opened shop said

[67] See E. E. Perkins, *A Treatise on Haberdashery and Hosiery* (8th ed., 1853) p. 198.
[68] B.3. 562.   [69] B.3. 5725.   [70] B.3. 2430.
[71] *B.P.P.*, *Select Committee on the Agriculture of the United Kingdom*; Mins. of Ev., 1821 (668) ix, p. 180.
[72] *Select Committee on Manufactures*, Q. 1462.   [73] Ibid., Q. 1463.

that 'it was entirely unusual for a retail draper to go to Manchester in those days'.[74] Retailers' written orders to the manufacturer were probably comparatively rare: in the majority of cases direct buying was arranged through the manufacturer's commission agent, although the big drapers were in a position to place job-lot orders with manufacturers for the fast moving lines.

Our examples also indicate that retailers bought stock from retail/wholesale tradesmen.[75] Invariably, the 'monster' drapery shops had large wholesale departments. Hutton & Co. was one such firm, with a rather unusual history. It was founded as a smallware manufacturing firm in Yorkshire around 1760, but manufacturing was abandoned 'on the introduction of steam power looms at Manchester' in favour of developing the retail/wholesale warehouse in the City of London. The retail trade was given up in the early 1850s, however, 'in consequence of the increasing requirements of space for their wholesale trade'.[76] The smaller High Street tradesmen also developed wholesale trades with town and country shopkeepers and hawkers. For example, W. & H. Hart of Holborn sold to firms in St Albans, Hatfield, Hornchurch, Chelmsford, Norwich, Nottingham and Winchester.[77] Froggott and Lilleyman, a Doncaster drapery firm, had customers in Everton, Wakefield, Barnsley, Hull, Derby and York.[78] A Bristol draper described how a woman came to his shop with £200 looking for stock to open a country shop:

We did our best for the widow, and everything she had—quarters of dozens of hosiery, and such goods—were all neatly papered up for her, and the descriptions outside plainly written in the text hand, and a dozen yards of linen and similar goods were put into neat rolls, ready for retailing, and this person became a steady customer to us afterwards.[79]

The retail drapery trade was characterized by extremes: extremes in size, from the 'monster shops' of the cities to the

[74] *Reminiscences of an Old Draper*, p. 203.
[75] Much of the previous analysis with respect to wholesale/retail trading in groceries applies equally to the drapery trade.
[76] Puseley, *Commercial Companion*, p. 121.
[77] B.3. 2430.   [78] B.3. 1756 and 7.
[79] *Reminiscences of an Old Draper*, pp. 145–6.

small back street and country shops; in quality from the high class tradesmen selling the finest damasks, muslins and shawls by the most unobtrusive methods, to the cutting shops of working class districts, selling off job-lots of cheap goods by the most brazen techniques.[80] Contemporaries who commented upon radical changes in retail trade referred mainly to the drapery trade. It was the first trade to manifest unmistakable characteristics of modern retailing: the retailer had few processing functions; price ticketing and cash trading spread quickly in association with more careful stock control; drapery shops led in the introduction of plate-glass fronts, in attention to window displays, and in the use of gas lighting for exterior advertisement. Above all, it was the first trade in which a significant range in the size of retail units emerged.[81] The most important factors defining the unique position of the drapery trade were the growth of factory textile production, the emergence of large urban mass markets, and the freedom of the distributor from heavy processing responsibilities. In the drapery trade, capital and entrepreneurial energy could be focussed exclusively upon improving distribution techniques, and these served as a model followed by all the consumer goods trades as, very gradually, production and distribution functions were disentangled.

2. *Tailors, Dressmakers, and Clothes Dealers*

It was only after 1850 and the development of the sewing machine that clothing came to be produced in factories for distribution in retail shops. Before then production and distribution were normally aggregated in one entrepreneurial unit, whether it be the bespoke shops of tailors and dressmakers, or the ready-made shops of the clothiers.

A big bespoke tailoring firm might employ twenty or more men, and hence considerable working and living space was essential. The premises were a combination of living quarters, sales and display area and cutting rooms. The cutting room would be used for measuring the customer and cutting the cloth; the workshop was where the garment was assembled; and the front shop was devoted to displaying drapery and any made-up clothing.

[80] Ibid., p. 82. [81] These problems are discussed in Chapter VII.

Measuring and cutting were the most skilled aspects of bespoke tailoring, and these tasks were invariably performed by the master tailor, his foreman or senior journeyman, who then supervized the assembly and finishing of the garment by the less skilled workmen. The foreman's position was a responsible one and often very well paid. For example, in the late 1830s and 1840s, Thomas Peters, a Cambridge tailor, paid his foreman £150 a year.[82] In a high class Jermyn Street shop, the articles of agreement between the master and his foreman provided that the latter would have 'by way of Salary or compensation for his labour one fifth of the profits'.[83] This amounted to about £500 a year.

Tailors purchased much of their materials directly from the West Country and Yorkshire manufacturers and merchants. Job-lot buying of the standard woollen cloths was a common practice,[84] often resulting in very substantial levels of indebtedness. For example, at bankruptcy in 1827, a London tailor, William Emmott, was indebted to one Wiltshire clothier alone for £450.[85] Both London and provincial tailors bought woollen drapery and the lighter textiles for linings, waist-coats and dressing gowns from warehousing firms in the City and specialist wholesale shops located on and around St Martin's Lane in London. These firms also supplied the necessary articles of haberdashery, but it was not uncommon for tailors to bring in supplies of smallwares and 'toys' directly from the manufacturer or from local drapery and haberdashery shops.

Tailoring was primarily a bespoke trade, but clothing was made in slack periods for 'off the rack' sales. For example, at bankruptcy Martin Clark of Newmarket had in stock some 12 Ruff Great coats, 5 Drab Great coats, 5 Shooting coats and 10 other coats; 14 waist-coats, 8 Snow jackets, 5 jackets, 7 pairs of trousers, 1 pair of overalls, 7 pairs of drawers, and 10 pairs of gaiters.[86] Some tailors also brought in stocks of ready-made clothing: Robert Claxton, a Norwich tailor, bought regularly from Isaac Moses, one of London's largest clothiers.[87] Most

[82] B.3. 4142.
[83] P.R.O., Chancery Master's Exhibits, 'Hopkinson v. Roe', C. 103, no. 42.
[84] *Select Committee on Manufactures*, Q. 1465.
[85] B.3. 1574.   [86] B.3. 983.   [87] B.3. 1219.

tailors kept stocks of gloves, hats, and hosiery which they bought from manufacturers, specialist wholesalers and local tradesmen.

The tailor's main function was to produce new clothing, but he also cleaned and repaired old garments. A tailor in Kent in the 1840s, for example, entered such transactions in his ledger as 'trousers lined', 'repairing coat', 'repairing trousers', 'altering waistcoats', and 'cleaning and trimming satin vest'.[88] Some tailors also made up garments for hire, particularly cloaks.[89]

The milliner and dressmaker was the counterpart in the women's trade of the tailor. The typical dressmaker was an unmarried or widowed woman, working on her own or with sisters and sometimes employing young female workers. The typical firm was probably on average smaller than the typical tailoring firm, but some were fairly large. For example, Jane Tait, who had a shop on Bold Street in Liverpool, had an average annual turnover of £5000 in the mid-1820s, and her stock was valued at £3225 at bankruptcy in 1828. She had customers in Liverpool, Manchester, Preston, Lancaster, Wigan, Bolton, Macclesfield, Birmingham, Coventry, and she even exported clothing to Ireland and the West Indies.[90] In contrast to the men's trade, the light cloth used for much women's clothing meant that garments could be made at home, and the development of the portable sewing machine intensified home and small shop production in the second half of the century.

The ready-made clothing trade underwent a rapid transformation during the early decades of the nineteenth century and this makes its analysis complex. Men engaged in the trade were known variously as slopsellers, clothiers, clothes sellers and outfitters. Its early history was associated closely with the navy and merchant marine, and this aspect of the trade still remained. In the 1830s, for example, a London slopseller by the name of William Prince defined his trade as buying 'cloth and other materials and working up the same into slops or clothes for the use of sailors and selling the clothes when so made up to East India captains and others'.[91] The marine connexion

---

[88] Kent County Archives, Q/Cl. 2.   [89] Ibid., Q/Cl. 399/1.
[90] B.3. 5028.   [91] B.3. 4083

is also manifest in the fact that many of the big London slop-sellers were involved as well in shipping and marine insurance.

The clothes sellers made up new garments and bought used articles which they cleaned and repaired for sale in the domestic market. They also bought clothing from small tailors and the big city sweatshops. For example, a Chichester clothier bought hats in Bristol and London, garments from two London sweatshops operated by Robert Popplewell and James Bousfield, and materials for new clothing from London warehousemen and local tradesmen.[92] Another clothes dealer, William Twaddle of Hertford, purchased cloth from wholesalers and from manufacturers in the North, hats and hosiery from London firms, and made up garments from William Bousfield.[93] Joseph Parry, a Houndsditch draper and clothes dealer, bought garments from Hervey Hawkins, a clothes salesmen on the Commercial Road, and had an arrangement with a Bloomsbury tailor to supply him with new clothing and to repair used garments. The tailor detailed his business with Perry as follows:[94]

1823	Work Done			
Sep. 27	Trowsers	£1	16	0
Oct. 4	Scowering & repairing a Great coat & a new collar & new buttoned		14	0
Nov. 22	A pr. black Milled Caps. Trowsers	2	2	0
Feb. 14	Scowering, finishing & repairing a pr. Trowsers		3	6
28	An extra Supr. blue Cloth Coat, gilt buttons	4	6	0
	A stripe Toilinett waistcoat		18	0
Mar. 27	Repairing a blue coat with new cuffs		4	6
	An extra Superfine black cloth coat, silk buttons	4	4	0
	A fine black Caps. waistcoat		18	0
Apr. 17	Altering a waistcoat		2	6

[92] B.3. 2090.   [93] B.3. 4984.   [94] B.3. 3984.

Much of the clothing bought from the London sweatshops was probably refurbished clothing, and extending the useful life of garments was essential so long as the country lacked large scale factory industries in woollens and clothing.

'Outfitter' and 'Clothier' were terms used increasingly in the nineteenth century as retailers attempted to trade up and throw off the stigma surrounding the older trades in slops and refurbished garments. These clothing firms, invariably a city phenomenon, differed from the typical tailoring shop mainly in size and the extent to which they produced or bought ready-made clothing, for most also maintained bespoke departments. The blurring of distinctions between bespoke and ready-made and the conscious attempt at trading-up are clear in many advertisements dating from the early 1840s. For example,

Gentlemen's superior Clothing, at prices much lower than any respectable house has hitherto offered the public, where cut and quality, the true test of real economy, are considered—J. Albert & Co., Tailors, 52 King William-street, City, established upwards of 26 years, respectfully invite families and gentlemen to an early inspection of an extensive and fashionable stock of entirely new articles for gentlemen's and youth's outer garments ... made to order in a superior style, for cash, at prices that perhaps may not astonish the public, but will prove by the superiority of wear much cheaper than those by which they are too often deluded by perambulating advertisements, pamphlets etc. issued by slop-sellers and hosiers, offering their slovenly made up rubbish at prices that would barely pay for the labour of a well-made garment.[95]

Probably the largest clothing firm in England at this time was E. Moses & Son, tailors, wholesale woollen drapers and outfitters, with shops in the Minories and Aldgate. Their advertisements usually displayed a two column price list, one for ready-made articles, the other for made to measure, with the assurance that 'Any article purchased, or ordered, if not approved of, exchanged, or the money returned'.[96] In the early 1840s Moses & Son also introduced their 'Self-Measurement' plan. Upon request, the firm posted free of charge a pamphlet with 'a wood-cut and full directions' for measure-

[95] *The Illustrated London News*, 14 October 1843.
[96] See for example, *The Illustrated London News*, 6 January 1844.

ment. The scheme was aimed at the provincial market, for 'Residents in the country cannot do better than avail themselves of so favourable an opportunity of purchasing at the greatest Tailoring Establishment in the Kingdom'.[97] Clothing firms of this kind were not restricted to London, however, for in the North there was Harrall and Company, 'Tailors, Clothiers, Hatters and General Outfitters' operating in several industrial towns. Their advertisements also emphasize quality as well as price:

Harrall and Co., take this opportunity of reminding their Friends and the Public, that the extent of their numerous establishments which embrace some of the principal towns in the country, affords them a very important advantage over other houses; possessing an unlimited command over the best markets in the world, for the production of woollen and other kinds of manufactured goods, and by employing upon the premises the ablest talent which this country can furnish, for cutting and making up every garment; they flatter themselves in being able to offer clothing of superb quality, choice material, and unsurpassed workmanship, at least 40 per cent lower than is usually charged.[98]

By 1850 a few manufacturers were sufficiently well known to brand articles sold in outfitter's shops, but these were mainly manufacturers of water-proof outwear: it was more common for retailers to attach their own labels to any goods bought from manufacturers.[99]

The retail clothing firms which had emerged in the cities and industrial towns by the 1840s were a new and important phenomenon. They catered to the more prosperous sector of the working class who could not afford bespoke tailoring, or were impatient with the time which bespoke production took, but who could afford better clothing than the slops and refurbished garments of the clothes sellers. They were a product of the new urban mass markets, and they could operate on no other principle than fixed prices and cash sales. The organizational gap between these firms, still relying upon sweatshop production for their stocks, and the retail clothing firms of the

[97] Ibid., 20 January 1844.
[98] Advertisement in P. Whittle, *Blackburn As It Is*.
[99] *Select Committee on Trade Marks*, Q. 1094 and 1101.

second half of the century, stocking factory, machine-made clothing, was not as wide as the gap between them and the traditional tailoring shop.

3. Boot and Shoemakers

The technical basis for a mass production footwear industry was provided by the sewing and riveting machines developed in the second half of the nineteenth century. Before then the trade was dominated by the producer/retailer, although there were many small manufacturing firms, like Clark's of Street which was founded in the 1830s. The producer/retailer looked to both the small manufacturing firms and journeyman outworkers located in Yorkshire, Northampton and the cities to provide him with ready-made footwear and components which were assembled and finished in the shop.

A national scale of sizes and fittings developed, in the main, with the factory footwear industry and before its advent fitted boot and shoes could be had only by placing bespoke orders with the producer/retailer. Thus, the records of Peal Brothers, a high class firm of London shoemakers, include the foot tracings of their regular customers.[100] The critical task of measuring the customer's foot and cutting the leather was assumed by the master or his foreman. Sewing and finishing the shoes was done either by journeymen and apprentices in the shop or was passed on to male and female outworkers. In 1829, for example, Peal Brothers put out work to a Mrs Thompson, who earned anywhere between 10s. and 20s. a week, and she returned the assembled components to the shop for finishing and polishing.

The shoemaker assembled his materials and components from a wide range of sources. Leather was purchased from leather dressers, curriers and manufacturers. Drapers and warehousemen were the usual sources for lining materials and sewing silks. By the early nineteenth century it was also normal for shoemakers to buy pre-cut soles, tops and tips from leather cutters and footwear manufacturers. The Peal Brothers bought many soles, tops and tips, but in turn they had something of a national reputation for their water-proof tops and they shipped large consignments of these to all parts of the country: between

100 County Hall Record Office, London, uncatalogued.

1811 and 1815 one firm alone, Samuel Fisher & Son, bought between £30 and £90 worth of tops each month. Thus, while measuring and cutting remained an essential skill for most shoemakers, it is true that the shoemaker was increasingly an assembler of ready-made components.

Manufacturing footwear from components carried the assumption that every pair of boots and shoes need not be uniquely devised for a particular customer. Hence, the boot-maker normally carried a large stock of ready-made footwear which he either purchased or made up in the shop from components. In 1824, for example, Frederick Noyce, a Richmond shoemaker, had in stock some 340 pairs of boots, shoes, slippers and clogs for men, boys, women and children.[101] In all but the high class shops, stocks of ready-made footwear might include refurbished footwear which had been received as 'trade-ins' on new footwear or refurbished stocks purchased from Northampton and city manufacturers.[102]

Many bootmakers retailed from both shops and market stalls. In 1851, for example, bootmakers were one of the best represented trades in Leicester market (Table 2:1). Frederick Noyce of Richmond estimated that his annual cost 'in attending the different markets' was £30, exclusive of the cost of maintaining a horse and cart for transporting the stock.

Good footwear was expensive: between 1811 and 1820 Peal Brothers charged about £4. 10s. 0d. for their water-proof boots, £2. 10s. 0d. for common leather boots, £3. 13s. 6d. for water-proof Hessians, £2. 6s. 0d. for common leather Hessians, and £1. 4s. 0d. for shoes and pumps. Since prices were high relative to most incomes, a significant proportion of all customer transactions in any bootmaker's shop was concerned with repairing footwear and refurbishing discarded articles.

4. *Hosiery and Hats*

Hosiers dealt in stockings, braces, belts, purses and watch chains, and usually in yarn caps, waistcoats, drawers and petti-coats. Specialist hosiery shops were to be found mainly in the

[101] B.3. 3740.
[102] *Select Committee of the House of Lords on Sunday Trading*, Q. 316.

larger towns and cities; elsewhere hosiery items were sold by haberdashers, drapers, tailors and general shopkeepers.

Hosiery production was no longer integrated with retail distribution, notwithstanding the fact, as one writer pointed out, that a hosier 'may employ one or two weavers, weaving near his shop door, to attract silly customers, who make about as many goods in a year as their employer sells in a day'.[103] Stockings were manufactured in three qualities from worsted, lambswool, cotton, angola and silk yarn, in a range of sizes (denoted by small holes under the foot or the ribbed part of the top) for children, youths, men and women.[104] The retailer retained a manufacturing aspect to his trade with respect to braces, belts, purses and watch chains, in so far as he assembled the metal components from 'toy' manufacturers and the cloth, leather, silk and webbing components from manufacturing hosiers, leather sellers and warehousemen.[105]

Drapers and general shopkeepers enjoyed a large share of the market in hats and caps of the more utilitarian and less fashionable kind. The high class hatter, on the other hand, traded in a very fashion conscious market, as is suggested by a letter received in 1804 by Mouys and Jarrit, Pall Mall hatters:

Mrs. Densley is sorry she is obliged to return the Hat—but it is so very unbecoming she cannot think of wearing it, or *any*, that ties *under the chin*—she therefore begs to have the most fashionable one that *does not*—something in the style of last years hat you sent her if they are now worn—it must not be very large in the Verge—the size of the hat return'd suits extremely well—have the goodness to send it *immediately* as Mr D—— is going a Journey.

N.B. Mr Densley likes his hat very much begs to have a bill of both—when he will immediately send an order for payment.[106]

In 1819, when a Halifax hatter was asked if he considered himself to be a retailer, he replied 'Entirely, I may say; but I manufacture the principal part of what I sell'.[107] But the manufacturing element in the producer/retailer complex was

---

[103] Several Tradesmen, *London Tradesmen*, p. 82.

[104] Perkins, *Treatise on Haberdashery*, p. 83.

[105] See the bankruptcy file relating to Francis Greasley of London, B.3. 2004.

[106] Preserved in 'Mouys v. Jarrit', P.R.O., Chancery Master's Exhibits, C. 103, no. 191.

[107] *Select Committee on Shop Windows Duty*, p. 15.

becoming increasingly circumscribed at this time. The less fashionable hatters bought finished caps and hats from manufacturers, and most purchased a machine made foundation from a hat manufacturer which left the retailer only the trimming and finishing. For example, Thomas Brown, a Norwich hatter in the 1830s, bought caps from a Norwich cap maker, his hat foundations from a manufacturer near Manchester, and his trimmings from Norwich haberdashers and jewellers.[108] Trimming and finishing, however, were crucial skills in the high class trade, and consumers would go to considerable trouble in order to deal with tradesmen whose skills they knew and trusted. For example, in 1803 a customer of Mouys and Jarrit resident in Edinburgh wrote to them:

Gentlemen,
    I will thank you to send me down here another hat of the same description size etc. to my last which I got previous to my leaving London. I shall now give you my address which is at Mrs Baillies, bottom of Warislaus Close High street Edinburgh, you may send it by Leith smack they set off from Wapping. I shall be in Town soon myself and will either pay you then or send the money.

As with other tradesmen in the clothing trades, the hatter earned revenues other than by selling new articles. Mouys and Jarritt provided a hat rental service; they took in old hats in exchange for new and stripped them down for remanufacture; and a very large part of their business involved cleaning and repairing hats.

5. *Conclusions*

The production of the lighter articles of women's clothing and all undergarments and nightwear was, to a significant extent, centred in the home. This can be attributed to the absence of a factory clothing industry, to the low incomes of working class families, to the extensive employment of domestic servants in middle class homes, and to the socially restricted alternatives for work and diversion available to middle class women. The materials for this home production of clothing were retailed by drapers, haberdashers and general shopkeepers. The production

[108] B.3. 771.

of heavy woollen garments, particularly men's outer clothing, and footwear, however, demanded skills and tools which very largely eliminated the possibilities for home production. Overwhelmingly, customers for bespoke and ready-made new clothing and footwear relied upon the producer/retailer, manufacturing the entire article or assembling and finishing it from components provided by specialist manufacturers and outworkers. The manufacturers and outworkers also made cheap, ready-made goods for sale in producer/retailer's shops, general shops, outfitter's and shoe seller's shops. While it is true that factory production had yet to be developed in the clothing and footwear trades, it is still very evident that tradesmen's reliance upon components and ready-made articles produced by outworkers and sweatshops had gone a long way towards dissolving the classic producer/retailer organisation.

Supplementing the new clothing industry was the trade in used clothing and footwear. It was collected by itinerant traders and shopkeepers for refurbishing by the collector or manufacturers for eventual resale in shops and markets. This emphasis upon extending the useful life of clothing and footwear was manifest in the producer/retailer's willingness to take in old articles in exchange for new ones and his obligation to clean and repair clothing and footwear.

C. THE DURABLE GOODS TRADES

The middle and upper classes and the better off working class families were the major consumers of durable goods, such as kitchen utensils, heating and lighting hardware, cutlery, pottery, furniture and furnishings. A. J. Taylor has suggested that working class families on the edge of relative prosperity were inclined to divert expenditure from increased food consumption to the new consumer goods industries;[109] but it was cloth and clothing, not durable goods, which figured in the emerging mass market. The quality of much urban working class life militated against significant expenditure on kitchenware and furniture and furnishings. Many husbands ate their cooked meal at the cookshop rather than at home; on weekends

[109] A. J. Taylor, 'Progress and Poverty', op. cit.

the Sunday dinner was often prepared by the baker. Long working hours limited the amount of time spent in the home, and among the poorest the home was no more than a crowded room. Under these conditions the incentive to spend any margin of income above subsistence on furniture and furnishings was not very great, and many poor families fashioned kitchenware and furniture from discarded metal containers and wooden boxes or bought used articles in the street markets. The poverty of the home meant that many people, to a much larger extent than now, spent their few leisure hours on the streets and in the public houses.

Consumer expenditure on consumer durables was limited in other ways. Durables, for one thing, were manufactured by skilled craftsmen to last and to be handed down to successive generations. Obviously, this limited the demand for new durables. Secondly, although population was growing there was probably a lower ratio of independent households to population than today. This was so because it was common for several families to share accommodation and for apprentices, journeymen and domestic servants to live with their employers. All this would suggest that there was a much more intensive use of consumer durables than is the case now.

1. The Metal Goods Trades

In the seventeenth and eighteenth centuries the West Midlands was a recognized production centre for nails, saddlers' ironmongery, cutting tools, and locks. In the course of the eighteenth century the region added to its list of products, firearms, glass and 'toys', wrought-iron hollow-ware, plated goods and papier-mâché products. In the early nineteenth century the new gas industry, with its demand for fittings and gauges, provided a strong impetus to the development of the Midlands brass trade, and the fall in brass prices after 1815 stimulated a demand for domestic brass and copper fittings and metal bedsteads.[110] The cutlery trade underwent a similar localization of production. The main cutlery producing centres in the seventeenth and eighteenth centuries were London, Birmingham and

[110] See G. C. Allen, *The Industrial Development of Birmingham and the Black Country* (1929), Part I, Ch. 2.

Sheffield. But by the nineteenth century only Birmingham for edge tools and London for precision instruments could compete seriously with Sheffield products. Almost the entire output of pen and pocket knives, tableware and razors was Sheffield produced in 1850.[111]

Working braziers, tinmen, cutlers, and ironfounders, however, could be found in all towns of any size. The Clerkenwell area of London was described in the 1850s as 'a second edition of Birmingham' with its many watch and clock makers, jewellers, japanners, brass and iron founders, wiremakers and metal turners producing for the fancy goods trade.[112] Ironmongers in both town and country had small foundries in which they manufactured fittings and hardware on special order from builders, plumbers and other trade customers. Especially in country areas, ironmongers were called upon to manufacture and to repair farm tools and equipment. But there were also ironmongery firms making pots and pans, fire irons, fenders, grates and even kitchen ranges on special order and for 'off-the-floor' sales. But the long term trend away from the producer/retailer structure was visible by the mid-eighteenth century, when Campbell had noted that,

The Brazier, or Ironmonger, neither makes nor is supposed capable of making all the different Articles in his Shop: It is sufficient that he is so much of a Working Brazier as to be Judge of all Works of that Kind, and so much of a Smith as to know when Goods are turned out in a workmanlike Manner. ...[113]

This trend was intensified in the nineteenth century. More and more, ironmongers and hardwaremen assumed the role of retail and trade distributors of Birmingham and Sheffield goods.

This departure from the producer/retailer structure was most marked in the cutlery trade. Specialist cutlers, dealing in tableware, pocket- and pen-knives, razors, scissors, steel combs, files and the finer cutting instruments used in the trades and professions, could be found in all of the cities and the larger

---

[111] G. I. H. Lloyd, *The Cutlery Trades* (1913) p. 98.
[112] Burn, *Commercial Enterprise*, p. 14.
[113] Campbell, *London Tradesman*, p. 177.

towns in the nineteenth century.[114] Theoretically, the working
cutler hafted instruments made by forgemen and finished by
grinders, but the working shopkeeper was an exception, even
in old cutlery producing centres like London. In 1862 a member
of the Select Committee on Trade Marks asked,

> Is it not the constant custom, with regard to some of the principal
> articles of manufacture in Sheffield, that is, table knives and forks,
> to affix not the mark of the maker but the name of the vender of
> the goods?[115]

This practice dated from at least the mid-eighteenth century
and was very widespread by the early nineteenth century.
Campbell had noted that 'frequently cutlers, who have a great
Demand for Goods, have them made in the country, put their
own Marks upon them, and sell them for *London* made'.[116]
In 1810 William Halls of Holborn described himself as a working cutler, but it is doubtful if much manufacturing was controlled from the shop. Although he had blades forged for him
by a Holborn smith, most of his stock was bought in Sheffield,
from general cutlers, scissor makers, penknife cutlers, file
makers, and steel refiners.[117] Grinding old cutlery was the
retailer's principal remaining link with the working trade.[118]

In the smaller towns cutlers were usually obliged to move
into compound trading. For example, Charles Goodman of
Northampton in the 1840s traded as a cutler, china dealer and
tobacconist, buying his metal goods from a local ironmonger
and a Sheffield cutler.[119] Trading in general hardware provided
the most common compound link, but in London old established cutlery firms like Tidmarsh and Co. of Holborn might
move into wholesaling and production at Sheffield.[120] Other
London firms began to specialize in the precision instruments
used in trades and professions. For example, in the 1820s
Charles Blackwell of Covent Garden attempted to build up a
surgical instruments trade, selling to surgeons and druggists

---

[114] See Tables A:1 to A:11, Appendix.
[115] *Select Committee on Trade Marks*, Q. 1102.
[116] *London Tradesman*, pp. 238–9, and also, *Book of English Trades*, p. 117.
[117] B.3. 2176, 77 and 78.   [118] *Book of English Trades*, p. 118.
[119] B.3. 2109.   [120] Puseley, *Commercial Companion*, pp. 211–12.

and to the West London and Salisbury infirmaries.[121] In the cities the market for cutlery was sufficiently large to support a few high class retail firms; but the mass market in town and country was serviced primarily by hardwaremen, ironmongers and shopkeepers.

The retail hardware trade was a modern one with especially strong linkages with the burgeoning Sheffield and Birmingham light metal goods trades. At this time hardwaremen dealt primarily in cutlery, household furnishings and ornaments and 'toys', the latter being sold both to retail customers and to tailors and hosiers. Hawes and Moore, for example, a London firm of wholesale hardwaremen in the 1820s, stocked Sheffield cutlery, Birmingham, Sheffield, and London made pewter, silver- and tin-plate, Birmingham and London made jewellery and toys, and a smaller range of tools, pots, pans, and fire-irons.[122] William Cole dealt in a comparable range of goods at his Covent Garden retail shop—cutlery, silver- and tin-plated goods, metal buttons, toys, and japanware.[123] In effect, the hardwareman was the retailer of regionally produced metal goods which, in previous centuries, had been made and sold by local craftsmen. The tradition of the trade, being fairly recent, was not deeply rooted in the producer/retailer pattern, but many hardwaremen employed workmen to make toys and jewellery and to grind and refinish old cutlery. For example, William Cole employed a 'shopman' and a 'workman', although he also sub-contracted work to independent metal workers.

Ironmongers were the most important of all the metal goods tradesmen. Since the trade demanded an enormous stock range to service both the household and trade sides, it was not uncommon for ironmongers in the larger towns and cities to specialize in one or the other. The 'furnishing' ironmonger, dealing in household durables, dealt in many of the goods sold by hardwaremen, apart from 'toys' and jewellery, as well as all the metal goods and furnishings required for the middle class home. This included stoves, ranges, fenders, chimney pieces, cowls, firescreens and fire irons, iron bedsteads, baths, gates and ornamental garden ware and a great variety of iron furniture. In addition, the furnishing ironmonger stocked the com-

[121] B.3. 599.   [122] B.3. 2442.   [123] B.3. 1068.

plete range of kitchen utensils, brass goods, such as candlesticks, ink-stands, etc., Britannia metalware, and Japanware and the common household oils and chemicals.[124]

There was a strong producer/retailer tradition in the ironmongery trade which influenced even the furnishing side. In 1848 Poole and Alderton, general and furnishing ironmongers at Folkestone and Dover, maintained a small brass and iron foundry in which they produced stoves, ranges, grates and other articles.[125] On the other hand, a high class tradesman like William Dainton of Piccadilly was concerned only with 'buying various Articles of Ironmongery used in furnishing and fitting up and decorating' houses.[126] In these high class shops the producer/retailer structure was usually abandoned. Location on the best shopping streets did not lend itself to small manufacturing: shop space was expensive and required for warehousing and display. At most, the high class tradesman would sub-contract work to independent metal workers.

The furnishing ironmonger bought stock in Birmingham, the Black Country and Sheffield. For example, Henry Downer, an ironmonger on the Strand in the 1820s, dealt with several cutlers, a Britannia metal manufacturer and a stove grate ornament maker in Sheffield. From the West Midlands he bought japanware, fire irons, steel 'toys' and locks. But a very large proportion of his stock was drawn from the workshops of London metal workers. He dealt with wire workers, lamp manufacturers, blind makers, tinplate workers, fender makers, silver platers, and numerous founders and braziers.

By the 1850s Birmingham and Sheffield goods enjoyed a reputation with consumers which the producer/retailer of furnishing items found difficult to match. Thomas Wright, a Birkenhead ironmonger and 'Manufacturer of all kinds of Smiths' Work' stressed in advertisements that his stock was drawn from Sheffield and the West Midlands, including 'the Manufactory of Messrs. Jennens, Battridge & Sons' of Birmingham, London and Paris.[127] The small ironmonger had neither

[124] See the stock list in Kemp, *Shopkeeper's Guide.*
[125] Advertisement in *The New Illustrated Hand-book to Folkestone* (1848).
[126] B.3. 1412.
[127] Advertisement in *The Strangers' Guide Through Birkenhead* (1848).

the capital nor the skills to manufacture a significant part of his furnishing stocks, although many retained sufficient equipment to manufacture special orders for brass and iron work and to do repair work.

The typical ironmonger, however, was not the furnisher but the 'general and furnishing' ironmonger who served both trade and retail customers. He offered a narrower range and choice of furnishing articles than the high class specialist, and his trade stocks were oriented towards the industrial characteristics of the area in which he was located. In agricultural areas, for example, the ironmonger's principal trade market was with farmers and agricultural labourers. John Rous, a Colchester ironmonger, testified to the effects of agricultural depression on his trade:

... it used to be a regular thing, at my shop, in 1813, 1814 and 1815, that I used to take from six to seven or eight pounds at my shop, on a Saturday, from the farmers; and now we do not take twenty shillings of a Saturday. ...

Rous dealt in spades, shovels, plough wheels and 'locks of all descriptions'. He said, 'I used to be in the habit of giving an order for 30 dozen of spades and shovels at a time, and now one-third of the quantity will do.'[128] Ironmongers serving carpenters, coopers, bricklayers, masons, plumbers, and other tradesmen kept stocks of 'black', 'cabinet' and 'shipping' ironmongery, such as nails, screws, wire, brackets, hinges and locks, and tools appropriate to the trades, including 'Lancashire tools', such as braces and bits, callipers, spanners, wrenches, turning tools, and vices. The very diverse trade side of the ironmongery business can be illustrated through the activities of William Barnes, an Andover ironmonger in the 1830s. He sold goods to farmers, carpenters, carriers, whitesmiths, braziers, tinmen, tanners, shoemakers and to a local silk factory. In order to service this demand he drew stocks from Sheffield cutlers, edge tool makers, and reap hook manufacturers. He bought in the West Midlands from brass and iron founders and factors, steel manufacturers, nail ironmongers, and sickle manufacturers. In London and Bristol Barnes dealt with

---

[128] *Select Committee on Agriculture*, pp. 179–80.

braziers, wireworkers, founders, iron merchants, coffin makers, and tin plate workers. He also bought agricultural equipment from Samuel Jellicoe's Shirley Mills spade factory and John Fussell & Co.'s edge tool works at Wells.[129]

The general ironmonger was normally both retailer and metal working craftsman. For instance, James Love of Havant in the 1830s defined his occupation as 'Ironmonger, Brazier, lock and White Smith' and James Durtnall of Dover in 1821 as 'Ironmonger, Brazier and Tinman'.[130] Sometimes the working side of the trade is reflected in records of shop wages: William Austin of Woolwich, for example, paid on average £145 a year to 'working servants in trade' and G. & B. Billows of Poole around £200.[131] Bulk purchases of iron and other metals is another probable indicator of a working ironmonger: in 1809 Thomas Wetherby of London was indebted to two iron masters for very large sums; G. & H. Stratton of Blackfriars bought from the Carron Company; and James Cooper of Blackfriars dealt with several iron merchants and scrap metal dealers.[132]

We have suggested that the ironmonger's forge and foundry continued to turn out furnishing items on special order and for off-the-floor sales; but the growth of the Midlands furnishing traders made this an increasingly less important trade function. On the other hand, the ironmonger did provide a local metal goods repair service for householders, farmers and tradesmen. It was very important for farmers and tradesmen in particular to have a local metal manufacturing unit which would turn out, on short notice, one or a small number of brackets, hinges, tools and castings to a specific design and measurement.

A striking characteristic of the ironmongery trade, compared with, say, grocery and drapery, was the comparative unimportance of the specialist wholesaler. To be sure, ironmonger's accounts payable schedules show that they bought from wholesalers based in London and other cities and from local retail/wholesale firms, but purchases from manufacturers and metal working tradesmen were more prominent. The Birmingham and Sheffield factor, moreover, undertook many of the marketing

[129] B.3. 745.
[131] B.3. 152 and B.3. 764.
[130] B.3. 3138 and B.3. 1350.
[132] B.3. 5639, B.3. 4461 and B.3. 899.

functions which in other trades were left to urban based specialist wholesalers. Apart from the outworker's industries, the typical metal goods manufacturer, and the brazier, founder, or tinman, was a small producer who could effectively market the output of his workshop with, at most, the assistance of a commission agent. A wholesale ironmonger, moreover, was confronted by problems of standardization. The wholesaler had no function if every article demanded had to possess unique characteristics. Articles like nails and screws were more-or-less standardized, and for most furnishing articles uniqueness was not a matter of concern, but there is no doubt that the ironmonger's frequent resort to the small shops of founders, braziers, and tinmen was in part necessitated by his requirements for articles with unique specifications. Finally, apart from the furnishing trade in the cities, ironmongery was not a retail trade of the pure type. The retailer's paramount concern—stock control and rapid turnover—was not yet highly developed in a trade which did not enjoy a mass demand for its products and was still very largely bound to small scale production.

2. *The Furniture Trades*

London and Buckinghamshire had emerged by 1850 as the great furniture manufacturing region for the whole of Great Britain. It was noticed in 1858 that,

> Strange as it may appear, nearly the whole of the furniture sold in Dublin is of London manufacture. Bed-room chairs of London make can be purchased either in Edinburgh or Dublin at the same price they are disposed of in the retail market in town.[133]

Manufacturers in Soho and the East End were narrowly specialized into chair, table, bed, and cabinet production, a stratification which enabled London producers 'not only to get up their goods in a superior style, but also to undersell their provincial rivals in every part of the United Kingdom'.[134] The output of these workshops was sold to wholesale dealers and directly to London and provincial furniture retailers.

Furniture retailers were known as 'cabinet makers', 'uphol-

[133] Burn, *Commercial Enterprise*, p. 22.   [134] Ibid., p. 21.

sterers' and 'furniture brokers'. The cabinet maker was normally a producer/retailer, while the upholsterer, originally 'a Species of Taylor'[135] dealt in furnishings and furniture, advised on the decoration of homes, and sometimes worked as an appraiser, estate agent and funeral director. The small cabinet maker and the high class upholsterer exploited very different markets, but there was a middle ground as well occupied by men styling themselves 'Cabinet Maker and Upholsterer'. It was the latter group which led one observer to suggest in 1821 that the 'business of cabinet-maker, and of an upholsterer, are now so generally united together, that any observation on either of these branches may, with propriety, be comprehended under one general head'.[136] The furniture broker was more distinctly a retailer: at most, he assembled materials for lining furniture or stuffing pillows, couches and chairs.[137]

The upholsterer's stock range was often very wide, overlapping with many articles sold by furnishing and general ironmongers. An inventory of stock taken at a Brighton shop in the 1830s included: a wardrobe, chests of drawers, commodes, dressing tables, card tables, reading stands, liquor stands, paper stands, mirrors, beds and cribs, and some seventy five chairs of various designs. The stock of furnishings included mattresses, carpets, lamps, shades, candlesticks, snuffers, iron and brass fenders, coal scuttles, fire irons, trays, coffee pots, ewers, canisters, kettles, pots, pans, and saucepans.[138] In a going concern the 'feather room' would be stocked with drapery, feathers, and horsehair for stuffing and covering furniture and mattresses. In contrast to the upholsterer, the small cabinet maker lacked the capital and warehousing facilities, as well as the aesthetic skills demanded for furnishing houses, to trade in furnishings or to hold large furniture stocks for off-the-floor sales. In general he manufactured on order from retail or trade customers, undertook furniture repairs and other wood-working jobs, and tried to sell any finished stock to wholesalers and upholsterers. Typical transactions recorded in the account

[135] Campbell, *London Tradesman*, p. 170.   [136] *Book of English Trades*, p. 60.
[137] See the bankruptcy records of Edward Pearson, York Street, Westminster, Furniture Broker, B.3. 4094.   [138] B.3. 5392.

books of William Launer, a Tonbridge cabinet maker in the
1820s and 1830s include, 'restoring matting', 'repainting and
restaining', 'dozen chair buttons sold', 'chair frames', 'altering
2 bed pillows', 'cleaning and repairing gold chairs', 'turning a
stool leg', 'repairing stable rack', 'handbill handle', 'a new
rolling pin', 'turning pulley wheel', and 'making hand barrow'.[139]

The input of materials varied with the type and quality of
furniture which was being made. William Walter of Crawford
Street, Marylebone for instance, manufactured plain cabinet,
chair and table furniture, and his accounts payable schedule
lists debts only with timber merchants and ironmongers.[140]
Upholsterers' schedules reflect inputs of many more materials:
they dealt with drapers, mercers, warehousemen, upholsterer's
warehousemen, fringe and tassel makers, leather sellers,
braziers, and tinmen.[141]

In the large upholsterer's shop the labour force was highly
skilled and specialized. The workmen carried out activities as
diverse as making, covering and stuffing furniture, cutting
carpets and arranging window drapery; but a great deal of
work had to be contracted to specialists. For example, John
Blease of Dover Street in London, sent out work to painters,
locksmiths and tailors; while John Davis, a high class London
upholsterer, contracted work to painters and glaziers, a herald
painter, and a turner.[142]

In the producer/retailer context, demand for furniture and
furnishings can easily outstrip the physical and labour capacity
of the shop/household unit, and the obvious short run solution
is to send out work, in this case to journeymen cabinet makers
and upholsterers. John Davis, for example, sent out work to at
least three journeymen upholsterers and two journeymen
cabinet makers. But a more fundamental solution, and the only
practical one in towns without a floating labour force of furniture craftsmen, was to buy stock. This was done extensively
even by relatively small cabinet makers. For example, Richard

---

[139] Kent Country Archives, Q/Cl 179/1 and 2.
[140] B.3. 5676.
[141] See for example a file relating to John Davis of London, B.3. 1421.
[142] B.3. 274 and B.3. 1421.

Aman, a small Northampton cabinet maker in the 1830s, bought from several Northampton cabinet makers and upholsterers, a Buckinghamshire chair manufacturer, a Spitalfield cabinet maker and a Finsbury wholesale upholsterer.[143] This is one indicator that the long term trend for furniture dealers to specialize either in production or distribution was already very visible. Once the cabinet maker had extended his business into upholstery items and began retailing furnishing ironmongery, hardware, glass, china, and fancy goods the pressures to abandon furniture production became very great.

A rounded view of the trade in country areas can be had by analyzing the accounts of an upholsterer in Kent in the late 1830s.[144] He sold articles such as chairs, sofas, tables, beds and mattresses, chests of drawers, mirrors, picture frames, mats and carpets, kitchenware, fire irons, fenders and ornaments. He bought and sold used furniture and repaired and refinished articles brought to his shop. He also rented furniture, such as an easy chair at 3s. a week, a small sofa at 6d., a tent bedstead at 9d. and a bolster at 3d. In a small way he was a decorator and remover, and he accepted orders for many small woodworking jobs, such as making a pair of bell pull handles, a tea pot handle and blind rollers. And he also carried out funeral arrangements: for the executor of the estate of Mr Hopper, he arranged to line the coffin, provide flannel for the shroud, supply a mattress and pillow, crape hat bands, seven pairs of gloves and a pall, hire five bearers, a minister, sexton, clerk and undertaker, all for £9. 11s. 3d.

3. Conclusions

A minority of ironmongers and furniture dealers specialized in either consumer or trade goods, but the typical tradesman served both markets, and for him the distinction between the two was neither very clear nor important. The producer/retailer structure was strongly entrenched in all but cutlery, hardware and high class ironmongery and upholstery, although there was a growing trend towards independent production units. Tradesmen manufactured for off-the-floor sales, but mainly they were involved in turning out special orders and

[143] B.3. 160. [144] Kent County Archives, Q/Cl/498, Bapchild accounts.

repairing tools, equipment, furnishings and furniture. If a special order demanded the application of unusual skills and equipment, it was contracted out to a working tradesman, but most ironmongers and furniture dealers inherited both a strong craft tradition and a manufacturing plant, and thus most special orders were handled in the shop. The long term trend towards disentangling production and distribution is visible in these trades, but with important exceptions in London and other large cities, the general absence of aggressive pricing and promotional devices—notable in the clothing and drapery trades—suggest that the mass consumer market and retailers serving that market, had yet to emerge.

VI

The Economic and Social Organization of Work and Trade in Shops

A SIGNIFICANT proportion of England's labour force in the early nineteenth century was engaged either full-time or part-time in distribution. For most, especially the petty hawkers, earnings were not high, but there was a dearth of alternative employment opportunities. Shops employed a great deal of labour as well, partly because in many trades production was still tied to small workshops, partly because processing duties were heavy in some of the retail trades, and partly because unskilled labour was cheap. The population of the typical tradesman's household was large, consisting of journeymen, apprentices, domestic servants, children, and perhaps kinsmen of the tradesman and his wife.

It is difficult to generalize about tradesmen's entrepreneurial attitudes and to construct the system of goals and behavioural norms which defined their actions. Behavioural norms were changing very rapidly throughout this period and are therefore not amenable to static definition. Moreover, entrepreneurial attitudes differed between and within town and country situations, and the historian, more than the social scientist, must be conscious of the subjectivity of human action.

In so far as generalizations have any validity, there is evidence to suggest that in the country throughout this period and in the town and city in the early decades of the period, there was a widespread live-and-let-live attitude among tradesmen. In small country towns the community of tradesmen was small and intimate, and its members can sometimes be seen adjusting their individual actions in the interest of the group. For example, a grocer described in his diary a meeting of Ashford tradesmen in 1816, and there is no implication in his report that such meetings and attempts to define a common policy were in any way unusual:

Monday the 10th 1816 a meeting held at the George Inn Ashford, consisting of 29 of the most principle (sic) Tradesmen. Danl. Nickalls first took the chair and began the business but when Mr Hutton cam he risinged it up to him viz. Mr Hutton and after a good deal of pro & con, it was agreed not to take any French Silver there being more than enough of the English silver for change abt that being shortly to bee called in and at a great loss to the holders and it was deemed impolitic to sadle ourselves with the loss of French Silver. and there being no where to get it off French Silver in large Quantities only by laying it out with smuglers and that would not do to pay our Lenders. So a paper was drawn up to that effect. and I believe Danl. Nickalls was one of the first to sign it. and money was put down to strike off 150 hand Bills. which was done by Mr Elliott. But the copy that was given to the printer was so very incorrect, that I was ashamed to put mine up in publick. But Observe to my great astonishment some thing was moved by Mr Rickard whether Mr D Nickalls would strickly stand to it, Mr Hutton rose and said that whatever Mr Nickalls agreed to He Mr Hutton knew Mr Nickalls so well. and so long was confident that whatever he agreed to would strickly adhered to, and I agreed with Mr Hutton in confidence of Mr D. Nickalls and after a few glasses of ale the meeting broke up all unanimous.[1]

The Journal entry reveals that Ashford tradesmen had developed a policy-making organization which was formalized in several respects: there was a recognized leadership—Hutton and then Nickalls—a developed procedure for discussing issues, arriving at decisions and communicating those decisions to Ashford residents. Yet it is clear that group solidarity was not perfect, and the fear expressed by Rickard that Nickalls would not stand by the common decision proved to be justified:

Astonishing the very next day ... D. Nickalls got what he could of the Trade together again to intreat them to take the french silver again. ... Mr Nickalls sent a note to me at Miss Bushells sale for me to come down to the George as they was again Met on the french silver. I read one line of it. and beg of Lurock to go back and tell them I wd. have nothing to do with Shuttlecocks so to the astonishment of me J.S. and Mr Hutton broke his word in a very few Hours.

[1] John Sills, *Diary*, Kent County Archives Office, U 442 Z6/3.

A tradesmen's organization such as this could be useful in reducing conflict over extraordinary issues, such as accepting French silver. But tradesmen's behaviour in normal day-to-day situations was governed more by the behavioural norms internalized during education in trade as apprentice and journeyman. As a master tradesman, actions were constrained by the formal legal code and, equally important, by the informal social sanctions of fellow tradesmen and the general public. But conformity to social norms is never perfect, and their very existence is best revealed when they are broken and when they are questioned during periods of intense situational change. This was happening in England during this period, particularly in the cities, when debate arose over the problem of what constituted 'fair trading'.

As late as 1853 Robert Kemp suggested that the shopkeeper must be 'frugal in his own expenditure, that, in deriving profits from trade, he may not trespass unduly upon the interests of others; but so holding the balance between man and man, that the eye of his soul should discover no bias in the beam to reprove his conscience. ... '[2] Lurking behind all this piety is the very old economic assumption that demand curves are inelastic, and that competitive pricing will not increase sales sufficiently to maintain profit margins; or, looked at from another point of view, that the size of the retail market is fixed, and that increased sales in one shop means losses for others. These assumptions are not always irrational, for in traditional societies their maintenance contributes to social welfare by providing a measure of protection for the less efficient. But in societies undergoing rapid economic growth the assumptions must be relaxed if that growth is to be sustained. The very intense concern of some contemporaries in Industrial Revolution England about the relaxation of these norms was not simply obscurantist: if only the efficient production and distribution units were to survive—that is, if welfare was to be disentangled from production and distribution units—then welfare would have to be provided through some other agency of the social system. In England and elsewhere the state has assumed this function, but during our period its assumption of the role

[2] Kemp, *Shopkeeper's Guide*, p. 55.

was very imperfect. It was this interim situation which brought so much hardship to individuals and which caught the attention of contemporaries and historians.

Traditional fair trading concepts were abandoned first in the cities. A London trained draper, operating for a time in the provinces, was surprised to find that a 'good trade' there was one with a regular patronage rather than an impersonal trade based on many customers and high turnovers. A regular patronage trade did not require aggressive pricing and advertising, and in the shop which he managed in Bristol,

... they had never been in the habit of displaying any quantity of goods in the windows and my style of window-dressing was looked upon as a decided innovation. A roll or two of cloth, with a few men's hats in paper in the background, would constitute all the show that was originally made. People seemed to depend more upon their connexion and usual customers than to seek for new ones.[3]

A technically more efficient operation could not guarantee success for the newcomer in this social context:

... a man commencing business in the country, unless he had lived in one town a number of years as assistant, and had made a connexion or succeeded to some old-established trade, or become a partner in a house, did not stand a very good chance in a country town, unless he went to very great lengths to make himself known. ...[4]

In other words, much of the countryside had yet to be converted to the impersonally competitive trading norms of the emerging industrial society.

Abandonment of the traditional norms of fair trading was a subject of much discussion among tradesmen even in the cities, and especially during the first two decades of the century. A tradesman who had established his son in a shop in London reported to a friend in 1810,

... I proceeded to London to see how things were going on, when judge of thy friend's surprise, when arrived in Cheapside, no longer able to discern the neat but unadorned shop which formerly bespoke the habits of its dweller, which was now entirely changed; the windows were such as Gulliver would describe as a glass case in

---

[3] *Reminiscences of an Old Draper*, p. 142.   [4] Ibid., p. 191.

Brognibog, each pane being no less than plate glass a yard square, and instead of his name in plain Roman capital, with his trade of chemist and druggist; after a quarter of an hour's decyphering, I could make out —— and Co. Chemicals & Galenicals in that kind of distorted characters which are pourtrayed on the Egyptian monuments of antiquity.[5]

But this was to question the changing situation only on its surface level: much more direct attacks were launched against the first shops to introduce price ticketing, and thereby price competition. 'Several Tradesmen' warned the public in 1819 that price ticketing was 'one of the most usually deceptive practices', that '*Cheap shops* are a great evil, and a much greater eye-sore to the *regular* Trader … because cheap *selling* is usually a mere pretence. … ' These 'Imposter shops' could be known 'by the vehemency and number of their placards, signs and tickets' but the public should understand that 'manufactured goods of nearly every description have standard prices, at which they are retailed in the market. … ' The tradesmen argued that price differentials among shops selling the same goods were justified only when one shop sold on cash terms and the other on credit.[6] In 1825 another writer suggested that 'Putting up prices in windows *at all* is far from respectable. … '[7] The biographer of Samuel Budgett, the Bristol wholesaler who began trade as a country grocer, felt obliged to make the naïve apology that 'I am not prepared to say, that the expedient called in the trade "leading articles" was not sometimes resorted to. …'[8]

Business survival in this period, however, particularly in the cities, involved continuous reassessment of 'fair trading' concepts. Despite some initial opposition, price competition and advertising were quickly accepted as normal business practice. In 1833 parliamentary commissioners asked a City wholesaler why ticketing was 'so generally prevalent now'; and was it not a fact 'that some of the oldest established retail houses in London have been obliged to have recourse to the system of

[5] *The Tradesman*, 3, no. 1, July (1809), p. 31.
[6] Several Tradesmen, *The London Tradesmen*, p. 120 and p. 118.
[7] 'Price-Ticket Shops', *The Economist and General Adviser*, i, 26.
[8] W. Arthur, *Successful Merchant*, p. 142.

ticketing the prices of their goods. ...' In answer, the wholesaler suggested that three out of four retail shops on Oxford and Regent Streets ticketed their goods, and he thought the practice arose 'from an entire change in the mode of carrying on the retail business, that is, that it has now become more casual and less dependent upon regular constant customers to particular shops. ...'[9]

We have noted that production and distribution functions were being disentangled in this period. 'Tradesmen', according to one definition, were those

... who *buy* and *sell* only, and are either *wholesale* or *retail*: those to whom goods are sold in a state fit for sale, and who perform little more than cut out, pack, or divide and dispense the articles confined to their care. In this view not only drapers and grocers, but haberdashers of hats (hatters), of gloves (glovers), stationery, and umbrellas, as well as oilmen and cheesemongers, are Tradesmen, and not any of them manufacturers, because they change not the shape and appearance of the articles of their respective trades; but having, *at most* bought their goods in a merchantable state of half preparation, they employ various submasters to finish or alter the same; but should they do this work themselves, the case is not altered in the least.[10]

This disaggregation of functions meant that tradesmen's energies were oriented increasingly towards developing retailing skills. In addition to techniques of sales promotion, the retailer needed at least an elementary understanding of business arithmetic. For some, and possibly many, business arithmetic was a formidable mystery. Aaron Woolf, a Brighton upholsterer and cabinet maker who, in the 1830s, moved into retailing in a big way, replied with obvious anguish to questions about his turnover, margins and costs:

A. I don't know how to do it. I don't understand. I did not put down my profits. I have no book or papers from which they can be seen.
Q. From what source did you obtain the amount of profits shown upon the balance sheets?

[9] *Select Committee on Manufactures*, Q. 1415–21.
[10] Several Tradesmen, *London Tradesmen*, p. 82.

A.   From calculations which I draw from memory. I estimated my
     expenses and then calculated what my profits were.
Q.   What were your Expenses from which you calculated your
     profits?
A.   I am no scholar and do not understand and have been obliged
     to get an accountant to make out my account.[11]

Informal accounting procedures did not usually lead to ruin:
the volume of trade in many shops was small; the tradesman
was intimately involved in all aspects of production and distribution and was highly sensitive to business changes. In so far
as income was derived from manufacturing or processing skills
and the personal connexion established in a community, fine
attention to turnover, margins, profits and costs might not be
too important. But as this old environment slowly gave way to
the competitive retailing developed in the cities, tradesmen were
obliged either to master the new skills or face the possibility of
going under.

1. *Turnovers, Margins and Credit*

The account books from retail shops have survived in very small
numbers, and few of these provide data for estimating annual
turnovers. However, calculations from the Journal of Mouys
and Jarritt, high class London hatters, suggest that turnover in
1804 amounted to no more than £780.[12] A running balance
of receipts and expenditure made by Peter Burdell, an Italian
warehouseman at Sheerness, indicates that in the year March
1833 to February 1834 his turnover amounted to little more
than £650, falling to £520 in 1834–5 and £490 in 1835–6, in
which year business ceased.[13] The receipts of a village shop in
Berkshire in 1801 were as little as £150.[14]

   Although caution is required in their use,[15] the Court of

[11] B.3. 1421.
[12] P.R.O., Chancery Master's Exhibits, C. 103, no. 191.
[13] Kent County Archives, Q/Cl 188/1 & 2.
[14] Berkshire Record Office, D/ESv (M) B23/1–2.
[15] In this chapter quantitative information derives principally from Court
of Bankruptcy records, supported where possible from other sources. Considerable
caution is necessary in using bankruptcy sources, because generalizations which are
true for this population will not necessarily be true for the general trading population. Nonetheless, to ignore this source of information or to assume that any
generalizations from it are invalid, would be insupportable. On a practical research

Bankruptcy files offer the historian a wider range of turnover estimates than surviving account books. A selection of data from this source, for the period 1800–42, is presented in Table 6:1. James Yovens, a London grocer, is recorded as estimating

TABLE 6:1. Estimated Shop Annual Average Gross Profits, Turnover and Profit Margins, 1800–42

Annual Gross Profits	Average Sales	Approximate Gross Profit Margins	Trading Period	Firm
£	£	%		*Grocers*
640	11 340	5½	1838–40	J. Yovens, London
625			1815–25	J. Booty, Newport
525	10 000	5½	1806–15	J. Smith, Faversham
500			1820–9	T. Walter, Wilstone
395			1810–29	J. Lyon, Cambridge
375			1830–2	C. Hayles, Portsmouth
335	3 360	10	1825–7	W. Hillier, Salisbury
300	4 000	7½	1836–42	T. Bumpus, Northampton
275			1829–32	T. Smith, Birmingham
260			1837–8	G. Hind, Bishops Waltham
240			1830–5	W. Towers, Nottingham
220			1829–41	E. Bumpstead, Halesworth
150	2 000	7½	1832–4	J. Gibbs, Ramsey
140			1825–9	W. Lambourne, Aylesbury
125			1828–31	J. Ward, Coventry
115			1819–25	E. Weaver, London
110	1 300	10	1835–8	R. Rose, Sutton Valence
100			1813–16	H. & T. Biven, Mortlake
100			1817–19	V. Barford, Romford
60			1830	H. Clackett, Dover
50			1823–5	A. Hawkins, Saint Albans
				Drapers & Haberdashers
2 270			1820–6	W. & H. Hart, London
1 665	22 175	7½	1818–27	Stephens & Croft, London

level, the records provide a voluminous and detailed source of primary material which can be tested against the relatively scanty surviving volume of account books and published material. Moreover, in surveying many hundreds of these files, I have formed the impression that bankrupts in this period cannot simply be dismissed as a category of people who had insufficient skills to meet the competition. It was an unusual tradesman in this period who did not, at some period in his career, either come very close to insolvency or actually experience it.

TABLE 6:1 *cont.*

Annual Gross Profits	Average Sales	Approximate Gross Profit Margins	Trading Period	Firm
£	£	%		
1 200	7 335	16	1820–6	Froggott & Lilleyman, Doncaster
900	6 000	15	1823–4	J. Thomas, London
300	2 000	15	1795–1800	J. Thomas, London
450	3 000	15	1800–09	J. Thomas, London
600	4 000	15	1809–12	T. Broad, Penzance
750	5 000	15	1812–21	T. Broad, Penzance
600	4 000	15	1821–4	T. Broad, Penzance
450	3 000	15	1824–7	T. Broad, Penzance
500			1813–32	S. Burrell, Saint Ives
480			1820–5	W. Fuller, Boston
480	6 625	$7\frac{1}{2}$	1816–18	Ronalds & Singleton, Wholesalers, Cheapside, London
400	8 200	5	1810–11	J. Stead, Wholesaler, Cheapside, London
390	5 200	$7\frac{1}{2}$	1810	R. Ball, Lambeth, London
240			1815–21	W. Bewley, Manchester
235			1835–9	J. Bond, Gt. Yarmouth
225			1828–9	S. John, London
100	4 000	$2\frac{1}{2}$	1823–4	R. Grimwood, Rochester
				Tailors, Clothes Dealers
1 130	4 595	25	1826–8	J. Tait, Liverpool
800			1827–30	C. Darby, London
600			1834–9	T. Davies, Lewes
460			1828–34	W. Hiscock, Southampton
450			1809–12	G. Kemp, London
245	800	30	1825	Dovey & Cox, London
235			1835–41	T. Peters, Cambridge
175			1819–21	W. Dixon, Portsmouth
160	1 585	10	1822–24	J. Perry, London, clothes dealer
				Ironmongers, Hardwaremen, Cutlers
460			1821	J. Patterson, London
910			1822	J. Patterson, London
1 510			1823	J. Patterson, London
715			1824	J. Patterson, London
810			1823–7	Hawes & Moore, London
700			1816–19	C. Ashford, London

TABLE 6:1 cont.

Annual Gross Profits	Average Sales	Approximate Gross Profit Margins	Trading Period	Firm
£	£	%		
650			1811–31	W. Austin, London
600			1835–7	G. Collis–Romford shop
200			1835–7	G. Collis–Dunmore shop
540	1 265	42½	1836–42	C. Goodman, Northampton, Cutler, tobacconist etc.
350			1824–8	C. Blackwell, London cutler
300			1825–35	W. Barnes, Andover
105			1808–21	W. Long, Warminster
260			1821–38	W. Long, Warminster
255	1 280	20	1829–31	J. Adam, London
225			1824–6	W. Dainton, London
				Furniture Trades
2 975	11 900	25	1823–7	J. Davis, London
250			1815–31	E. Pearson, London
50	100	50	1831–5	R. Aman, Northampton
100	300	33	1835–7	R. Aman, Northampton
				Stationers
1 040			1820–4	S. Wilkins, London
290	1 030	28	1828–32	W. Penley, Portsea
50	170	28	1830–2	A. Penley, Portsmouth

Source: Commissions of Bankruptcy, Public Record Office, B.3. Figures are rounded to the nearest £5.

his annual average turnover between 1838 and 1840 at £11 340, and John Smith, a Faversham grocer, £10 000. Stephens and Croft, Oxford Street haberdashers, calculated their average annual turnover to be £22 175, and Froggott and Lilleyman, Doncaster drapers, at £7335. John Davis, a high class London upholsterer, calculated his annual average turnover at £11 900. In most cases the figures cited in Table 6:1 are averages over two or more years and the averaging may mask substantial annual variations. But the largest turnover figures cited in Table 6:1 are not for exceptionally large shops. The 'monster shops' enjoyed annual sales approaching, and exceeding, £1M per annum; and tradesmen on the principal shopping streets of

London and the provincial cities anticipated turnovers exceeding £20 000: in the 1830s, for example, a draper rented a big shop in Holborn on the understanding that the previous owner had enjoyed sales of £1200 per week, or about £60 000 per annum.[16] But turnovers exceeding £50 000 were enjoyed only by the comparatively few big shops in the cities and larger market towns. Grocers like John Smith of Faversham, with annual turnovers of £10 000 would be recognized as substantial High Street shopkeepers. Table 6:1 would suggest that there were many small shopkeepers struggling along on annual sales of £1000 a year or less.

The profit figures listed in Table 6:1 are gross profits. Gross profits are a function of two variables: sales and gross profit margins. In retailing the gross profit margin represents the value added by the distributor, or alternatively, the cost to final buyers of retail services. In some twenty cases listed in Table 6:1 the bankrupt either stated his average margin or provided sufficient data for it to be calculated. Among the grocers and shopkeepers the highest margins were quoted by William Hillier of Salisbury and Richard Rose of Sutton Valence, in both cases 10 per cent. The lowest margins, in both cases 5½ per cent, were quoted by the two tradesmen with the largest turnovers in the sample, James Yovens of London and John Smith of Faversham.

Among drapers and haberdashers, Stephens and Croft of Oxford Street in London cited their average margins as 7½ per cent, and Richard Ball of Lambeth also worked on margins of 7½ per cent. Froggott and Lilleyman of Doncaster traded on margins of about 16 per cent, and Thomas Broad, a draper at Penzance for over thirty years, also believed his average margins to be 15 per cent over the entire period. If Robert Grimwood of Rochester traded on gross margins of 2½ per cent then his bankruptcy is hardly surprising; but this figure may be a net rather than a gross profit margin. Finally, the two wholesale margins of 7½ per cent and 5 per cent were cited by London warehousemen for 1816–18 and 1810–11.

There is little information available on margins in the clothing trades. Jane Tait, a Liverpool dressmaker, estimated

---

[16] *Reminiscences of an Old Draper*, p. 203.

her margins at 25 per cent and Dovey and Cox, tailors in London's Soho district, worked on 30 per cent margins. Joseph Perry of Houndsditch in London cited margins of 10 per cent, but he was a retailer of clothing rather than a manufacturer.

In the metal goods trades profit margins were cited in two cases. Charles Goodman, a working cutler and a retailer of tobacco and china in Northampton, believed his gross profit margins to be 42½ per cent on average, and James Adam, a City of London ironmonger, set his at 20 per cent.

In the furniture trades, John Davis, a high-class London upholsterer, stated his average gross profit margins at 25 per cent. Richard Aman of Northampton was, in contrast to Davis, a small cabinet maker who manufactured most of the goods he sold. He informed the bankruptcy commissioners that between 1831 and 1835 his returns amounted to no more than £100 per annum; but when he married he attempted to increase his trade and the average margins on the goods he sold fell to 33 per cent.[17] Finally, in the partnership of William and Aron Penley with stationery shops at Portsmouth and Portsea, the average margins in both shops were set at 28 per cent.

There is little supporting evidence for these figures which can be found in either published or unpublished sources. Thomas Danks, a shopman with Joseph Higgs, a Dudley woollen draper, testified that around 1816 his employer marked-up Irish linens by about 22 per cent, narrow cloth from 7 to 14 per cent, broad cloths from 7 to 10½ per cent, handkerchiefs around 6 per cent and muslins at cost when fresh in stock and up to 16 per cent on old stock.[18] The average mark-up on these five items would range from 10½ per cent to 13½ per cent, which is compatible with the figures listed in Table 6:1.

A village shopkeeper in Berkshire in 1801 entered in his Journal some rough calculations of expected profits. On 26 yards of flax tape he planned for a mark-up of 14 per cent; on 9 yards of blue tape 12½ per cent; but he planned to retail Holland tape and stockings at cost. He priced barley, soap,

---

[17] B.3. 160. It is probable that he began buying furniture for resale, and the average margins, as a per cent of retail sales, would thus be lower.
[18] B.3. 2236.

cheese, and sugar either at a loss or 'to cover the break of the scale'. In general his margins were cut very finely, and presuming that personal expenditure was included in 'Disbursements' it can be seen that the business barely met its costs:[19]

Disbursements	£202	2	6	Stock	£58	0	$0\frac{1}{4}$
Losses		1	4	8	Receipts	149	12	$4\frac{1}{2}$
	£203	7	2		£207	12	$4\frac{3}{4}$

The accounts of William Doubleday, an Essex shopkeeper, include some mark-up calculations on consignments of china. On Blue Printed china his mark-up in 1833 and 1834 was 25 per cent; on Willow between 25 and 30 per cent; on Painted 35 per cent; Dipped between 40 and 45 per cent and on 'C. C. Ware' between 50 and 55 per cent. On two consignments received in 1833 and one in 1834 he calculated his costs and adjusted his mark-up for an expected *net* profit of about 2 per cent; but on a stock order received in 1832 he anticipated a small net loss.[20]

Table 6:1 indicates that retailers in the same trade applied different margins: for example, James Yovens' margins in the grocery trade were $4\frac{1}{2}$ per cent lower than those applied by Richard Rose. This might reflect a different competitive position resulting from the location of the two shops; or competition based on personal connexion rather than price; or it might reflect differing cost structures, sources of wholesale supply and sales composition and varying ability to control leakage.

Table 6:1 also indicates that margins varied among trades as well as within them. In general, relatively high margins are found in trades where the product is varied and large stocks are carried, and low margins where turnover is comparatively rapid and little or no 'free' service is given. The margins in the grocery trade were probably lower than in the drapery trade, while in the tailoring, furniture and metal goods trades the comparatively high margins reflect shop production costs as much as retail distribution costs.

[19] Berkshire Record Office, D/ESv (M) B23/1–2.
[20] Essex Record Office, D/DQ 27/1–5.

The margins listed in Table 6:1 are low in comparison with present day margins, and certainly in comparison with margins prior to the post-war 'revolution' in British retailing. In 1938 it was calculated that margins averaged 9 per cent on sugar, 14 per cent on tea, 15 per cent on butter, 33 per cent on men's outwear, 34 per cent on haberdashery, 35 per cent on cutlery and ironmongery, and 41 per cent on furniture.[21] It is known that retailers' margins have accounted for an increasingly larger share of the total value of consumer expenditures in recent times. Harold Barger has shown that in the U.S.A. retail margins rose between 1869 and 1947 in most trades. For 1869 Barger calculated that average margins in the independent grocery store were 18 per cent, in the country general store 17.5 per cent, in dry goods (drapery) shops 18.7 per cent, in furniture 30 per cent, hardware 25.2 per cent and stationery 22 per cent.[22]

It is possible that the margins listed in Table 6:1 are unusually low (particularly for groceries and drapery) and not representative of the trades as a whole. All of those who cited their margins were necessarily somewhat inexact. When Joseph Gibbs was asked by the commissioners what profit he allowed on the cost of goods sold, he had to reply, 'No regular profit on the cost price.' The existence of price haggling could mean that tradesmen's estimates of average margins were at best informed guesses rather than calculated fact. It is also impossible to be certain that the profits and margins cited are gross of all trade expenses. For example, John Davis the upholsterer offered the commissioners three different gross profit margins—25, 15, and 10 per cent—each one being gross of certain trading costs. In other words, some of the low margins cited may be closer to net profits as we understand them rather than gross profits. Finally, it should not be forgotten that many tradesmen carried on a wholesale trade, and if this was at all extensive then the average margins cited would be below actual retail margins.

On the other hand, there are reasons for believing that retail

[21] P. Bareau and J. B. Jefferys, *Consumer Goods*; *The Methods and Cost of Distribution* (News Chronicle Publications, N.D.), Chart II.
[22] H. Barger, *Distribution's Place in the American Economy Since 1869* (1955) p. 81, table 24.

margins were comparatively low in this period. The final prices of consumer goods probably reflected the absence of large-scale factory production more than retail distribution costs. Costs in retail shops will be examined in detail in later sections, but it can be said here that tradesmen made extensive use of cheap apprentice and family labour. Rents were comparatively low, except on the major shopping streets of the cities, and little capital equipment was used in retail shops. Price competition between shops began to develop strongly around the 1820s, but the distribution system as a whole was never lacking in price competitiveness, since markets, fairs and itinerant distributors did provide consumers with an alternative retail service, even in the remoter country areas.

Price haggling in shops declined very rapidly in this period, although it was still to be found in drapery and haberdashery shops, especially in the country.[23] When prices were not ticketed the tradesman resorted to private shopmarks. The mark was formed by choosing any ten letter word, each letter of the word representing a numeral. If the word was COMPATIBLE and the tradesman had purchased a piece of cloth for 4s. 6d. a yard and the assistant was to ask 7s. and no less than 6s. a yard, the cloth would be marked 'PT' to represent the cost price, 'I' to indicate the asking price, and 'T' to denote the lowest asking price.[24]

High class shops were never seriously troubled by price haggling. The accounts of Mouys and Jarrit, Pall Mall hatters and Peal Brothers, London bootmakers, indicate that standard prices were charged on all goods, though it is doubtful if the stock was ticketed.[25] Price haggling frustrated the drive for large turnovers, reduced the productivity of the sales staff and obliged the shopkeeper to have confidence in the honesty and bargaining power of his assistants: it also made the simplest forms of business budgeting a major problem. Fixed pricing was essential to the success of the 'monster shops' and the 'cutting shops'. A draper who had worked in an East End

[23] Kemp, *Shopkeeper's Guide*, p. 6.

[24] 'On the Private Shopmarks of Tradesmen', *The Tradesman*, x, no. 5, N.S., 462–463.

[25] P.R.O., Chancery Master's Exhibits, C.103, no. 191. County Hall Record Office, London, uncatalogued.

'cutting shop' sometime before 1820 recalled that in the corner of each window was a 'No Abatement' sign:

In old-fashioned times people used to chaffer and haggle about the price ... and the healthy system of sticking to one price was just coming into vogue, and was the means of saving much time, ours being a pushing and ticketing shop. ...[26]

By maintaining a single price system this shop was able to operate on large turnovers while employing relatively inexperienced shopmen.

Cutting shops were found in the provisions trade as well as drapery and haberdashery. They forced the neighbourhood shops to cut their margins very close to costs and to compete mainly on the basis of service. Edward Peacock, an Islington shopkeeper in the 1840s explained to a Select Committee that,

... I endeavour to sell articles at the same price that they are sold at in the most respectable shops, certainly considerably under what they are sold at at the West End; but in every neighbourhood like mine there are a number of what are termed cutting shops, that dispose of an article under the cost price. The article of sugar is disposed of by grocers, and the article of soap is disposed of by oilmen, at a price that I cannot purchase it for. It is a well-known fact that it is done, and the consequence is that they draw an influx of trade for other articles by selling some article or other at a very low profit. Now my shop is surrounded by shops of this description, except the article of tobacco, and in that I carry on a greater trade in the week days than on Sunday, because I sell at the same price as my neighbours; in some articles I am rather above.[27]

Peacock's explanation of how he survived in trade would be a familiar one for any small neighbourhood shopkeeper today: '10 out of 12 of my customers in six days of the week do not expend more than 1d. ...;' but on Sundays 'I have a greater concourse, and respectable women will come in and say, "Oh, dear me, I am so glad your shop is open; I do not know what I should have done if I had not found it open; I want several things" and the consequence is, that I made a good bit of money on Sunday.'[28]

[26] *Reminiscences of an Old Draper*, p. 6.
[27] *Sunday Trading (Metropolis)*, op. cit., Q. 2039.
[28] Ibid., Q. 1952.

We have seen that tradesmen commonly provided a wholesale service for hawkers and small shopkeepers. As one retired draper noted a wholesale trade 'swelled up a return very much and was very useful'.[29] At his shop in Bristol in the 1820s 'to save inconvenience, and prevent the necessity of young men continually running to me to ask what this or that article could be charged, I began a plan of marking all goods two prices, the top price with ... a capital T, to denote trade price.'[30] It was essential, however, to separate the trade and retail counters in order to prevent retail customers hearing prices quoted to trade customers:

... we felt at the time as if we were committing an act of injustice almost by making such a distinction, although now it is clearly understood and expected that a difference should be made betwixt the wholesale and retail prices.[31]

Jonathan Pedlar, the St Austell grocer mentioned earlier, did a small trade business with shopkeepers. It is possible to compare the prices he charged J. Robbins, a grocer, with those charged to retail customers on or near the same date. The wholesale discount in Pedlar's case does not seem to have been a fixed percentage of the retail price. Robbins' discount on barley ranged from 0 to 13.6 per cent, and retail credit prices seem to have been fixed. Between October 1841 and October 1842, Robbins received discounts of up to 16.6 per cent on bran, 15.4 per cent on meal, 14.3 per cent on pepper and 9.5 per cent on flour. Possibly, wholesale discounts fluctuated with stock levels at the time of sale, or with Pedlar's estimate of stocks held by rival grocers.

On the question of the ratios of cash to credit sales there is little available information. Joseph Gibbs, a Ramsey grocer and draper, testified that between 1832 and 1834 he received about £15 to £20 in cash on average weekly sales of £34, or cash sales of about 43 to 57 per cent of total sales.[32] Peter Burdell, a Sheerness shopkeeper with average monthly sales of about £50 in 1833, received £25 and £24 in cash sales in March and April, or about 50 per cent of sales.[33] In high class

[29] *Reminiscences of an Old Draper*, p. 223.   [30] Ibid., p. 145.
[31] Loc. cit.   [32] B.3. 2095, testimony of 23 January 1835.
[33] Kent County Archives, Q/Cl 188/1 & 2.

shops the ratio of cash and short credit sales to total sales was probably still less favourable. In 1837 a commentator pointed out that butchers and greengrocers serving the upper classes needed large capitals in order to finance long term retail credit.[34] Robert Taylor, a high class London bootmaker, testified in 1823 that,

... a gentleman will perhaps come in and get a pair of boots and a couple of pair of shoes, and I never see any more of him; and if I do find him out, when I press him for the money, he feels angry, because the sum is so small. There are others that go away, and when they come back, they forget those small sums, and they feel angry because they forgot it; and I also feel angry, because they get thus far into my debt, and do not have any thing more.[35]

Table 6:2(A) shows that Mouys and Jarrit, high class hatters on Pall Mall, London, received payment in cash or fifteen days for only about 22 per cent of the total value of their 1804 sales, and only about 30 per cent within one month.[36] Only a further 7 per cent was recovered within one to three months, and the final 63 per cent was either uncollectable or outstanding for long periods. Table 6:2(B) is an analysis of the Ledger (long

TABLE 6:2. Payment for Goods sold by Messrs. Mouys and Jarritt, 1804

Date of Payment	(A) Amount	% of Total	Cumulative %
Cash or 15 Days	£146. 1. 5	21.6	21.6
16 Days—1 Month	59. 14. 0	8.8	30.4
—2 Months	21. 15. 6	3.2	33.6
—3 Months	24. 1. 6	3.5	37.1
Bad & over 3 Months	427. 2. 11	62.9	100.0
	£678. 15. 4	100.0	

[34] Whittock, *Book of Trades*, pp. 82 and 242.
[35] *Recovery of Small Debts*, op. cit., p. 18.
[36] Mouys and Jarritt adopted the following procedure: if a debt was not paid in six months an account was set up in the Ledger. Most short term accounts are therefore to be traced in the Journal. The total value of debts accounted for in Table 6:2 falls short of turnover for 1804 by about £100. It has been impossible in some cases to trace when, or if, an account was paid; sales to army regiments have been excluded from Table 6:2; and account has not been taken of returned goods when totalling annual sales.

TABLE 6:2 *cont.*

(B)
Ledger Accounts Unpaid After Three Months

Date of Payment	Amount	% of Total	Cumulative %
Four Months	£16	3.8	3.8
Five Months	—	—	3.8
Six Months	39. 6. 6	9.6	13.4
Six Months—1 Year	86. 3. 6	20.8	34.2
Over 1 Year & Bad	271. 10. 5	65.8	100.0
	£412. 19. 17	100.0	

Source: Public Record Office, 'Mouys v. Jarritt', Chancery Master's Exhibits, C. 103, no. 191.

term) accounts. The Ledger accounts for all but £14 of sales recorded in the Journal but not collected within three months. It indicates that of £413 outstanding at the end of three months, only 13.4 per cent was collected within six months, 34.2 per cent within one year, and 65.8 per cent remained outstanding at the end of a year. In other words, if the firm did not receive payment in cash or fifteen days the probability of collecting the account within a year was less than 50 per cent. Their position was not exceptional among firms of this class. Robert Taylor told the small debts inquiry that, 'I have about £18 000 upon my books, and I have not £100 above paying my bills: all the money I have saved in my life is on my books.'[37]

Tradesmen's accounts receivable ledgers were filled overwhelmingly with small debts. Donald Currie, a Regent Street hatter, said, 'I have about 560 accounts upon my books, and out of these there are 253 for sums under £5.'[38] The accounts receivable of 26 bankrupted tradesmen have been analyzed in Table 6:3 to show the value dispersion in terms of cumulative percentages. It is possible that the dispersions are distorted by bankruptcy: with approaching insolvency tradesmen probably concentrated on collecting large accounts. But the results of the analysis do support the evidence given to the small debts inquiry.

Among the grocers, drapers and ironmongers, Table 6:3

[37] *Recovery of Small Debts*, op. cit., p. 19.   [38] Ibid., p. 14.

TABLE 6:3. Analysis of Accounts receivable for Value Dispersion

	No.	Cumulative % of Debts Under Class Limits								
Trade	Debts	£1	£2	£3	£4	£5	£10	£15	£25	Over £25
Grocers										
J. Booty	154	44	57	66	75	80	89	97	99	100
J. Smith	141	32	46	60	67	73	78	83	88	100
C. Hayles	119	50	70	80	84	88	94	97	99	100
T. Smith	117	26	48	63	72	75	89	95	99	100
W. Watts	111	58	73	78	83	86	91	96	98	100
W. Towers	106	38	58	70	73	76	87	92	97	100
B. Lyon	78	26	53	58	68	71	84	89	97	100
W. Alcock	77	66	84	93	94	97	100			
W. Holmden	75	65	77	88	92	96	100			
J. Lowman	70	19	38	58	64	68	84	89	93	100
J. Ward	56	30	62	73	78	83	99			
W. Johnston	55	9	16	40	45	60	80	89	93	100
V. Barford	46	63	78	82	88		97			100
H. Clackett	38	21	42	58	71	74	90	95	97	100
H. &. T. Biven	30	13	40	50	60	70	87	90	97	100
A. Hawkins	27	70	92	96		100				
Mean %	1 300	40	58	67	76	80	90	94	97	100
Drapers										
Froggott & Lilleyman	365	24	39	48	54	59	74	81	90	100
W. Fuller	155	40	59	70	78	86	99			100
Stephens & Croft	130	31	50	62	68	72	88	92	94	100
G. Brearey	43	47	70	91			98			100
Mean %	693	35	55	68	73	77	90	94	95	100
Ironmongers										
W. Long	240	39	59	70	78	83	94	95	98	100
G. & B. Billows	200	55	69	78	82	87	95	98	99	100
W. Austin	125	46	57	67	76	80	88	92	97	100
W. Dainton	80	36	51	66	72	75	91		97	100
Nettleford & Reid	63	58	74	81	84	86	92	93	95	100
J. Adam	51	40	50	62	72	78	86		94	100
Mean %	759	46	60	71	77	81	91	92	97	100

shows that between 95 and 97 per cent of the total number of
debts were for individual sums valued at £25 or less; but 90 per
cent of all debts were accounted for by individual debts of £10
or less, and between 77 and 81 per cent for £5 or less. As much
as 35 to 46 per cent of the total debts were for an individual
value of £1 or less.

The Select Committee on the Recovery of Small Debts
reported that 'every witness whom the committee have examined
agrees in stating, that no prudent tradesmen ever thinks it
for his interest to sue for any debts below £15.'[39] One of the
witnesses, a shopkeeper on Regent Street in London, went as
far as to suggest that 'with persons of the worst credit' we prefer
'to give them credit beyond £15 rather than restrain our
accounts under that sum, that we may thereby have a more
summary way of suing and recovering'.[40]

The accounts receivable of 24 bankrupt tradesmen have been
examined in Table 6:4 to show the percentage of good debts and
of bad and doubtful debts to the total *value* of accounts receivable. As an indicator of the bad debts situation the table has
serious limitations. In most cases some portion of the doubtful
debts would prove collectable. One would also expect that a
higher percentage of bad debts might be more typical of
bankrupt tradesmen than successful. Moreover, if a tradesman
was in business several years prior to bankruptcy, the value of
bad debts accumulated over these years, expressed as a percentage of *accounts receivable* at bankruptcy, would diverge widely
in significance from the value of bad debts as a percentage of
total sales over the same period. If carefully interpreted, however,
the table provides some insights into the bad debt situation.

[39] Ibid., p. 3.   [40] Ibid., p. 13.

TABLE 6:3 *cont.*

Source: Public Records Office, Court of Bankruptcy, B.3.
Notes: (1) The figures represent the per cent number of debts falling within the
designated classes and not the percentage value.
(2) All calculations are rounded to the nearest 1 per cent, and hence the cumulative figures do not always total 100 per cent.
(3) Class limits were defined, for example, as all debts falling within the range
£1.1.0. to £2.0.0.
(4) A blank indicates there were no debts due within that class.

TABLE 6:4. Analysis of Good, Bad and Doubtful Debts (Rounded Figures)

Case	Value A/R	Good Debts % of Total	Bad & Doubtful % of Total
Grocers	£		
R. Heale (?–1828)	3 835	46	54
J. Yovens (1838–40)	2 045	68	32
J. Booty (1815–25)	1 640	23	77
B. Coxhead (1816–26)	1 150	37	63
W. Watts (?–1842)	275	89	11
J. Lyon (1810–29)	850	57	43
Drapers & Haberdashers			
Froggott & Lilleyman (1819–26)	4 065	66	34
A. & H. Hart (1819–24)	3 200	18	82
Stephens & Croft (1819–24)	1 580	8	92
S. John (1828–9)	1 165	81	19
W. Bewley (1814–21)	910	44	56
T. Broad (?–1824)	865	60	40
J. Thomas (1823–4)	710	93	7
W. Fuller (1820–5)	525	53	47
J. Pinck (1822–4)	450	11	89
G. Brearey (1826–7)	110	59	41
Ironmongers			
G. & B. Billows (1834–8)	745	70	30
G. Collis (1835–7)	710	83	17
W. Cole (1821–6)	585	8	92
W. Austin (1811–31)	510	90	10
W. Dainton (1824–6)	445	58	42
Nettleford & Reid (1829–31)	360	43	57

Source: Public Records Office, Commissions of Bankruptcy, B.3.

George Brearey, a Manchester draper trading between 1826 and 1827 accumulated bad debts in one year valued at 41 per cent of his accounts receivable. In a similar length of time Seymour John, an Oxford Street draper in London accumulated 19 per cent bad and doubtful debts. In one year of trading, J. Thomas, with a fashionable West End of London trade, accumulated only 7 per cent of his accounts receivable as bad or doubtful. It is likely that William Watts, a Kings Lynn grocer, traded for only about one year, and his bad and doubtful debts amounted to some 11 per cent of all accounts receivable.

It is obvious that a more satisfactory insight into the bad debt situation is achieved by calculating the value of bad debts as a percentage of turnover. Unfortunately the relevant figures are available in only a few cases.

TABLE 6:5. Bad and Doubtful Debts as a per cent of Turnover

Case	Turnover	Bad and Doubtful	
		Value	Percentage
	£	£	
J. Yovens, Grocer	17 000	660	3.3
Froggott & Lilleyman, Drapers	44 500	1 365	3.0
Stephens & Croft, Haberdashers	192 000	1 450	0.8
J. Thomas, Draper	6 000	50	0.8

Source: Public Records Office, Court of Bankruptcy, B.3.

Table 6:5 offers a much less pessimistic interpretation of the bad debt situation than Table 6:4. James Yovens' bad and doubtful debts were calculated to be 32 per cent of his accounts receivable, but only prove to be 3.3 per cent of his turnover. The contrast is more striking still in the case of Stephens & Croft: their bad and doubtful debts accounted for over 90 per cent of the value of their accounts receivable, but amount to only 0.8 per cent of their turnover. By way of comparison, bad debts in British department stores of all sizes and types in 1961 accounted for less than 0.1 per cent of sales.[41] The four firms listed in Table 6:5, however, cannot be regarded as occupying a typical position. James Yovens was a high class grocer, and James Thomas' shop in Piccadilly was patronized by customers like the Earl of Essex and Lord Althorpe. It is likely that long credit rather than uncollectable accounts was their major problem. Froggott and Lilleyman of Doncaster had a large wholesale trade, and Stephens and Croft were a comparatively large, mainly cash sales shop on Oxford Street. Undoubtedly many firms were confronted by more severe bad debt problems than these.

Shopkeepers dealing with the working class were especially vulnerable to the accumulation of bad debts. Their accounts receivable were composed overwhelmingly of what were

[41] McClelland, *Costs and Competition in Retailing*, p. 239.

officially small debts; but a debt of £5 to £10 was not small in relation to a labourer's ability to settle it. The problem of controlling credit extended to labourers can be illustrated through the account which John Bear, a miner, had with Jonathan Pedlar, the St Austell grocer.[42] Bear purchased a weekly basket of provisions and household goods, and paid on account each month between £1. 10s. and £3. 3s. But the balance of his indebtedness with Pedlar rose from 6s. 6½d. on 14 September 1839 to £5. 16s. 9½d. on 14 November 1844. In effect, Pedlar's credit facilities allowed Bear to increase the average value of his weekly purchases while maintaining the same average payment on Account. Bear's account was dangerously out of control by 1845 and Pedlar appears to have withdrawn further credit.

Consumer credit was granted extensively by shopkeepers, but not indiscriminately. Jonathan Pedlar, for example, imposed interest charges on some of his overdue accounts. In 1843 John Boyle owed Pedlar £24. 10s. 4½d. and Pedlar added an interest charge of 1½ per cent. Peter Merifield owed Pedlar £15. 18s. 9d. in November 1844, and Pedlar added to his account an interest charge amounting to 5 per cent. Peal Brothers, the London shoemakers, printed on their invoices 'interest at the rate of 5 per cent per annum, charged after 12 months'. Many tradesmen offered positive inducements to prompt payment. William Cruden, a tailor in Kent in the 1840s, gave discounts ranging from 3 to 6 per cent on accounts which were settled promptly.[43] It was also common for prices to be adjusted to the credit worthiness of the customer. Donald Currie, a Regent Street hatter said that 'In a case where we are sure of the money, of course every tradesman will sell his goods cheaper than where there is a greater risk' and 'if we were sure of our debtor, we should not charge upon the general run the same quantity of profit'.[44]

Although they obviously preferred cash sales, many tradesmen felt obliged to give credit. Abraham Lancaster, a draper at Stratford in Essex, argued that,

[42] 'Geach v. Pedlar', op. cit.
[43] Kent County Records Office, Q/Cl. 2.
[44] *Recovery of Small Debts*, op. cit., p. 15.

There are many businesses in which it is absolutely impossible to avoid giving credit, and even we shopkeepers find it next to impossible, to avoid it, we are all obliged to live by the goodwill of our neighbours, and if we were not to accommodate them by giving credit, and very often we cannot do it with safety, we should get that ill-will, which would be very detrimental to our trade.[45]

There were, however, some elementary safeguards. William Hillier, a grocer at Salisbury in the 1820s, always 'demanded ready money for the first two or three orders'.[46] Abraham Lancaster of Stratford would not give credit to customers 'unless they are well known to us', and if he knew a customer was poor he would 'certainly run the chance of losing him' rather than give credit.[47] In Leicestershire in the 1840s, where the working classes were exceptionally poor credit risks, shopkeepers took in clothing, bedding and other possessions as security on credit sales of provisions. Many of the big clothing shops gave credit only if a deposit was placed on the articles purchased and guarantors were found for the regular payment of instalments: a customer purchasing a 50s. coat would deposit 10s. and,

... during the week he finds two respectable housekeepers, as security, and next Sunday morning he cuts a respectable figure; if he does not pay his instalments, a person waits upon him for them, or they go upon the security.[48]

By the 1840s, however, the big shops in central areas of the cities had eliminated credit selling, offering in exchange substantially lower prices. For example, Schoolbred & Co. of London, one of the largest tailoring firms in England, advertised that 'So many losses arising from long credits and bad debts, have induced S. & Co. to reduce their prices for ready money'.[49] The Hierokosma and Tailors' Company of Saville Row offered 'clothes of the choisest quality at an immense reduction for ready money only'.[50] The famous Panclibanon

[45] Ibid., pp. 43-44.
[46] B.3. 2456, testimony of 14 September 1827.
[47] *Recovery of Small Debts*, op. cit.
[48] *Sunday Trading (Metropolis)*, op. cit., Q. 409.
[49] *Illustrated London News*, 4 June 1842.
[50] Ibid., 2 July 1842.

Ironworks Bazar on Baker Street in London advertised iron-mongery 'of the BEST description, and offered at exceedingly LOW PRICES for CASH only'.[51]

The cooperative movement contributed to weaning the working classes from credit buying, but they did not introduce the cash sales principle. In the 1820s and 1830s the shops which introduced fixed prices and ticketing usually insisted upon cash payment. Until the 1840s ticket shops operating on cash sales were confined largely to drapery and clothing, but according to a police superintendent, credit sales in all Lambeth shops in the early 1830s were exceptional; tradesmen insisted on 'ready-money transactions, except at public houses or chandler's shops; where they know the man is in work, they will give him credit for a week'.[52] Edward Peacock, the Islington shopkeeper in the 1840s, sold only for cash, although he agreed that if he gave credit he would 'have a greater trade on working days' and he acknowledged that many of his competitors 'give credit ... and some of the large ones. ...'[53]

It is unquestionably true that small shopkeepers were pressed by the working classes for credit facilities, and even when they were careful in controlling credit it sometimes led to insolvency. W. Neild noted that shopkeepers were 'generally the first to feel reverses in manufacturing districts; and in all instances of considerable depression in trade numbers of them are ruined'.[54] J. R. McCulloch argued that the abolition of consumer credit would bring returns in the form of lower prices and a more efficient shop distribution service. Tradesmen's difficulties, and reluctance, in breaking the credit habit and controlling and financing large volumes of credit probably acted as an impediment to the more rapid introduction of new retailing techniques. But the cash sales principle was much more widespread by the 1840s than is generally acknow-ledged, and in any case tradesmen did provide a valuable, if imperfect, social service by financing working class people through periods of unemployment or low earnings. If much

[51] Ibid., 17 December 1842.
[52] *B.P.P.*, *Select Committee on the Observance of the Sabbath Day*; Mins. of Ev., 1831–32 (697) vii, Q. 223.
[53] *Sunday Trading (Metropolis)*, op. cit., Q. 2012–2014.
[54] W. Neild, *J. Stat. Soc. Lond.*, iv, 332.

of the credit extended (particularly in the high class shops) was unnecessary, in the sense that the consumer could pay cash, the widespread tolerance of the credit system offered some assurance to poorer people that periodic unemployment and low earnings would not necessarily mean a savage fall in customary living standards.

2. The Household

Lock-up shops were comparatively rare in the first half of the century. The very close physical relationship between the 'business' and the 'household' meant that for most tradesmen life was not clearly differentiated into family life and business life. Tradesmen did not normally regard the business as paying them a salary with which to maintain the home and family and net profits for allocation to retained earnings, to dividend payments or to investment outside the business. Rather, their ultimate concern was that sales, less trade expenses, should leave a margin to support the household at an accustomed, or expected, standard. The importance of this situational difference between the businessman now and then should not be exaggerated, but to a certain extent the intermingling of household and business meant that the business was viewed much more as a source of direct consumption—akin to the peasant subsistence farm—than as a distinct entity to be operated and developed almost for its own sake, and then, if successful, paying its 'manager' higher rewards in the form of income.

An indication of this is the fact that many tradesmen did not distinguish between household and trade expenses.[55] A domestic servant in the household of Joseph Gibbs, a Ramsey grocer and draper, was asked if housekeeping books were kept: 'None that I know of. We paid for everything as we had it at the time and I went to the Till for the money.'[56] Although Peal Brothers, the London bootmakers, ruled their expenditures book into trade and household columns, purchases of tea, household stores and meat were often entered in the trade column. Peter Burdell, the Sheerness shopkeeper, made a weekly

[55] Such distinctions could be difficult when domestic and family labour was extensively, but casually, employed in the shop.
[56] B.3. 2095, testimony of 10 December 1834.

cash allocation to a household account, but his books also record cash expenditure on food, beer and spirits.

Tradesmen did not necessarily require figures on turnover, margins, receipts on account and bills coming due in order to assess their solvency and adjust their standard of living. But the real short- and long-term position of the business could be obscured, if such accounting procedures were lacking, by the running down of stocks, buildings and equipment, or by a cash flow from low profit, ready-money sales. These factors, as well as the possibility of securing credit from wholesalers and loans, on little or no security, from family and friends meant that the solvency of the business could be undermined while the household continued on at its accustomed level of consumption.

Analysis of the accounts of John Patterson, a London ironmonger in the 1820s, indicates how insensitive household expenditure could be to turns in business profitability:[57]

Year	Profits £	House Exps. £	Business Exps. £	Balance £
1820	160	312	391	−543
1821	460	390	419	−349
1822	910	400	453	+ 57
1823	1510	410	475	+625
1824	1015	440	553	+ 22
1825	715	460	542	−287
1826	235	329	296	−390

Negative profits and the run-down of capital investment would, of course, eventually bring sharp reductions in personal and household expenditure. Hannah and Thomas Biven, Mortlake shopkeepers, invested £400 in their shop and estimated their mean gross profits to be £255 per annum over three years. They calculated their personal and household expenditure to be:[58]

Year	Household Exps.
May 1813–May 1814	£400
May 1814–May 1815	250
May 1815–Jan 1816	200

[57] B.3. 4012.   [58] B.3. 372.

In 1813–14 the Bivens' household expenditure was £150 in excess of their mean gross profits over the three years, and the sharp reductions in the following two years still left household expenditure accounting for the whole of the mean gross profits: the household was simply consuming the initial capital investment.

TABLE 6:6. Annual Average Housekeeping Expenditures
(Figures rounded to nearest £5)

Firm	Period	Amount	Firm	Period	Amount
1. *Grocers*		£			£
J. Lyon	1810–29	645	W. Holmden	1822–3	155
H. & T. Biven	1813–14	400	R. Rose	1835–8	140
	1814–15	250	T. Bumpus	1835–42	115
C. Hayles	1828–32	400	E. Weaver	1819–25	100
E. Bumpstead	1829–41	400	J. Ward	1827–31	90
J. Gibbs	1832–4	355	J. Smith	1830–1	60
T. Walter	1820–4	300			
J. Smith	1806–15	200			
H. Clackett	1830	195			
W. Lambourne	1824–5	150			
	1825–9	190			
2. *Other Food Trades*					
G. Baker	1830–7	550	J. Cumming	1820–3	260
J. White	1827	385	J. Collins	1829–31	200
J. Holland	1827–9	350	S. Chappel	1822–31	180
W. Jarrin	1821–8	350			
3. *Drapers*					
W. & H. Hart	1820–6	540	R. Bishop	1826–30	250
R. Grimwood	1823–4	310	W. Fuller	1820–5	230
J. Thomas	?–1824	310	G. Brearey	1816–27	220
Froggott &			J. Pinck	1822–4	200
Lilleyman	1819–26	300	T. Broad	1806–24	200
J. Higgs	1814–15	260	J. Bond	1835–40	190
			W. Bewley	1814–21	120
4. *Taylors*					
T. Peters	1835–41	300	R. Reynard	1824–6	180
T. Davies	1834–9	290	W. Hiscock	1828–34	170
G. Klugh	1808–10	200	W. Dixon	1819–21	155
C. Darby	1827–9	200			

TABLE 6:6 *cont.*

Firm	Period	Amount	Firm	Period	Amount
5. Clothes Dealers					
W. Lloyd	1816–17	880	J. Perry	1823–4	240
R. Cruden	1809–11	550	R. Farrar	1822–5	210
	1812–20	650	J. Gray	1821–3	120
6. Ironmongers					
J. Patterson	1820–5	400	G. Collis	1835–7	260
C. Ashford	1814–16	200	W. Dainton	1824–6	175
	1816–19	300	W. Cole	1821–6	160
W. Austin	1811–31	270	G. & B. Billows	1834–8	150
6. Furniture Trades					
A. Woolf	1833–9	200	E. Pearson	1815–31	150
W. Lewis	1813	185	R. Aman	1831–7	90
7. Household Stores					
L. Robertson	1830–1	200	T. Butler	1804–23	600
J. Haley	1833–6	170	J. Stott	1819–31	270
W. Ward	1821–6	150	S. Hall	1816–28	250
J. Reynolds	1819–26	400	J. Coleman	?	220
J. Coster	1822–4	160			
	1825–7	300			
8. Stationers					
S. Wilkins	1820–4	400			
W. Penley	1828–32	250			
A. Penley	1828–32	160			

Source: Public Records Office, Court of Bankruptcy, B.3.

Table 6:6 lists the estimated annual household expenditure of some seventy bankrupted tradesmen. The table suggests that tradesmen were part of the high consumption class, but even then the figures understate in several ways real household and personal expenditure. In most cases the expenditure estimates include food, household stores, lighting, heating and washing, but in only a few cases is medicine, education, clothing and travel included. The estimates do not include a rent charge for the household or the wages paid to domestic servants. In most cases the estimates are mean averages over two or more years, and therefore are possibly deflated by sharp reductions of expenditure in the months prior to bankruptcy. The mean household expenditure in this sample, however, was about £250, and it may be concluded that earned incomes among successful tradesmen were substantially above this figure.

It is misleading, however, to view the tradesman's household as something of a dangerous parasite on the business earnings and assets. A substantial business meant a large household and therefore large household expenditure. W. & H. Hart, the Holborn drapers, for example, spent on average £450 on the household; but their household consisted of fourteen shopmen and apprentices and two domestic servants. While it is true that household expenses were often charged to the business, it can also be seen that business costs were charged to the household. The business and the household can be separated only for analytical purposes: in reality they were interwoven parts of a single function.

3. *Labour Conditions and Wages*

It was estimated that 15 000 people were employed in Liverpool shops in 1841. This estimate was reached on the assumption that there were 9000 sales assistants in the drapery, provisions, shoe and chemists' trades and some 6000 porters and errand boys.[59] Practically all retail shop labour was housed on the premises, and even 'monster shops', like Schoolbred and Co. of London with 500 employees, provided boarding and lodging.[60]

Living-in was a logical element of the social and economic situation. The typical retail shop had at its centre a nuclear family; but if the nuclear and extended family network was unable to provide the shop with sufficient labour, then outsiders would be 'adopted' into the shop/household complex. Young men and boys comprised a very large part of this 'adopted' labour force, and parents and guardians drew up articles of apprenticeship wherein the tradesman assumed responsibility for educating the apprentice in the trade and for promoting

---

[59] *Proceedings of the Public Meeting on Behalf of the Shopkeepers' Assistants* (Liverpool, 1841), p. 6. This and other documents on labour conditions in retail shops is preserved in the Goldsmiths' Library, University of London.

[60] Burn, *Commercial Enterprise*, p. 56.

his moral and physical well being. The fact that social relationships between employer and employee had not everywhere
assumed an impersonal form is evident in advertisements such
as,

Wanted, in a First-rate IRONMONGERY Establishment at the
WEST END of the TOWN, a respectable well-educated
YOUTH as an APPRENTICE. He will be treated as one of
the family, and have every opportunity of thoroughly learning his
business.[61]

But the nuclear family structure of most retail shops and the
youthfulness of much of the hired labour force does not provide
a sufficient explanation for the living-in system. Working hours
were very long, and the living-in system provided the employer
with a more effective control over work attendance and those
leisure pursuits which might impair regular attendance.
Moreover, the absence of rapid public transport and the long
working hours made it impractical for employees to live very
far from the shop. It was also true—as large firms like Schoolbred's knew—that economies of scale in boarding and lodging
employees made for lower aggregate labour costs than if all
assistants maintained their own homes.

Certainly in many retail shops an intimate personal relationship existed between the employer and employee; but this did
not mean that employment conditions were ideal or that
employees generally were satisfied with their situation. Moreover, as retail shops grew in size in the cities the integration of
employees into the nuclear family society was weakened, and
something of a class, or at least group consciousness developed
among shop assistants which found expression in the formation
of shop employee associations. Their principal grievance—and
they had support on this issue from some employers—was the
very long hours of opening. Shopping hours varied among
towns, but most shops were open from twelve to sixteen hours a
day, and longer on Friday and Saturday. Assistants began to
prepare the shop for opening around 6 a.m. and very few shops
closed before 7 p.m. and many not until 10 p.m. They opened
earlier and closed later in the summer than in the winter, and

[61] *Illustrated London News,* 24 December 1842.

those which catered for the working class were open longer than those which serviced the middle and upper classes.[62] London shops usually opened for business on Sunday morning, but this was less common in the provinces, apart from the small neighbourhood shops.[63] Most shopkeepers allowed only 15 or 20 minutes for meals, and assistants rightfully complained that they had little chance to enjoy fresh air.[64] In urban drapery shops a dozen or more assistants might work behind a counter in a space of some 3 ft. by 30 ft., and poor ventilation and gas lighting fouled the air with fumes.[65] In the bigger shops household facilities were soon outstripped by the expanding labour force, and an apprentice in a cut price drapery shop in the East End of London wrote in later years that he was 'not at all surprised to find when bedtimes came that I was shown mine under the counter at the top of the shop'.[66] The stunted, sallow and tubercular shop assistant was a reality, not a sentimental creation of Victorian novelists.

The campaign for shorter working hours and better conditions (wages were not openly an issue) was led largely by drapery shop assistants, with the support of a few sympathetic employers. As early as 1825 Birmingham drapers attended a meeting at the Royal Hotel to consider an appeal from their assistants for shorter hours.[67] By the early 1840s the early closing movement had achieved national proportions with a measure of coordination among local groups. Leading the struggle were the Liverpool Association of Assistant Tradesmen and the Metropolitan Draper's Association of London. But similar groups were active in all the major provincial cities of England and Scotland and most of the sizeable industrial towns.[68] In the 1850s the movement published a journal, *The Early Closing Advocate and Commercial Reformer* but it collapsed after a half dozen issues. The history of the movement was uneventful between

[62] T. Davies, *Prize Essay on the Evils Which are Produced by Late Hours of Business* (1843) pp. 2–3.
[63] *Observance of the Sabbath Day*, op. cit., Q. 1328–34.
[64] *Proceedings of the Public Meeting*, op. cit., p. 5.
[65] E. Flower, *A Glance at the Present System of Business Among Shopkeepers* (1843), p. 7.
[66] *Reminiscences of an Old Draper*, p. 5.
[67] Langford, *Century of Birmingham Life*, ii, 465.
[68] *Fourth Annual Report of the Liverpool Association of Assistant Tradesmen* (1844) p. 13, and The Metropolitan Draper's Association, *The Late-hour System* (1844) p. 4.

the late 1850s and 1880s at which time it was revived under the leadership of T. Sutherst and his 'Shop-Hours Labour League'. The League persuaded Sir John Lubbock to introduce into Parliament the Factory Acts (Extension to Shops) Bill, but it was not until the early twentieth century that labour conditions came under effective legislative control.

It is not surprising that the shop assistants failed to secure any concrete gains in this period. Scattered as they were among thousands of shops, each one almost with a unique labour situation, collective action was impossible. It was this, as well as the assistants' feeling that they were socially superior to labourers, that led them to reject strike action and, less wisely, appeals to parliament for legislative protection. Their tactics were limited to canvassing retailers to adhere voluntarily to shorter hours and issuing appeals to the public not to patronize shops which remained open late into the night. Black-listing was sometimes proposed, but usually this threat was modified to the publication of a list of early closers.

Voluntary early closing agreements invariably failed over more than a few days or weeks because some shopkeepers expected favourable treatment. As one explained in a published letter,

... we are ready to sign for peace—to agree to close at seven in winter and eight in summer—provided the majority, the respectables, will close at five and six, so as to give the inferior shopkeepers, who keep but few hands, a small chance of picking up a few crumbs from customers who cannot get at the great drapers' counters in time.[69]

The persistent attempts by small retailers to gain a slight advantage resulted in an unnecessary prolongation of hours. Legislation could have modified the marathon characteristics of shop hours, and Sutherst's movement in the 1880s, after much hand-wringing and published debate, decided to work for a 'judicious state-interference on lines already laid down for other workers'.[70] But a radical reduction of working hours in retail trades ultimately depended upon the reduction of

[69] 'The Early Closing Question', *The Clothier and Draper*, i, no. 3, 97–8.
[70] The Earl of Wemyss and T. Sutherst, *Shop Hours Regulation* (1885) p. 3.

industrial working hours and the release of wives from employment.

The tradesman's family and domestic servants worked at least part-time in the shop, and there was seldom any attempt made to assess this labour as a business expense. For example, Thomas Broad, the Penzance draper, recorded in his balance sheet a gift to his son Thomas of £150 'in lieu of Annual Salary' for his services as a shopman between 1816 and 1823, and his second son received £140 for similar services between 1821 and 1825.[71] Charlotte Hill, a relative of Joseph Gibbs who operated a shop at Ramsey, said that she occasionally worked in the shop 'particularly in Market Days and Saturday Evenings', and the domestic servant, Alice Allured, 'occasionally assisted in it'.[72] The family and domestic servants thus provided tradesmen with a convenient pool of labour for peak hours, and thereby saved the costs involved in employing but under-working additional shopmen and apprentices.

The wages which some twenty tradesmen paid to their hired labour are listed in Table 6:7. In most cases the wages paid were only a part of the shopman's total earnings since they generally

TABLE 6:7. Annual/Weekly Wages paid to Shop Labour

Trade	Date	Annual Wage	Weekly Wage	Notes
1. *Grocers*				
J. Gibbs	1832–4	£ 25	9/6	Journeyman, brother
W. Johnston	1829	20	8/–	
J. Yovens	1838–40	10	4/–	Two clerks
		20	8/–	
2. *Cheesemongers*				
J. Holland	1827–9	£ 65	25/–	Parkes
		39	15/–	Williams
		39	15/–	John
		52	20/–	Johnson
		31	12/–	James
		15/10	6/–	Archer
		47	18/–	Gregory
3. *Butchers*				
S. Chappel	1824–31	£ 15/10	6/–	A basket woman

[71] B.3. 560.   [72] B.3. 2095, testimonies of 10 December 1834.

TABLE 6:7 *cont.*

Trade	Date	Annual Wage	Weekly Wage	Notes
4. Provisions Merchants				
G. Baker	1830–7	£ 62	24/–	Clerk
5. Drapers				
T. Broad	1798–1806	£ 12	4/6	Shop girl
	1806–27	15	5/8	Shop girl
Froggett &		40	15/4	Lockwood
Lilleyman	c. 1826	35	13/5	Phillips
		40	15/4	?
		35	13/5	Andrews
W. Fuller	c. 1825	30	11/5	Shopman
6. Tailors				
C. Darby	1827	£ 65	25/–	Shopman
T. Peters	1835–41	150	57/7	Foreman
7. Clothes Dealers				
T. Farrar	1818–20	£104	40/–	Shopman
J. Gray	1826–33	10	4/–	Housekeeper
		4/10	1/7	Girl
		60	23/1	Shopman
8. Shoemakers				
F. Noyce	1822–4	£54	20/–	Journeyman
	1821–4	67/6	26/–	Journeyman
9. Ironmongers				
C. Ashford	1817–19	£100	38/5	Shopman
		110	42/3	Shopman
G. Collis	1835–7	50	19/2	Shopman
W. Cole	1821–6	30	11/5	Shopman
		40	15/4	Workman
Hawes & Moore	1823–7	54/12	21/–	Porter
10. Chemists & Drysalters				
A. Davis	1831–6	£36	13/8	Assistant
J. Haley	1835–6	20	7/7	Shopman
11. Stationers				
E. Wilkins	1820–4	£ 78	30/–	Shopman

Source: Public Records Office, Court of Bankruptcy, B.3. Where weekly wages have not been cited, they have been calculated on the basis of a 52 week year.

received board and lodging. Shopmen commanding high wages, such as those employed by Charles Ashford, an ironmonger, and Thomas Farrar, a slopseller, possibly maintained their own homes. Journeymen's wages were probably lower on average in the retail trades than in the producer/retailer trades, but wages generally reflected the shopman's age, experience and management responsibilities. A young shopman in a small concern might receive no more than £20 or £25 in wages, whereas in larger concerns in the cities the senior shopmen, who were responsible for work supervision and wholesale buying, usually received £50 or more a year in wages. In the 1820s in London,

there were not separate buyers to each department ... but there were generally two or more. The 'fancy buyer' would invariably purchase all the goods that were contained on the shelves on one side of the shop, which embraced all the small and lighter articles; while the drapery and heavy goods generally would come under the supervision of the 'drapery buyer'.[73]

In this case, the shopman was in his early twenties and already in full charge of the haberdashery department and earning well over £50 in wages. When he moved to a high-class shop in the City he was paid a wage of £90 a year.[74] In the competitive situation of urban retailing, shopkeepers often paid assistants premiums for selling slow moving items. Buying 'in those days was often indiscretely done, and large quantities of unsaleable goods were bought in "lots" that were often difficult to sell, and hence the premium system'.[75] The shawl and dress men 'would generally make from 20s. to 25s.' on premiums each week.[76]

The wages paid to domestic servants were very low. Female servants were unlikely to receive more than £15 per annum in wages, and it was clearly advantageous to the tradesman if he could substitute the labour of his family and domestic servants for the more expensive shop labour. In table 6:8 the annual wages bill (which is not the real labour cost) is listed for some twenty five shops. In the producer/retailer trades the wages bill

[73] *Reminiscences of an Old Draper*, p. 29.
[75] Ibid., pp. 19–20.
[74] Ibid., p. 82.
[76] Ibid., p. 16.

TABLE 6:8. Tradesmen's Annual Wage Bills

Trade	Date	Shop Wages	House Wages	Total	Comments
1. Grocers					
T. Bumpus	1835–42			£ 50	
H. Clackett	1830			52	
B. Coxhead	1816–26	£ 75			2-shopmen
W. Holmden	1820–3		£10		2-servants
W. Lambourne	1825–9		10		
R. Rose	1835–8		14		
T. Smith	1831			135	
W. Towers	1831–4			37	
	1834–5			56	
T. Walter	1812–20			70	
	1820–9			70	
J. Ward	1827–31		10		
2. Confectioners					
W. Jarrin	1822–8			£430	10-employees
T. Lipsham	1815–20	£150			
3. Bakers					
J. White	1827	£280	£36	£316	
G. Henley	1825	75			2-men, boy
4. Butchers					
W. Blizzard	1817–25	£ 18	£ 8	£ 26	
5. Drapers					
W. Bewley	1814–21		£ 8		
R. Thompson	1827–30			£ 45	
J. Bond	1835			65/10	
	1836			119/10	
	1837			130/10	
	1838			152/10	
	1839			97/–	
W. & H. Hart	1820			£290/10	
	1821			340/15	
	1822			540/14	
	1823			540/16	
	1824			600/13	
	1825			600/13	
J. Pinck	1822–4			77	

TABLE 6:8 *cont.*

Trade	Date	Shop Wages	House Wages	Total	Comments
6. *Tailors*					
C. Darby	1827	£ 65			2-shopmen
	1828	117			2-shopmen
	1829	196/10			3-shopmen
G. Klugh	1808–10			£ 40	
7. *Shoemakers*					
F. Noyce	1821–4		£ 5		
8. *Ironmongers*					
W. Dainton	1824–6	£100	£ 9/9	£109/9	
J. Patterson	1820			56	
	1821			112	
	1822			146	
	1823			168	
	1824			168	
	1825			168	
9. *Furniture Trades*					
A. Woolf	1823–9		£10		2-servants

Source: Public Records Office, Court of Bankruptcy, B.3.

was usually high because the opportunities for substituting family and domestic labour were limited. Ironmongers like Dainton and Patterson paid out over £100 a year in wages, while by contrast, Thomas Broad, the Penzance draper, not only worked his sons without regular wages, but employed a shopgirl for £12 a year in wages between 1798 and 1806 and £15 between 1806 and 1827.

In comparatively large retail concerns opportunities for substituting cheap family and domestic labour were more limited. The physical connexion between household and shop was severed more often in the cities than in the country, and the intense competition among central area shops necessitated the employment of a professional sales staff at high wages. For example, W. & H. Hart, a drapery firm on Holborn in London, employed fourteen shopmen and apprentices in 1824 and 1825 at a total cost in wages of £600 a year, or over £40 a year for

each shopman and apprentice. In the producer/retailer trades
the typical shop employed fewer people but they were comparatively more skilled and expensive. There was, however,
some possibility of labour substitution as the retailing side of a
producer/retailer's business began to assume greater importance.
For example, William Cole, a working hardwareman in London, was obliged to pay a 'workman' £40 a year, but his
'shopman' only £30.[77]

4. The Tradesman's Premises

In all towns the tradesmen were the major users of available
house, shop and warehouse facilities. Their premises were more
or less self-contained living and working units. For example,
John Lyon, a Cambridge grocer and tallow chandler, held the
lease on premises containing 'Shop, Parlour, large Kitchin ...
good Drawing-Room ... and several excellent Bed Chambers,
ample cellaring running under the whole house. At the back is
a large paved yard, approached by a private entrance, with
colour shops, old-established chandlery premises and Loft over,
excellent 3-storey Warehouse and other buildings'.[78] In this
instance the shop, or retailing area, accounted for only a small
percentage of the total floor area leased, the largest areas being
given over to living quarters, warehousing facilities and production and processing buildings.

An extensive living area was necessary in order to accommodate the normally large household. A Boston draper, William
Fuller, had a household in 1825 numbering fifteen, including
nine children, two shopmen and two domestic servants.[79]
An ironmonger at Woolwich, William Austin, stated that
between 1811 and 1831 his household had averaged nine
people.[80] In 1837 George Collis, a Romford ironmonger, had a
household of eleven people, including four children, one shopman, two apprentices and two domestic servants.[81] Households
of a dozen and more people were not unusual, and we have seen
that with the growth of business units, particularly in the urban
drapery trade, adherence to the living-in pattern led to
employee grievances about overcrowding. But in some cases

[77] B.3. 1068.   [78] B.3. 3100.   [79] B.3. 1739.
[80] B.3. 152.   [81] B.3. 1069.

the need for processing, production, or warehousing space necessitated rental of premises additional to the consolidated shop/household complex. Grocers sometimes rented warehouses;[82] a confectioner might need an ice-house;[83] butchers frequently maintained slaughter houses which were spatially separated from their retail shops;[84] and ironmongers rented additional workshops.[85] In general, both the living-in tradition and the production and processing functions attached to many of the trades necessitated a high ratio of floor space to turnover.

Of course, it would be desirable to have information on the costs per square foot of space occupied by tradesmen, but such data is not available. The material in Table 6:9 is, admittedly, a poor substitute for such statistics: it lists the rents, taxes and rates (the composition of which is not always known) which were paid by some forty tradesmen. As one would expect, it does indicate that tradesmen paid heavily for a good location. In London, shops on Bond Street, Saint James's Street or important City thoroughfares were costly to occupy. Thus, Lipsham, a St James's Street confectioner, paid £400 a year in rents and rates; Reynard, a New Bond Street tailor, paid £375 a year in rents and rates. Shops on the Strand, Coventry Street, Piccadilly, Regent Street and Oxford Street were also expensive; but rents fell sharply off these main thoroughfares and in less fashionable areas, where a tradesman could rent good facilities for £100 or less.

Rents on the best streets of provincial cities were almost comparable to those in London: Thomas Roberts, a Manchester draper, for example, paid £215 in rent a year. In the smaller towns rents were highest for market square locations. Between 1826 and 1830 William Towers, a Nottingham grocer, paid £40 in rent a year for his shop at Carter Gate, but when he moved to a shop in the Market Place his rent more than doubled. Rents in country villages were low. Frederick Noyce, a Richmond shoemaker, paid only £21 a year rent between 1819 and 1824, while William Holmden, a Milton shopkeeper, actually paid more in rates and taxes (£24) than in rent (£15) during the early 1820s!

[82] B.3. 5408.   [83] B.3. 2739.
[84] B.3. 1228 and B.3. 1171.   [85] B.3. 3778.

TABLE 6:9. Tradesmen's Rents, Rates and Taxes

Trade & Location	Annual Rent	Rates & Taxes	Total
1. Grocers			
J. Yovens, Ludgate Hill, London	£180	£108	£288
W. Towers, Nottingham	40		
Market Place, Nottingham	95		
B. Coxhead, Cannon St., London			75
J. Ward, Coventry			60
W. Lambourne, London	40	22	62
Aylesbury	42		
T. Bumpus, Northampton	37	15	52
T. Smith, Birmingham	30	12	42
W. Holmden, Milton in Kent	15	24	39
2. Confectioners			
T. Lipsham, St. James's, London			£400
W. Jarrin, Bond St., London	£255	£ 60	315
Ice-house	100		
3. Cheesemongers			
J. Cumming, Borough, London			£133
J. Holland, Somers Town, London	£ 90		
Back Premises	10		
4. Butchers			
J. Collins, Brighton			£ 80
Slaughter House	£ 15		
S. Chappell, Honey Lane, London	52	£ 30	82
5. Drapers			
W. & H. Hart, Holborn Hill, London	£200	£118	£318
T. Roberts, Manchester	215	45	260
Froggott & Lilleyman, Doncaster	85	37	122
R. Bishop, Birmingham	60	15	75
J. Bond, Great Yarmouth			88
J. Pinck, Chichester			73
W. Fuller, Boston	45	16	61
W. Bewley, Manchester			40
6. Tailors			
R. Reynard, Bond St., London	£315	£ 60	£375
C. Darby, Cheapside, London	180		
W. Brown, Hanover Squr, London			174
G. Klugh, Coventry St., London	105	40	145

TABLE 6:9 *cont.*

Trade & Location	Annual Rent	Rates & Taxes	Total
T. Davies, Lewes	90	20	110
W. Hiscock, Southampton	55	20	75
7. *Shoemakers*			
F. Noyce, Richmond	£ 21		
8. *Haberdashers*			
Stephens & Croft, Oxford St., London	£167	£ 55	£222
9. *Ironmongers*			
J. Patterson, City of London			£250
W. Dainton, Piccadilly	£112	£ 25	137
G. Collis, Romford	108	16	124
C. Ashford, Paddington, London			110
W. Austin, Woolwich			85
T. Nettleford, London	80		
New Yard Inn	15		
10. *Hardwaremen*			
W. Cole, Covent Garden			£170
11. *Furniture Trades*			
A. Woolf, Brighton	£ 86	£ 13	£ 99
R. Aman, Northampton			36
12. *Chemists*			
L. Roughton, London			£130
H. Ward, Old Kent Rd., London			80
13. *Stationers*			
S. Wilkins, Holborn, London			£100

Source: Public Records Office, Court of Bankruptcy, B.3.

The small neighbourhood shopkeepers often lived and traded from cellars and ground floor rooms, and in objective terms their cost of premises were low. Edward Weaver traded from various London locations between 1819 and 1825 and it is possible to calculate his rental costs to yearly figures:[86]

[86] B.3. 2569.

Location	Period months	Annual Rent £
Houndsditch	6	36
Rosemary Lane	9	48
Rosemary Lane (New Shop)	9	40
Bethnel Green	6	27
Clare Market	3	40
Camberwell	12	18
Waterloo Road	6	19
Kenington	6	26
Lambeth	9	20
Westminster Road	3	44

Neighbourhood shopkeepers like Weaver carried only small volumes of stock and hence required little in the way of warehousing facilities; at most they employed a young shopman, and thus living space requirements were minimal.

Many early eighteenth century shops lacked glass windows, and their proprietors exposed goods on the pavement 'much as they appear', argued one writer in 1840, 'in the butchers' and brokers' shops at the present time'.[87] The famous Georgian shop, with its enclosed front, bow glass windows and well lit interior, was a distinct aesthetic advance on its predecessor, but the most radical change in the use and design of shops came in the first half of the nineteenth century. By mid-century the central area shop was much less a house from which its inhabitants traded than a commercial building in which its workers, in many cases, still happened to live. This commercialization of shop buildings, which were usually still basically Georgian in design if not in origin, was greatly assisted by the development of plate glass and gas lighting. For example, one shop in the City of London in the 1850s had covered the interior walls and ceiling with mirrors in order to give an appearance of brilliance and space. The Holborn branch of Moses and Sons, the ready-made clothes dealers, was gas lit on three sides with 'many thousands of gas-flames, forming branches, foliage, and arabesques'.[88]

[87] N. Whittock, 'Construction and Decoration of Shop Fronts', Appendix to *The Decorative Painter and Glazier's Guide* (1840) pp. 1–2.
[88] M. Schlesinger, *Saunterings in and About London* (1853), p. 17.

In the provincial cities and larger towns the central area shopkeepers followed trends established in London by fitting their shop fronts with plate glass and attaching gas lamps to the exterior to reflect onto the window displays. But there were still many conservative High Street tradesmen who avoided these 'pushing' styles of trade,[89] and the smaller shops were still very often dark, dirty and cluttered, with goods displayed on rails along the shop front or set on the pavement by the door.

Fitting-up a house for trade and maintaining it in good repair was an important business cost during this period, as a few examples will indicate. George Hind, a Bishops Waltham grocer, purchased a house for £130 in the 1830s. He hired a surveyor to draw plans for a shop and shop front, and this service cost him £95. He then engaged a builder to construct the shop, and the bill for this work was £152. Including the many small bills presented by plumbers, smiths, painters and glaziers, the cost of conversion was well over £250.[90] Hind's experience was not unusual. Robert Bishop, a Birmingham draper and tailor, spent £125 when he decided to lower the shop floor and put in a new front.[91] In the 1820s a Boston draper, William Fuller, fitted new windows to his shop at a cost of £200,[92] and around the same time Benjamin Coxhead spent £750 altering his grocery shop on Cannon Street in the City of London.[93] There is much evidence of this kind in surviving business records that for the substantial tradesman a modern shop front and gas lighting were essential for efficient trading and the attraction of customers.

5. *Furnishings and Equipment*

Tradesmen's shops were fitted with counters, showcases, shelving, cupboards, containers, cash boxes, weights and measures and the tools appropriate to the production and processing functions associated with the trade. Butchers, for example, fitted their slaughter houses with racks, hooks, blocks, saws and knives; and a working ironmonger might instal a small forge and foundry. Shoemakers required cutting, sewing

[89] *Reminiscences of an Old Draper*, pp. 160–1.
[90] B.3. 2606.   [91] B.3. 562.
[92] B.3. 1739,   [93] B.3. 1060.

and punching tools; and grocers needed many drawers and containers to protect bulk stocks from spoilage.

In the 1830s a draper who took possession of a well-appointed shop on Holborn in London (which was only beginning to decline as a major shopping street) paid £200 for the fixtures.[94] Both Alfred Davis, an Arundel chemist, and William Cole, a Covent Garden hardwareman, estimated the cost of fitting-up their shops at £200.[95] But the cost of furnishing a shop could be much higher. Greengrocery and confectionery shops in this period were often 'fashionable lounging places for the great and titled ones, and the places of assignation for supposed casual encounters'[96] and they were therefore fairly luxurious. Two West End confectioners, Lipsham and Jarrin, valued their fixtures and equipment at £420 and £755 respectively.[97]

Capital invested in furnishings and equipment naturally varied among trades and within them with respect to the size of the shop and the quality of its trade. But, at cost, a minimum investment in furnishing a High Street shop was probably well over £150.

6. *Miscellaneous Trading Expenses*

In bankruptcy proceedings, the balance sheets usually detailed household expenditure, rent, repairs and labour costs, while aggregating other important costs as 'trade expenses'. For most tradesmen, the cost of goods carriage would be an important component of trade expenses, but few kept records of the costs of in-transport of goods from wholesale suppliers or out-transport in the form of free delivery to wholesale and retail customers. A tradesman who bought a significant part of his stock from local wholesalers, rather than from suppliers at the main wholesale markets, however, would have a small, visible in-transport bill, since the costs of goods carriage would be absorbed in the price charged by the local wholesaler. The costs of in-transport of goods purchased in the major wholesale markets would vary with the distance of the shop from those markets and its positioning with respect to water and land transport routes. Out-transport costs varied with the amount of

[94] *Reminiscences of an Old Draper*, p. 203.   [95] B.3. 1494 and B.3. 1068.
[96] Whittock, *Book of Trades*, p. 242.   [97] Ibid., p. 242.

free delivery service required to sell in a market of a certain physical size and consumer density.

Annual costs of goods carriage (in-transport) as estimated by seven tradesmen, are listed in Table 6:10. The estimates

TABLE 6:10. Estimated Annual Transport Costs

Trade	Goods Carriage	Horse Hire	Horse Keep
1. Food Trades			
T. Bumpus, Grocer	£ 60		
T. Walter, Grocer		£50	
R. Rose, Grocer			£ 18
T. Smith, Grocer	103	9	
J. Bond, Grocer	10		
J. Smith, Grocer	100		
R. Rose, Cheese factor, 1824			30
1825			45
J. Holland, Cheesemonger (two horses)			100
S. Chappel, Butcher			85
2. Drapers			
Froggott & Lilleyman	£ 75	£18	
W. Fuller	20		
R. Bishop	125		
J. Bond		10	
3. Metal Goods Trades			
C. Goodman, Cutler	£ 12		£ 55
W. Austin, Ironmonger			70
G. Collis, Ironmonger			50
W. Long, Ironmonger			30
Nettleford & Reid, Ironmongers			36
Hawes & Moore, Hardwaremen			40

Source: Public Records Office, Court of Bankruptcy, B.3.

vary widely in absolute amount, but in four cases it is possible to express them as a percentage of annual turnover (from Table 6:1). The cost of goods carriage as a percentage of turnover for Thomas Bumpus of Northampton was 1.5 per cent; for Froggott and Lilleyman of Doncaster, 1.02 per cent; John Smith of Faversham, 1.0 per cent; and for Charles Goodman of Northampton, 0.95 per cent.

Both in-transport and out-transport costs are reflected in Table 6:10 in the estimates of the costs of hiring or owning a horse and cart. In many trades it was possible for porters to man-handle goods to the shop, and since bulk was broken into small units for retail sales, home deliveries could also be made on foot by porters and errand boys. A grocer or draper with a wholesale trade among town and country shopkeepers might own or hire a horse and cart; but ownership was apparently more common among ironmongers than other tradesmen. Man-handling of bulk iron or heavy furnishing items (such as stoves) was impractical, and it was also difficult to avoid providing a delivery service for trade and retail customers. Since the cost of maintaining a horse was equal, and in excess, of the wages paid to many journeymen in retail shops, it was not a cost which was incurred unless essential to the business.

The costs of commercial travelling and business trips to London and manufacturing centres were included among the miscellaneous expenses. In 1831 Thomas Smith, a Birmingham grocer, estimated his travelling costs in excess of £180; in the 1830s Henry Clackett, a Dover grocer, spent around £80; and in 1816 Joseph Higgs, a Dudley draper, about £50. These men were unusual since many tradesmen appear to have travelled hardly at all, and very few estimated their expenses (including family journeys) in excess of £25 a year.

The costs of legal and financial advice, licenses, stationery and packaging materials were minor expenses for most tradesmen, estimates seldom going above £25. Advertising, apart from shop decoration, was also a negligible item: two grocers, Thomas Bumpus and James Yovens, estimated their annual advertising expenses in the 1840s at £5 and £2. 10s. respectively. Printed advertising was limited to trade cards, bill-heads and hand-bills, and occasional newspaper notices and displays in guide books and directories. By mid-century, however, a few of the big London retailers, particularly in the household furnishing and clothing trades, advertised regularly in newspapers and weeklies.

7. *Initial Capital Investment*
In a Book of Trades published in 1837, Whittock suggested

that grocers could begin business with £400 to £600, particularly if they sold for cash.[98] A London butcher serving 'respectable' customers needed £500 to £1000 to buy on cash terms in the wholesale markets and to finance retail credit; but cash sales were the rule in the lower class trade and little capital was required to begin.[99] In the haberdashery trade the stock turnover rate on many items was very slow, and Whittock suggested that a higher ratio of capital to turnover was required in this trade than in most others. Business could not be started with less than £400 and £800 was needed to begin 'on a tolerable scale'.[100] If an ironmonger limited his stock range to items of 'prime necessity' it was possible to enter trade with £400 to £500; but if he wanted 'to serve builders and others, who take long credit' he would need a much larger capital.[101] In the book and stationery trade £500 was considered 'a fair capital'.[102]

In effect, Whittock argued it was possible to begin business in most trades, at some point on a size and quality scale, with a capital of £400 to £600. To purchase a really good business as a going concern, however, involved access to £1000 or more. For example, an advertisement in 1843 read:

> To be disposed of by Private Contract, an Old Established Woollen-Drapery, Tailoring, and Ready-Made Clothes Establishment, which has been carried on prosperously upwards of half a century, in a large, populous, Manufacturing Town in the West Riding of Yorkshire. The Shop is decidedly one of the best situations in the Town. The Amount of Capital required would be from £1000 to £1800.[103]

Similarly, a firm of ironmongers located near Fitzroy Square in London 'with a good connexion' and premises 'well situated' with 'every convenience for carrying on an extensive trade' was for sale to any man with a capital of £1000 to £1500.[104] The size of the initial capital investment, then, broadly determined a tradesman's entry point on a business size and quality scale, but men did manoeuvre themselves into big shops with comparatively little capital. For example, in the 1830s a draper

[98] Ibid., pp. 264–65.
[99] Ibid., p. 82.
[100] Ibid., p. 290.
[101] Ibid., p. 301.
[102] Ibid., p. 43.
[103] *Illustrated London News*, 13 May 1843.
[104] Ibid., 5 August 1843.

negotiated for the purchase of a business on Holborn in London
with a reputed annual turnover exceeding £60 000. The seller
expected a premium for goodwill and £300 for the fixtures,
and the prospective buyer estimated that £2000 to £3000 would
be needed to stock the shop at all adequately. However, the
buyer was able to persuade the owner to forfeit his goodwill
claim and to accept £200 for the fixtures and £10 additional
rent a year. He lacked £2000 to buy stock, but went up to
Manchester for bargains and thereby pressured the London
wholesalers to 'cut the trade as fine as possible with me'. An
illusion of a good stock was furthered by making-up dummy
packages and drapery rolls, and by leaving the shop drawers
empty. Seven shopmen were hired, hand-bills were distributed
on the streets and at tradesmen's homes, and the shop was
opened for business. In this way, the draper successfully
manoeuvred entry into a shop with a big potential on very
little capital.[105]

Table 6:11, compiled from balance sheets and testimony in
bankruptcy proceedings, lists the capital invested by over 60

TABLE 6:11. Capital Invested in Shops

Trade	Capital	Trade	Capital
1. *Grocers*	£		£
J. Lyon, Cambridge	2 200	J. Smith, Faversham	250
B. Coxhead, London	2 000	C. Cooper, London	250
J. Yovens, London	1 635	J. Ward, Coventry	220
J. Bowles, Balsham	880	V. Barford, Romford	200
J. Lowman, London	750	W. Lambourne, Aylesbury	200
W. Johnston, London	700	T. Smith, Birmingham	200
T. Walter, Wilston	500	W. Towers, Nottingham	190
J. Gibbs, Ramsey	500	J. Bond, London	180
E. Bumpstead, Halesworth	500	W. Hillier, Salisbury	100
H. & T. Biven, Mortlake	400	H. Clackett, Dover	100
T. Bumpus, Northampton	340	G. Hind, Bishops Waltham	60
A. Hawkins, St. Albans	260	E. Weaver, London	25
2. *Butchers*		3. *Confectioners*	
S. Chappel, London	280	W. Jarrin, London	1 000
J. Collins, Brighton	50	T. Lipsham, London	1 120

[105] *Reminiscences of an Old Draper*, pp. 195–209.

TABLE 6:11 *eont.*

Trade	Capital	Trade	Capital
4. *Cheesemongers*	£		£
J. Holland, London	1 070	G. Henley, London	790
R. Rose, Marlborough	790	J. Cummings, London	500
5. *Drapers*			
Stephens & Croft, London	4 380	Hawthorn & Lloyd, Burton-	
W. & H. Hart, London	2 300	on-Trent	600
Froggott & Lilleyman,		R. Weaver, Plymouth	400
Doncaster	2 000	J. Bartlett, Barnstaple	350
I. Worthington, Manchester	1 050	J. Higgs, Dudley	200
T. Roberts, Manchester	980	W. Bewley, Manchester	180
J. Bond, Gt. Yarmouth	700	W. Fuller, Boston	110
		R. Bishop, Birmingham	100
6. *Tailors, Clothes Dealers*			
R. Reynard, London	450	J. Tait, Liverpool	200
G. Kemp, London	200	C. Darby, London	150
J. Gray, Chichester	200		
7. *Ironmongers*			
G. & B. Billows, Poole	2 000	J. Patterson, London	1 000
W. Barnes, Andover	2 000	Nettleford & Reid, London	710
C. Ashford, London	1 500	W. Austin, Woolwich	600
8. *Hardwaremen*		9. *Furniture Trades*	
Hawes & Moore, London	2 500	J. Davis, London	2 500
W. Cole, London	500	A. Woolf, Brighton	1 760
		E. Pearson, London	150
		R. Aman, Northampton	40

Source: Public Records Office, Court of Bankruptcy, B.3.

tradesmen. In most cases the figure indicates the initial capital investment. All of the trade groups, except butchers and tailors, include at least one case of a capital investment of £1000 or more. Stephens and Croft, Oxford Street haberdashers with an annual average turnover of some £20 000, invested over £4000, the largest among all the retailers. Three grocers, one in Cambridge and two in London, invested over £1500; the two high class London confectioners invested around £1000;

and John Holland, a Somers Town cheesemonger, invested over £1000 in his shop. Two drapery firms, one in London and the second in Doncaster, had invested around £2000, and Isaac Worthington of Manchester, over £1000. Among the iron-mongers and hardwaremen there were three firms with capital investments of over £2000, and two other firms had invested £1000 and £1500. John Davis invested £2500 in a high class London furniture business, and Aaron Woolf, who claimed ignorance of the most elementary accounting procedures,[106] had nonetheless had access to £1700 for investment in a Brighton furniture shop.

Table 6:11 also shows that many tradesmen began business with much less capital (trade credit apart) than Whittock recommended. The table is compiled from bankruptcy sources and it is possible that there is a bias towards under-capitalized firms, but most of these shopkeepers traded for three or more years. Edward Weaver, a London shopkeeper began business with as little as £25; Joseph Collins, a Brighton butcher, had only £50; and Robert Bishop, a Birmingham draper, around £100. Richard Aman, a Northampton cabinet maker, began business in 1832 with '£40 or less'. He worked from a shop with a yearly rent of only £4 and lived at a boarding house for £33 a year.

It was normal to work some years as an apprentice and journeyman before entering trade as a master. Ideally, the journeyman saved from his wages to accumulate capital to buy a shop, and one tradesman argued that 'nearly all young men in the drapery trade' could accumulate sufficient capital from their wages 'if they are careful and economical, as their living and lodging are found for them. ...'[107] There is no doubt that many tradesmen did enter business in this way: William Hillier, a Salisbury grocer, was asked:[108]

Q. What was your capital (on starting business)?
A. £100 and no more.
Q. Have you since added to your capital in any way?
A. No.

[106] See p. 223.
[107] *Reminiscences of an Old Draper*, p. 185.
[108] B.3. 2456, testimony of 24 August 1827.

Q. From what source did you get the £100?
A. I saved it out of my salary—from that source only.

On the other hand, there was a certain naïvety in the surprise which Bankruptcy Commissioners showed when they learned that Joseph Gibbs had entered trade entirely on borrowed capital:[109]

Q. What money had you when you began Business?
A. I had £350 of Mr Wasdale and £150 of Mr Gordon.
Q. Had you any other borrowed money at that time?
A. No.
Q. Had you any money of your own at the time you began Business?
A. I might have £15 or £20.
Q. How long had you been a Journeyman ... ?
A. Ever since I was out of my Apprenticeship, which was about the year 1813.
Q. Do we understand you to swear that during the 19 years you were Journeyman that you saved no wages ... ?
A. I had not saved any more money.

It was expected that a journeyman would accumulate some capital from his wages; but for most this would be an unnecessarily delayed procedure, and it was very common for men to enter trade on borrowed capital or money received as gifts from kinsmen and friends. John Lyon of Cambridge entered the grocery trade by borrowing £1200 from his father and £1000 from his father-in-law.[110] Daniel Wright, a corn factor, loaned Joseph Higgs £100 to open a drapery shop at Dudley.[111] Thomas Walter used a £200 legacy in order to open his grocery shop at Wilstone in 1820.[112] When he opened a grocery shop in Northampton in 1828 Thomas Bumpus had no capital of his own, but 'My Father advanced £342 which he gave me to furnish my house and put up the fixtures in the house and shop. ...'[113] A Bedford shoemaker, Thomas Hanson, testified that he had only £2 or £3 when he began business in 1824. The bankruptcy commissioners asked,[114]

Q. You of course began business with some stock in trade and some household furniture, how did you acquire it?

[109] B.3. 2095, testimony of 16 January 1835.　　[110] B.3. 3100.
[111] B.3. 2236, testimony of 23 April 1816.　　[112] B.3. 5319.
[113] B.3. 741.　　[114] B.3. 2358, testimony of 20 November 1824.

A. Through Mr Wilson (a yeoman farmer).
Q. In what way thro Mr Wilson—explain?
A. He gave security to my 2 sisters for their 2 shares of the property they were entitled upon the Death of my Father. ...
Q. What was the amount of your Stock in trade when you began business?
A. £300 was the Amot. of my Stock in Trade and £100 my Furniture, and I believe Mr Wilson became secty. to my Father's executors for that amot. ...

Succession to a business through a kinship network was, from the capital point of view, unquestionably the least difficult way of entry into trade. Business succession from father to son was the most likely path, but not the only one: William Twaddle became a draper and clothier at Hertford by marrying a widow with £800 in stock and £455 in accounts receivable.[115] It was also possible for a young man with limited capital resources to buy a junior partnership in a good shop with the eventual goal of complete ownership. An instance of this situation occurs in an advertisement directed to 'Grocer's Assistants':

An Opportunity is now offered to any Young Man having at his Command not less than £300, of going into Partnership with a person of long standing, having a shop, well situated, in a populous county town, and also a good connexion. He will be expected to take an active part in the business.[116]

Good opportunities of this kind, however, were probably not very common.

It was not impossible or even remarkable for a young man to save from his wages and open his own business; but for anyone following this path more than average abilities were necessary in order to emerge with a substantial business. Most of the substantial tradesmen either inherited a business or were able to buy one because they had access to capital through kinship and friendship networks.

8. *Stocks and Trade Credit*

Tradesmen's account books provide little information on the value of stocks held under normal, operating conditions. Most

---

[115] B.3. 4984.   [116] *Illustrated London News*, 1 October 1842.

of the available information on stocks may be misleading since it arose out of financial crisis and the demands of creditors for a valuation of assets.

Much of the incidental data on stocks is informative, but taken as a whole it defies generalization. Mouys and Jarrit, the high class Pall Mall hatters, took stock in May 1809, possibly with a view to dissolving the partnership. The value of their hats, materials and trimmings was estimated at £88. This is an unbelievably low valuation for a firm of such repute, but would not be remarkable for a more pedestrian firm in the producer/retailer trades. For example, the creditors of Thomas Addington, a bootmaker in Kent, forced a valuation of assets in 1840 or 1841. Addington's stock consisted of 234 pairs of footwear and materials which a licensed appraiser valued at about £30.[117]

The value of stocks held in the more strictly retail trades was probably higher on average, although many small shopkeepers held very little. Around 1801 a village shopkeeper in Berkshire compiled a balance sheet in which he valued his stock at about £65, but whether this figure represents costs or market prices it is not possible to say.[118] By contrast, William Doubleday of Essex maintained annual records of the value of his grocery, drapery and crockery stocks. The quinquennial average values were:[119]

Quinquennium	Average Value
1815–19	£3225
1820–24	2650
1825–29	2785
1830–34	1925
1835–39	2110
1840–44	2835
1845–49	2440

The average value of Doubleday's stock was about £785 lower in the quinquennial 1845–49 than in 1815–19, and was at its lowest in the decade 1830–39. It is probable that he valued his stock at expected retail value; but allowing for average margins

[117] Kent County Archives, Q/Cl/270.
[118] Berkshire Record Office, D/ESv (M) B 23/1–2.
[119] Essex Record Office, D/DQ 27/1–5.

as high as 20 per cent it remains obvious that a considerable capital was invested in stock, and possibly more than efficiency required. A rough estimate of Doubleday's stock turn ratio suggests that it was lower than was normal among reasonably efficient firms in this period.[120] The Holborn draper cited earlier[121] estimated his ideal stock requirements (at cost) to be between £2000 and £3000, and it is certain that Doubleday's turnover did not approach the volume anticipated for the Holborn shop. But a stock of £3000 would not be at all large for a retailer on a major city shopping street: in 1843 a firm of Holborn drapers, Hardwick and Ford, advertised a sale of stock 'amounting to upwards of £28 000 Value. ...'[122] Only a few of the 'monster' shops would have stocks in excess of this figure.

Table 6:12 lists the value of stocks held by some sixty tradesmen at bankruptcy. In fourteen cases the valuation was made at cost prices, and in all other cases the estimates probably represent auction values. It is also likely that tradesmen randown their stocks in the months prior to the issue of a commission of bankruptcy. For example, in 1834 Joseph Gibbs' stock was valued at £330, but when he bought the grocery and drapery shop the stock was valued at £464 and under his management it had reached £600. It is likely, therefore, that the estimates of Table 6:12 are lower than the actual value held under normal trading conditions.

Within this sample, 1 grocer, 11 drapers and haberdashers, 2 clothes dealers, and 5 ironmongers held stocks valued at over £1000. The stock values held by tailors and shoemakers, however, were comparatively low. This reflects the craft character of the clothing and footwear trades, the small size of the average producing and distributing unit, and the normally high margins on low sales volumes. The median stock value in the grocery trade sample was £300, compared with £810 for ironmongers and hardwaremen and £1800 for drapers and haberdashers. It is not statistically valid to suggest that these median figures are descriptive of the population of bankrupts or the

---

[120] Stock turn ratios are discussed later in this section.
[121] See p. 278.
[122] *Illustrated London News*, 25 November 1843.

TABLE 6:12. Values of Stock held at Bankruptcy (Rounded to nearest £5)

Trade	Date	Stock	Notes
1. Grocers			
G. Hind, Bishops Waltham	1835	£1 075	
E. Bumpstead, Halesworth	1841	585	
T. Dunlap, Pontefract	1828	440	
W. Watts, King's Lynn	1842	420	
C. Hayles, Portsmouth	1832	355	
T. Smith, Birmingham	1831	340	Cost
Booty & Son, Newport, I of W	1825	300	
R. Rose, Sutton Valence	1843	285	
J. Yovens, Ludgate Hill, London	1840	260	
J. Bowles, Balsham	1829	260	
J. Smith, Faversham	1815	230	
T. Walter, Wilstone	1829	180	
H. & T. Biven, Mortlake	1816	70	
2. Drapers			
E. & J. Marriott, Northampton	1840	£5 350	
I. Worthington, Manchester	1825	4 260	
Froggott & Lilleyman, Doncaster	1826	4 160	Cost & fixt.
J. Higgs, Dudley	1816	3 740	
S. John, Oxford St. London	1829	2 500	
W. Fuller, Boston	1825	2 030	Cost
R. Grimwood, Rochester	1824	1 960	
T. Roberts, Manchester	1826	1 770	
J. Bartlett, Barnstaple	1830	1 500	Cost
J. Thomas, Piccadilly, London	1824	890	
J. Pinck, Chichester	1824	810	Cost
J. Bond, Great Yarmouth	1840	640	
J. Reed, Regent St., London	1826	465	
R. Ball, Lambeth, London	1810	450	
W. & H. Hart, Holborn, London	1826	335	Cost
3. Haberdashers			
Stephens & Croft, Oxford St.	1827	£1 920	
Dickinson, City of Lond. (whsle.)	1825	1 830	
G. Kirtland, London	1815	660	
4. Tailors			
M. Clark, Newmarket	1824	£ 270	
W. Hiscock, Southampton	1834	250	
T. Davies, Lewes	1839	200	
R. Reynard, London	1826	200	

TABLE 6:12 *cont.*

Trade	Date	Stock	Notes
W. Brown, London	1812	135	
W. Dixon, Portsmouth	1821	80	
5. Slopsellers & Clothes Dealers			
J. Tait, Liverpool (Dress Mkrs.)	1828	£3 325	Cost
W. Twaddle, Hertford	1825	745	
T. Farrar, Shadwell	1820	440	
J. Gray, Chichester	1833	360	
R. Cruden, Gravesend	1820	345	
Burne & Lightfoot, London	1830	280	
6. Shoemakers			
R. Hanson, Bedford	1824	£ 300	
F. Noyce, Richmond	1824	100	
7. Ironmongers			
H. Downer, London	1826	£1 940	
G. Collis, Romford shop	1837	1 540	Cost
Dunmow shop	1837	320	
Nettleford & Reid, London	1831	1 400	
C. Ashford, London	1829	1 020	
W. Barnes, Andover	1835	1 000	
C. & B. Billows, Poole	1838	825	
W. Austin, Woolwich	1831	600	
W. Long, Warminster	1838	560	
J. Patterson, London	1827	520	
W. Dainton, London	1826	260	Cost
8. Hardwaremen			
Hawes & Moore, London	1827	£ 800	Cost
W. Cole, London	1826	250	Cost
9. Chemists			
W. Ward, London	1826	£ 140	
J. Haley, Witney	1836	100	

Source: Public Records Office, Court of Bankruptcy, B.3.

trading population as a whole, but they do lend support to a situation that was widely observed at the time. Grocers retailed a range of foodstuffs with high rates of stock turnover, such as bread, eggs, butter, vegetables and fruit. The turnover rate was lower on grocery items, strictly defined, but small stocks were encouraged by the rapid deterioration which they suffered from being stored loose in casks, canisters, bowls and drawers in damp cellars and inadequately ventilated shops. Drapers and haberdashers, on the other hand, were obliged to offer a wide choice of goods in all departments, and changes in fashions left them with accumulating stocks of unsaleable goods, in part a consequence of buying in 'job lots'. A young haberdasher was advised,[123]

to be very guarded in his purchases, as although the articles separately are of small cost, yet their immense number would cause an aggregate of considerable amount; and as they have to be sold by retail for very small sums, the return would be found a very slow process. ...

Similarly, ironmongers held stocks for trade customers, such as builders, plumbers and masons, and for retail customers requiring household furnishings and fixtures. The range of stock required to service both sides of the trade was very large, and in the retail oriented furnishing trade, the unit values of fenders, grates, fire-irons and stoves was high.

There is virtually no published information on rates of stock turnover, although W. N. Hancock suggested that drapery shops in Dublin in the 1850s turned stock once in every four months on average.[124] From data provided in bankruptcy files, however, it is possible to make rough calculations, using the average annual turnover and average margins to provide a cost of sales figure which can then be compared with the bankruptcy stock level,[125] always recognizing the severe limitations of the data.

The average number of weeks' stock carried in the grocery trade in 1932 and 1961 were respectively 6 to 8 weeks and 3.6 weeks.[126] The average rate for 1932 was thus higher than the

[123] E. E. Perkins, *A Treatise on Haberdashery* (1853) p. 199.

[124] Hancock, *Competition Between Large and Small Shops*, p. 23.

[125] The rate of stock turn is the ratio of the cost of sales to stock, where the cost of sales represents the value based on the purchase price of the goods sold and stock is valued at cost or lower market value. A stock turn ratio of 6, for example, would mean that stock was turning over approximately once every two months ($12/6 = 2$).

[126] McClelland, *Costs and Competition*, table vi/1, p. 126.

TABLE 6:13. Estimated Stock-turn Rates

Trade	Stock-turn Rate
1. *Grocers*	
T. Bumpus, Northampton	once every 8 weeks
R. Rose, Sutton Valence	once every 12 weeks
J. Gibbs, Ramsey	once every 16 weeks
W. Holmden, Milton	once every 24 weeks
2. *Drapers*	
R. Ball, London	once every 6 weeks
J. Thomas, London	once every 8 weeks
Froggott & Lilleyman, Doncaster	once every 24 weeks
R. Grimwood, Rochester	once every 36 weeks
J. Higgs, Dudley	once every 52 weeks

Source: Public Records Office, Court of Bankruptcy, B.3.

best rate calculated for any of these four grocers; but a stockturn ranging between three and six months in the early nineteenth century is not an improbable conclusion. Comparatively low rates were the consequence of buying in job lots, the availability of wholesale credit for three and more months, and communications bottlenecks which restricted visits by commercial travellers to once in two or more months before railway development, as compared with once or more in a month after the 1840s.[127] Small shopkeepers in the cities, however, probably turned their stocks quite rapidly. They had little capital with which to finance large stocks, credit facilities were restricted and their trade was oriented towards fast moving necessities. In general, one would expect the stockturn rates to be higher among city grocers than remote country grocer-shopkeepers. The latter were probably slow to respond to the new entrepreneurial attitudes, but it was difficult for them to limit stocks to fast moving items, and uncertainty with respect to delivery dates of stock orders encouraged them to over-stock.

With respect to the drapers represented in Table 6:13 it may be more than accidental that the two London firms apparently had markedly more favourable stockturn rates than the three provincial firms, since metropolitan firms were advantageously

[127] A. P. Allen, *The Ambassadors of Commerce* (1885), p. 104.

located with respect to stock supply. Froggott and Lilleyman, by far the largest of the three country retailers, achieved the most favourable ratio among them, while Joseph Higgs, with the least favourable rate of stockturn, bought most of his stock from manufacturers, probably in job-lots.

However much railway development contributed to improved stock turn rates, it is evident that more efficient stock handling was not entirely a product of that development. The activities of two young London trained drapers operating in Chatham in the 1820s illustrate how the existing transport network could be utilized:

> We got through a great quantity of goods, and our stock had to be frequently replenished, so that a horse and cart were set up to bring quickly to us the articles that were wanted most urgently, besides those that were sent by waggon, and also by sailing vessel down the Medway.[128]

City wholesale firms also did much to encourage retailers to adopt more efficient stock handling procedures. In the early decades of the century many wholesalers did not insist upon a bill of exchange on delivery of goods, and conventions respecting payment on account at specific days of the month were not strongly developed. Even renowned firms could show a remarkable tolerance towards long outstanding accounts. For example, Josiah Wedgwood, the pottery firm, first sold goods to John Blease, a London upholsterer, in February 1808, and they continued to supply Blease over the next three years without once receiving any payment on account.[129] But by the 1820s the credit relationship between wholesalers and retailers, and, as we have seen, between retailers and their customers, was beginning to change. Thomas James, of Moore, James & Co., a London firm of wholesale drapers dealing mainly with provincial retailers, told the Select Committee on Manufactures in 1833 that retailers,

have been gradually improving their method of managing their business, and are now enabled to pay for their goods in about half

---

[128] *Reminiscences of an Old Draper*, p. 102.
[129] B.3. 274.

the time that they used to pay some twenty years ago, when I was first a partner in the house. ...[130]

He attributed this improvement not 'to a larger amount of capital being employed by the retail dealers' but to 'a better system of managing their business; the necessity of paying closer induces them to pay more attention to their stocks, and to turn their stocks round oftener'.[131] He said 'that the retail dealers now cannot obtain credit at the first houses without satisfying those houses that they have something like an adequate capital to begin business'.[132] In previous years Moore, James had given credit for six to nine months, but they now drew bills 'at three months from the beginning of the following month in which the sale has been made'.[133] James said that 'Our practice is to make our customers either accept bills or pay their accounts on the day that the bill would become due, and not to wait for our application for the money'.[134] Some wholesalers were more rigid than Moore, James: a West Country wholesale grocery firm required Bristol retailers to pay cash on delivery, and in the country,

Each customer was waited upon by a traveller once in four weeks. Each customer knew when to expect the visit. If Mr S——— had called on a tradesmen in Hereford on Monday at ten o'clock, that tradesman would expect Mr S——— four weeks after on Monday at ten o'clock. If he had given Mr S——— an order on his former visit, the cash would be expected now; if he had ordered any goods in the meantime the cash for them also would be expected now. ... If the tradesman was not at home or had not prepared himself with his cash, the traveller did not call again. ...[135]

However, wholesalers did not rely upon coercion alone to induce prompt payment: by the 1820s discounts were beginning to be introduced. For example, Goodwin and Hutchinson, a London firm of curriers, noted on all their bill-heads that 'Our terms are $2\frac{1}{2}$ per cent Disct. off for cash or three months

[130] *Select Committee on Manufactures*, op. cit., Q. 1351.
[131] Ibid., Q. 1357.
[132] Ibid., Q. 1394. He defined an adequate capital for beginning business to be £800 or £1000.
[133] Ibid., Q. 1352-3.
[134] Ibid., Q. 1355.   [135] W. Arthur, *Successful Merchant*, pp. 161-2.

credit'[136] and Samuel Pigg & Co., Norwich warehousemen, offered 'Nett first journey or $2\frac{1}{2}$ per cent for cash'.[137] A retailer who neglected a discount of $2\frac{1}{2}$ per cent in order to secure an extra month's credit was, in effect, borrowing money at 30 per cent per annum. Retailers were quick to realize this, and the Chatham drapers mentioned earlier attempted careful stock control in order 'to see how much discount we could get each month. The system of $2\frac{1}{2}$ per cent for cash, monthly payments, or net at three months, was then regularly carried out'.[138]

In the early nineteenth century many accounts between retailers and wholesalers were settled by remittances of cash. In 1868, however, a financial journalist, commenting on yearly fluctuations in the demand for currency, noted that the 4th of every month was the day on which the great majority of home trade bills fell due: 'It is the settlement-day between the great wholesale houses and the retail-dealers who purchase their goods.'[139] An analysis of 477 bills, drawn mainly between 1820 and 1842, indicated that this practice had a long history, as they were overwhelmingly drawn to fall due in the first week of the month.[140] Sixty per cent of these bills were due in two or three months. Among 50 bills drawn on grocers, 75 per cent were due in one or two months; 50 per cent of 237 bills drawn on drapers fell due in two or three months, but 35 per cent were payable only in six or more months. Among ironmongers the two month bill was the most common, but in the furniture trade 73 per cent of the bills were due only in three months or more.

Since a considerable proportion of remittances on account were in the form of cash, a sample of due dates on bills does not prove that the majority of accounts were being settled within three months. The analysis does suggest, however, that long credit was not as common in the grocery trade as in the drapery and furniture trades. Drapers and haberdashers were subjected to the same coercion by wholesalers as grocers, but they also

[136] Invoice preserved in, Kent County Archives, Q/Cl/241/4.
[137] Ibid., Q/Cl/2.
[138] *Reminiscences of an Old Draper*, p. 109.
[139] R. H. Patterson, *The Science of Finance* (1868) pp. 211–12.
[140] This analysis was made from the record of dishonoured bills which accompanied claim sheets in bankruptcy proceedings.

dealt extensively with small manufacturers whom they could bully into granting very long credit. London drapers and haberdashers in this sample accepted bills drawn by Spitalfields weavers, for example, which fell due in instalments of nine, twelve and eighteen months. Upholsterers and ironmongers enjoyed a similar bargaining power over the small craftsmen who supplied them with finished or semi-finished goods.

At the present time, discounts of $2\frac{1}{2}$ and $1\frac{1}{4}$ per cent are offered in the food trades for payment within seven or fourteen days. In the non-food trades the rates may be $3\frac{3}{4}$ or 5 per cent, or $2\frac{1}{2}$ per cent for the same or longer periods.[141] The credit terms offered by the major wholesalers in the first half of the nineteenth century were thus more generous than is general today. But the evidence does indicate more efficient management of trade credit and stock control by 1850 than had existed in 1800.

9. *Loan Capital*

We know that country banks played an important part in financing local retail and wholesale trade.[142] But bankers' claims against insolvent tradesmen were few compared with the losses suffered by trade creditors and private lenders. They were probably more selective in providing loans than private lenders, and their more certain knowledge of the borrower's solvency enabled them to wind-up overdrafts before bankruptcy was declared. This was apparently the case with Joseph Higgs of Dudley and his bankers:[143]

Q. Who are your Bankers?
A. Dixon, Dalton & Coy.
Q. What induced you to give them a Bill for £224.12.6 on the 25th Jany.?
A. Mr Dalton said he wanted Money.
Q. Did you know at this time you could not go on?
A. I was very short of money & could not make my Payments good.
Q. Did Mr Dalton threaten to arrest you?
A. He did not—he said he must have the money.

[141] W. G. McClelland, *Costs and Competition*, p. 29.
[142] L. S. Pressnell, *Country Banking in the Industrial Revolution* (1956) pp. 356–360.
[143] B.3. 2236, testimony of 23 April 1816.

In 1840 the East of England Bank was creditor to an insolvent draper at Great Yarmouth for almost £1500,[144] but losses on this scale by country banks in their dealings with retailers seem to have been relatively rare.

Tradesmen depended heavily upon their kinsmen to provide loans on easy terms. If the terms of repayment were formally set out, they were not usually strictly enforced. For example, a Balsham grocer borrowed £100 at 5 per cent from his sister in 1824, but he made no payments on the principal or interest prior to his bankruptcy in 1829.[145] Thomas Bumpus of Northampton borrowed £150 from his father in 1829 and £100 in 1833 at 5 per cent, but the principal and interest were unpaid in 1842.[146] It is likely that tradesmen's fathers did not press for payment because the loans were, in effect, advance payment on an eventual legacy. No doubt this was the case with Bumpus's father and with Thomas Froggott, a Lancashire gentleman, who lent Froggott and Lilleyman over £270 at various times.[147] Similarly, Robert Hart, a Somerset gentleman, supplied over £500 in loans to W. & H. Hart the London drapers.[148] If a tradesman's father was dead, he might draw on the savings of his mother or a legacy left to an unmarried sister. For example, Robert Bishop of Birmingham borrowed over £450 from Mary Bishop, a Rugby spinster.[149] Harriet Dainton, a Pimlico spinster, loaned William Dainton, a Piccadilly ironmonger, some £100.[150]

The tradesman's shop was a focal point in a flow of capital from the country into the towns, from agriculture into trade and industry. The investment mechanism was probably very simple. On the one hand, a farmer might seek advice from a solicitor or scrivener as to local outlets for his savings; or, on the other, tradesmen seeking loans might approach farmers who patronized their shops. Many examples could be given of such loans: Joseph Bond, a Somers Town grocer, borrowed from a St Albans farmer;[151] John Lyon of Cambridge borrowed from several local farmers;[152] and a Dover ironmonger, James Durtnall, borrowed from two Kentish farmers.[153]

[144] B.3. 773.   [145] B.3. 649.   [146] B.3. 741.
[147] B.3. 1756 and 1757.   [148] B.3. 2430.   [149] B.3. 1350.
[150] B.3. 1412.   [151] B.3. 306.   [152] B.3. 3100.   [153] B.3. 1350.

The major classes of private lenders in the towns were professional men, such as doctors and lawyers, and wholesale and retail tradesmen in particular. In bankruptcy proceedings claims from manufacturers, merchants, wholesalers and retailers for 'goods sold and money lent' were very common. For example, Francis White, a Hounslow grocer, claimed for almost £110 against Charles Cooper, a grocer near Gray's Inn Road in London; James Harman, a London ironmonger, owed Edward Walters, a merchant, some £600; and George Kirtland, a Leicester Square haberdasher, owed Jonathan Delver, a Whalebone merchant in London, over £220. Neighbouring tradesmen were also willing to provide small loans.[154] John Lowman, a grocer on Crawford Street in London, owed John Levendge, a cheesemonger on the same street, some £15.[155] When asked if he had ever provided Joseph Gibbs with small loans, Joseph Mead, a Ramsey chemist, replied: 'Various sums, sometimes a sovereign sometimes 5 or 10 or 15£.'[156]

Rates of interest charged on long term loans in this period were normally 5 per cent, although occasionally 6, 7½ and 10 per cent despite the usury laws. Most loans were in the form of unsecured notes or bills, but if the loan was a large one the borrower might be asked to sign a bond. Lenders, and particularly trade creditors, sometimes demanded security on real property, as was the case with William Johnston, a grocer on the Old Kent Road who was in debt to a wholesale cheesemonger:[157]

Q. Do you hold the lease ... of the Bankrupts Premises?
A. Yes: an Agreement.
Q. At what time was the Agreement placed in your Hands ... ?
A. On the 24th Febry. last. ...
Q. For what purpose ... ?
A. In consideration of my letting him have £100 extension of credit more than I had let him have.
Q. Did you in consequence give the Bankrupt further credit to the extent of £100?
A. Yes nearly to £200.

[154] B.3. 961, B.3. 2198 and B.3. 2835.
[155] B.3. 3036.
[156] B.3. 2095, testimony of 10 December 1834.
[157] B.3. 2754, testimony of 24 November 1829.

Q. What was the Amount of your Debt against the Bankrupt at the time he gave you the Agreement?
A. Between £70 & £80 for which I had no security whatever.

Bill discounting was another important source of short-term funds for tradesmen. If a trade supplier demanded cash or would accept bills drawn by the tradesman as a creditor only at a high rate of discount, then the tradesman would have the bills discounted by bankers, professional men, tradesmen, and even customers and relatives. The loss of discounting facilities could force bankruptcy on a business with a sound long-term position. Benjamin Coxhead, for example, was ruined during the financial crisis of the mid-1820s:[158]

Q. When did you first have reason to think your affairs were getting wrong?
A. At the time I had some returned bills ... and the difficulty I had in getting discounts.
Q. Were they your own Bills which had been sent you?
A. Some my own and some lent me.

Q. Give me the name of any person from whom you experienced difficulty in getting discounts?
A. My Bankers Hanbury & Co. and Mr Fry (a Clements Lane grocer with whom he had discounting arrangements).

Q. Did your facilities of discounts improve between Xmas and the time of your becoming Bankrupt?
A. No—they got worse.
Q. Did your trade get better or worse in that time?
A. There was no falling off in trade in the business—it was the falling off in discounts that occasioned my embarassments. There was a better sale in my business. If I had more facilities in discount I could have done more Business.

Coxhead was unable to secure loans from friends or relatives, and he attempted to overcome the crisis by disposing of an estate. This last resort proved unsuccessful, and he was forced into a declaration of bankruptcy.

[158] B.3. 1060, testimony of 25 July 1826.

10. *Contributions to Commercial and Industrial Development*

It would be misleading to leave the impression that a tradesman's economic activities were concentrated exclusively upon
the problems of distributing, and if necessary manufacturing
and finishing, some particular range of consumer goods. It was
an unusual tradesmen who was not, at this time, involved in
some way in many peripheral financial and commercial activities.

In the first half of the century there were few institutions
dedicated to the mobilization of small savings for productive
investment. Tradesmen's shops were, in fact, very important
in drawing out these savings, and since many tradesmen were
producer/retailers, this meant that small savings were being
invested in production as well as distribution. In so far as a
particular business prospered, the supply of investible funds was
multiplied. For example, it is possible to trace the steady expansion of William Doubleday's investment portfolio during his
fifty years as a grocer and draper in Essex. In 1811 he purchased
a freehold estate for £200—apparently the first investment he
made outside his business—and a second estate, valued at £100,
was added in 1817 with a third, valued at £300, in 1819. In
1828 he purchased some 'Tropical Shares' and by 1837 his
assets included stock holdings in gas and railway companies.
While his stock portfolio continued to grow, he added to his
property holdings by buying the 'Poorhouse Estate' for £135 in
1839. Like most tradesmen of a substantial kind, he also provided
his community with financial services, taking bills and notes in
exchange for short-term loans.[159]

Many tradesmen were involved in financing and marketing
agricultural produce. A Romford grocer, Valentine Barford,
was heavily engaged in the potato trade, buying them while
they were still in the ground and arranging for their carriage
to London and sale through a commission agent.[160] John Lyon,
a grocer in Cambridge, bought and marketed hops, and was
also in partnership with his brother in a feltmongery trade.[161] A
Gravesend slopseller, Robert Cruden, was a cattle dealer, and
probably used his farm at Chalk as a grazing ground.[162] A

[159] Essex Record Office, D/DQ 27/1–5.   [160] B.3. 416.
[161] B.3. 3100.   [162] B.3. 951.

village shopkeeper at Milton in Kent was a dealer in horses;[163] and Edward Weaver, a small London shopkeeper, speculated on livestock in the Camberwell area.[164]

In some areas of the country tradesmen were involved in managing and financing mining ventures. For example, Jonathan Pedlar, the St Austell grocer, was the principal financier of the Wheal Ruby Iron Mine, and he assumed responsibility for marketing the ore through London.[165] Between 1795 and 1827 a Penzance linen draper, Thomas Broad, was a partner in 'Sundry Tin and Copper Mines'.[166]

In coastal areas tradesmen were sometimes involved in shipping. Thomas Broad, in addition to his mining interests, had substantial investments in shipping, losing £344 in wrecks and damages and £528 through 'Captures by the Enemy'. The Isle of Wight grocery firm of James Booty & Son owned a share in the ship 'Four Friends';[167] and the large Portsea provisions firm, George Baker & Son, owned the Sloop 'Jane', valued at £275, and an eighth share in the Sloop 'Prosperous', the share being valued at £100.[168]

Real estate investments were particularly popular with tradesmen, including the financing of new housing. Joseph Collins, a Brighton butcher, bought two unfinished houses and spent £200 to bring them to completion.[169] A St Albans grocer, Abraham Hawkins, began the construction of seven houses on freehold property which he bought in 1823, but these 'buildings costing more money that I was possessed of was the occasion of my failure. ...'[170] James Booty & Son owned property on the Isle of Wight of some £3000 in value.[171]

Tradesmen provided many small towns with services which could not be supported on a specialist basis. They supplemented professional factors in marketing agricultural produce; they acted as small deposit bankers, discount, loan and investment agents. Some acted as representatives for insurance companies, like John Lyon who earned over £300 as a Cambridge agent for the Phoenix Fire Office. Certainly one of the

[163] B.3. 2330.
[164] B.3. 2569.
[165] Chancery Master's Exhibits, op. cit.
[166] B.3. 560.
[167] B.3. 500.
[168] B.3. 759.
[169] B.3. 1228.
[170] B.3. 2371.
[171] B.3. 500.

more important services they provided the community—and they were paid for it in the form of labour and premiums—was that of educating new generations in trade and entrepreneurial techniques. At a time when the public provision of education was virtually non-existent, this was a very important function indeed.

PART IV

VII

Conclusions

IT IS ESSENTIAL at this point to draw together the conclusions which have been reached and to consider the contribution which the distribution system made to the British economy during the Industrial Revolution period.

It is inconceivable that such a massive growth of population, rapid urbanization and accumulating changes in transport, communications, and techniques and organization of production, could leave unchanged the ways by which producers marketed their goods and consumers purchased them. There were, in fact, major structural changes in the distribution system in this period, but perhaps because these changes were less dramatic than, say, the development of a new source of power, or the emergence of great centres of factory production, historians have tended to ignore them, or at least to underestimate them. But it is logical that a distribution system organized to service a predominantly rural society with a high level of personal self-sufficiency would necessarily undergo major changes as that society became increasingly urban and industrial.

For most of the eighteenth century England's distribution system was comprised of a system of fairs and markets, of rural itinerant distribution and of producer/retailer type shops centred in small market towns. There was a considerable degree of consumer self-sufficiency and a large proportion of exchange transactions were direct between producer and consumer. The relative primitiveness of the distribution system was manifest in the reaction of many consumers as that network, through necessity, began to develop a more complex structure: initially consumers were suspicious of the growing chain of middlemen who fitted themselves in between producer and consumer, but by the mid-nineteenth century the necessity for

this extended chain was more generally recognized and complaints about 'engrossing middlemen' tended to disappear.

The system of agricultural and industrial fairs was the major
casualty of the old distribution system. Even the greatest of
the retail fairs, such as Sturbridge, were disintegrating by the
mid-eighteenth century. The wholesale fairs struggled on rather
longer, although their usefulness was increasingly compromised
by improvements in transportation and by the emergence of
large consumption centres, other than London, which required
less periodic and more tied and guaranteed sources of supply.
As early as the seventeenth century middlemen from London
were travelling into the country contracting with producers,
both agricultural and industrial, for regular supplies, and by the
late eighteenth century the same pattern had emerged in
Lancashire, the West Riding and the Midlands. By the mid-
nineteenth century only the livestock fair, which effected the
transfer of lean stock to grazing areas near the large consumption centres, remained of any economic significance, and even
its position was undermined by railway organized meat packing
in country areas.

Unlike the fairs, the markets did not disappear as economic
institutions; but in both the old market towns and the emerging
cities and industrial towns they were obliged to undergo a
massive adaptation to changing circumstances. By the mid-
nineteenth century the inhabitants of market towns could no
longer rely exclusively upon growers from the surrounding
countryside to provide them with necessary food supplies. To be
sure, market women and farmers continued to attend the nearby
weekly market, but a large proportion of agricultural output
was now flowing into the wholesale markets of the great cities,
and from there some of the produce flowed back to the country
towns. In the cities, markets came to be structurally differentiated into wholesale and retail; in London and the provincial
cities the consumer now rarely purchased directly from the
producer, and even the retail traders dealt increasingly with
market salesmen rather than farmers. The disappearance of
direct exchange between producer and consumer and the
enormous increase in the volume of trade, led to a greater
bureaucratization of market trading. City markets were

greatly enlarged and their facilities improved, and the authorities defined and enforced a code of trading procedures. This trend towards the bureaucratization of market trading was also noticeable in middling sized towns like Leicester; and the benefits which it brought to both distributor and consumer were confirmed by instances where, as at Coventry, reforms should have been introduced and were not.

There was a continuing role for itinerant distribution, but this was of a radically different kind than had characterized the rural society of the early eighteenth century. With improved transportation town and country were more closely integrated, and for country people reliance upon the periodic visits of packmen was no longer necessary. Statistical evidence indicates that the licensed country pedlars ceased to grow in number in the first half of the nineteenth century, and the perambulating hawker was reduced to an increasingly marginal role as a retailer of novelties at the Spring and Autumn markets and fairs. The retail market was growing much faster in the cities and industrial towns, and here the numbers of street traders were very large and their contribution to urban distribution very important. Although in some cities, such as Liverpool, the corporation built suburban markets, in London and many other cities and towns the growing suburbs were increasingly distant from the centrally located markets and normally, for some years, they were inadequately provided with shops. It was one of the functions of the hawker to extend the distribution range of the central markets by carrying produce into the suburbs, where it was retailed either from house to house or in recognized street markets. In addition, hawkers from both the city and the nearby towns, carried produce from the central wholesale markets to those nearby towns and villages which had been robbed of their proximate sources of direct supply. Above all, it was the function of itinerant traders, dealing both in foodstuffs and manufactured goods, to break bulk into those small units which the poverty of so many consumers demanded and for which the time of the shop was too valuable.

But the adaptation of markets and itinerant distribution to the new urban and industrial culture had a social as well as an economic aspect, in so far as they provided a social bridge for the newly urbanized between the rural and the urban ways of life. The incomes of most inhabitants of the cities and towns left no margin for error in expenditure, and they searched for distribution channels with which they were familiar rather than confront the city shopkeeper and his assistants. But with rising incomes and greater familiarization with city life—and the self confidence which both would produce—working class consumers committed themselves increasingly to retail shops. In this respect the small neighbourhood shop performed a valuable socializing function. There was an enormous growth of shops between the 1820s and 1850s, and much of this growth was dominated by the small general shop which tended to be operated by men and women of a similar social background to the urban poor. To some extent it was the experience gained by working class people in dealing with this channel of distribution which enabled them, with rising incomes, to venture into the bigger, less personal shops of the central area.

There were enormous changes in shop retailing in this period, but the extent of the change can be missed because it was taking place within an old, inherited shell which had not visibly disintegrated before 1850. This inherited shell was made up of such elements as the intermingling of shop and household, the use of household labour and the partial survival of producer/retailer structures. Something of the live-and-let-live attitude remained—the assumption that the market should be shared—but such an attitude was limited increasingly to the rural towns and villages, and by 1850 was largely alien to shop retailing in the cities. The new entrepreneurial concepts, which arose in London and other cities and spread gradually over many decades through the country, were aggressively competitive. Prices were marked, and thus became competitive; periodic sales offering 10 or 20 per cent 'off regular price' were familiar to city shoppers; more and more shops abandoned the financial and administrative constraints on growth imposed by retail credit (other than fixed instalment plans) by demanding cash and striving for rapid turnover on narrow margins; and concern with maintaining an optimum stock level and making quick payments to wholesalers in return for discounts—these were the marks of the new retailer. Big shops with turnovers reaching a million pounds a year, with plate glass windows, gas lighting displays, regular periodical and newspaper advertising, were, of course, a city phenomenon; but the drift of city trained tradesmen into country towns and the much tougher attitude of wholesalers towards sleepy country retailers meant that by 1850 the difference between city and country retailing was one lying along a continuum rather than across an unpassable chasm. But to a certain extent all of these changes were only surface signs of a much deeper transformation: tradesmen by 1850 were more distinctly shopkeepers, or retailers, than they had been a hundred or fifty years before. In the cities in particular, the producer/retailer structure had been very largely eroded by the mid-century, despite the fact that there was not yet factory production of most consumption goods. In the grocery trade much of the sorting, grading, processing, and packaging was being assumed by the wholesaler and by specialists in food preparation. Bread production was still tied to the distribution point, but there were experiments with centralized factory production and in the cities many bakery outlets had been absorbed into chains owned by flour millers. The city butcher was able to buy animal sections from wholesale and cutting butchers, thus obviating the need for a slaughter house and all but minimal cutting facilities. Drapers and haberdashers, of course, had always been retailers with only limited processing responsibilities; but in the clothing trades there was a marked trend towards the disaggregation of production and distribution. Shoemakers bought made-up goods and assembled footwear from pre-cut components; hatters confined themselves to the trimming of factory produced shells; and the bespoke tailoring trade was being challenged in 1850 by the new 'clothier and outfitter' who retailed the ready-made goods produced in city sweatshops. The demand for ready-made clothing was enormous by the mid-nineteenth century, even among 'respectable' consumers. There was an equally impressive disentangling of production and distribution in the metal goods and furniture trades, particularly in the cities. City ironmongers, hardwaremen and upholsterers bought the vast proportion of their stocks, and if a workshop was retained it was there mainly for doing repairs, turning out special orders and satisfying the strong craft instincts of its owner. The disentangling of production and distribution in this period made it much easier for men to enter the trades, since capital requirements were reduced and long years spent developing craft skills were no longer necessary. Shopkeepers turned towards developing retailing and management skills which in the old producer/retailer shops had been subordinated to concern over the quality of their limited volumes of output.

It was noted earlier that the performance of the distribution system in this period had received two contradictory assessments. J. H. Clapham thought that the essential features of the nineteenth century distribution system had emerged in the first five decades, whereas J. B. Jefferys argued that the system changed very little between 1750 and 1850 and that it 'still bore the marks of a pre-industrial economy'. Recently, Jefferys' interpretation has been given still greater emphasis: Dorothy Davis felt that 'so much of the nation's energy and imagination was being drawn into industry and foreign commerce that none was left to fertilize the retail trades with new ideas'. It would be surprising if there were not large residues of conservatism in the retail trades, since they were part of an earlier industrial structure undergoing transition. The inheritance of buildings, and in some trades the inheritance of industrial plant, such as a foundry in the ironmongery trade, meant that the run down of the producer/retailer complex was bound to be a gradual one if the capital assets of the economy were to be utilized to their fullest extent. It should be recognized that a great deal of the industrial skill of the country was located in these small producer/retailer shops, and that the master tradesmen passed on these skills to succeeding generations for further development. The redeployment of labour skills—and this is what was involved in the disentangling of production and distribution —is not achieved suddenly, especially when that redeployment is directed solely by market forces. The inheritance of a centuries old craft tradition inevitably meant that there would be some resistance by some shopkeepers to changing methods of production, buying and selling. It must also be remembered that in large areas of the country there was little pressure to change traditional methods. The market opportunities afforded by a growing population—and the corresponding responsibility to adapt methods in order to get goods to that population at the place and in the volume and price demanded—was a phenomenon which faced shopkeepers to a dramatic degree in perhaps a hundred cities and towns at most. Elsewhere the pressure for radical change in methods was less insistent, and it is doubtful if consumer welfare was seriously imperilled by the comparatively leisurely rate of change.

Clapham was right to argue that the essential features of the nineteenth century distribution system emerged in this period. We have seen that by the 1820s tradesmen were beginning to develop improved techniques of stock control; they introduced cash buying and selling, price cutting and ticketing; they refashioned their shop fronts and interiors and some began to advertise; there were experiments in intra- and inter-city multiple shop retailing; and in some trades there emerged a significant range in the size of retail units. But Jefferys was equally perceptive in noting that the distribution system 'still bore the marks of a pre-industrial economy'. This characteristic was most noticeable in the market and itinerant channels of distribution. Unemployment or underemployment is a characteristic of economies with an insufficiency of co-operant resources—land, capital, technical and entrepreneurial skills—to put people to work, and in these circumstances surplus labour may well find its way into the distribution system. This was true for England in the first half of the century, and the massive labour input had the effect of keeping down the capital requirements of the system as a whole and providing consumers with their essential needs at a low cost, since the itinerants charged very little for their services. The possibility of substituting capital for this labour, and thus achieving greater technical efficiency in distribution, was not very great, and not necessarily very desirable. Some investment of public and private capital in markets, shops and shopping streets was essential to meet the demands of a growing population; but investment of scarce capital in transport and the heavy- and consumer-goods industries offered higher returns in terms of labour productivity and higher incomes. As the industrial and commercial economy took a firmer hold on England from the 1840s, much of this labour was gradually absorbed into better paid occupations; but until that time the employment of surplus labour in distribution was an economically efficient use of the economy's real resources, as well as, in effect, the most important form of 'welfare' relief in a society which did not, and perhaps could not, provide it in any other way.

The performance of the distribution system is notoriously difficult to measure, and in any case the volume of statistical information for this period is not large. The conclusions reached, in the final analysis, are largely impressionistic. There is certainly no evidence that the distribution system acted as a constraint upon development. The costs of distribution services, as reflected in retail margins, appear to have been low, and judged by the long-term optimism of producers and the growing materialism of the society as a whole, distributors were successful in marketing the increased output and, among the slowly growing body of better-off consumers, transforming a latent demand for new consumption goods into a manifest demand. These accomplishments were achieved, moreover, at an apparently low capital cost, transport excluded. This was an important achievement when scarce capital was urgently required in developing the industrial, transport and housing needs of the country, and on the whole it would seem that the distribution system served England very well in this period.

APPENDIX I

Table Series A:1 to A:11

TABLE A:1. Numbers of Tradesmen—London

TRADES	1822	1834
A. *Book and Stationery*		
Booksellers	477	742
Newspaper Advertising Agents	—	7
News Vendors	51	201
Stationers—Retail	344	518
—Wholesale	62	118
—Fancy	—	41
B. *Chemists and Druggists*		
Retail	297	442
Wholesale	38	51
Merchants	1	8
Brokers	19	27
C. *Cloth and Clothing*		
Boot and Shoemakers	896	2 054
—Wholesale	11	39
Clothiers—Army	12	15
Clothes Salesmen	—	323
Slopsellers	74	84
Dress Makers	—	525
Tailors	1 131	2 459
Linen Drapers—Retail	546	649
—Wholesale	30	66
Woollen Drapers	155	165
Silk Mercers	49	69
Silkmen	29	13
Men's Mercers	40	20
Haberdashers and Hosiers—Retail	302	291
—Wholesale	24	66
Hosiers and Glovers	174	320
Hosiers—Wholesale	57	51
Glovers—Retail and Wholesale	66	84
Hatters	259	462
Lace Dealers—Retail	174	320
—Wholesale	21	65

TABLE A:1 *cont.*

TRADES	1822	1834
D. *Pottery*		
China and Porcelain Dealers—Foreign	2	11
China, Glass and Earthenware	259	419
E. *Food Trades*		
Bakers	496	2 216
Confectioners	192	338
Butchers	—	1 824
Cheesemongers	656	1 058
Corn Dealers—Retail	233	389
Fishmongers	152	438
Fruiterers	54	124
Greengrocers	—	1 152
Grocers and Tea Dealers	899	1 702
—Wholesale	38	66
Ham and Tongue Merchants and Dealers	13	65
Provisions Merchants	39	33
Milk Sellers, Dairymen and Cowkeepers	—	656
Tea and Coffee Dealers—Retail	93	187
—Wholesale	63	95
Shopkeepers	—	2 192
F. *Metal Goods Trades*		
Cutlers	90	173
Hardwaremen	50	59
Ironmongers—Retail	309	443
—Wholesale	45	58
Birmingham and Sheffield Warehouses	23	38
G. *Leather Trades*		
Curriers, Leather Sellers and Cutters	164	196
Leather Dressers, Manufacturers and Sellers	91	126
Tanners	49	51
Saddlers	201	240
H. *Oil and Colour*		
Oil and Colour Dealers	437	686
Colourmen	20	28
Oil Dealers and Refiners	4	42
Italian and Oil Warehouses	59	138
I. *Tobacco*		
Tobacconists	177	755
Manufacturers	81	73

TABLE A:1 *cont.*

TRADES	1822	1834
J. *Miscellaneous*		
Drysalters	48	63
Furriers	51	124
Pawnbrokers	207	296
Tallow Chandlers	363	308
Toy Dealers—Retail	71	177
—Wholesale	13	95
Gold, Silversmiths and Jewellers	277	249
Silversmiths—Working	17	103

TABLE A:2. Number of Tradesmen—Liverpool

TRADES	1822	1834	1846	1851
A. *Book and Stationery*				
Booksellers	16	21	—	—
Booksellers and stationers	30	38	63	94
Stationers	—	25	74	75
B. *Chemists and Druggists*				
Chemists and Druggists	52	113	161	188
—Wholesale	1	8	8	9
—Manufacturing	3	16	13	16
C. *Cloth and Clothing*				
Boot and Shoe Makers	101	261	196	603
Clothes Dealers and Outfitters		14	102	142
Slopsellers	30	20	6	—
Milliners and Dress Makers	47	141	105	319
Tailors and Drapers	77	280	186	408
Drapers and Haberdashers	105	135	115	146
Smallware Dealers	18	73	127	156
Hosiers and Glovers	38	34	95	102
Hatters	35	23	44	52
D. *Pottery*				
China, Glass and Earthenware	33	50	44	65
E. *Food Trades*				
Bakers	—	130	209	272
Confectioners	47	76	100	131
Butchers	—	344	—	532

TABLE A:2 cont.

TRADES	1822	1834	1846	1851
Cheesemongers	10	25	—	—
Fishmongers	—	64	—	51
Fruiterers and Greengrocers	13	51	22	132
Grocers and Tea Dealers	91	155	206	243
—Wholesale	14	14	16	11
Poulterers	3	35	28	32
Provisions Merchants	12	36	53	61
—Dealers	35	80	510	324
Tea Dealers	58	64	51	43
Shopkeepers	—	571	—	738
F. *Metal Goods Trades*				
Hardwaremen and Cutlers	11	18	27	42
Ironmongers	43	60	78	87
G. *Leather Trades*				
Curriers and Leather Sellers	28	40	35	41
Leather Dealers and Factors	—	14	20	27
Saddlers and Harness Makers	15	29	32	47
Tanners	7	11	12	14
H. *Oil and Colour*				
Oilmen	3	—	—	—
Colour Manufacturers	—	14	25	34
Oil Merchants	—	12	17	19
Oil and Italian Warehouses	—	5	6	15
I. *Tobacco*				
Tobacconists	31	76	97	163
Cigar Merchants and Dealers	—	—	24	30
Tobacco Manufacturers	25	26	27	16
J. *Miscellaneous*				
Drysalters	13	21	25	23
Furriers	4	12	13	12
Pawnbrokers	67	84	101	99
Gold, Silversmiths and Jewellers	22	37	47	54
Tallow Chandlers	20	35	46	43
Toy Dealers	10	10	15	23

TABLE A:3. Number of Tradesmen—Manchester

TRADES	1822	1834	1841	1851
A. *Book and Stationery*				
Booksellers and Stationers	22	43	52	82
Stationers (repetitions from above)	—	25	—	121
B. *Chemists and Druggists*				
Chemists and Druggists	52	94	145	195
—Manufacturing	1	32	25	55
C. *Cloth and Clothing*				
Boot and Shoe Makers	41	226	371	694
Shoe Warehouses	20	14	18	18
Clothes Brokers and Dealers	22	40	33	37
Milliners and Dress Makers	—	138	177	473
Tailors (and Drapers)	39	208	318	430
Linen Drapers	77	110	140	190
Woollen Drapers	20	41	41	24
Smallware Dealers	17	72	112	162
Hosiers and Glovers	27	33	84	87
Glovers—Wholesale	—	5	6	8
Hosiers—Wholesale	—	8	13	11
Hatters	21	17	26	57
D. *Pottery*				
Glass, China and Earthenware	11	11	31	32
Earthenware Dealers	16	44	43	47
E. *Food Trades*				
Bakers and Flour Dealers	—	108	193	294
Confectioners	27	49	58	125
Butchers	—	446	463	641
Cheesemongers	11	10	10	10
Fishmongers	—	17	25	45
Fruiterers and Greengrocers	3	40	34	85
Grocers and Tea Dealers	92	123	174	319
Tea and Coffee Dealers	23	31	37	70
Poulterers	—	6	9	20
Bacon and Ham Dealers	—	—	—	20
Egg and Dried Fish Dealers	—	11	44	26
Provisions Dealers	11	49	—	—
Shopkeepers	—	723	1 037	1 482
F. *Metal Goods Trades*				
Cutlers	3	13	18	23

TABLE A:3 *cont.*

TRADES	1822	1834	1841	1851
Hardwaremen (Birmingham and Sheffield warehouses)	—	9	12	20
Ironmongers	24	37	48	72
G. *Leather Trades*				
Curriers and Leather Sellers	18	30	40	42
Leather Dressers	1	5	7	14
Tanners	—	7	10	16
Saddlers	19	34	33	38
H. *Oil and Colour*				
Oil and Colourmen	—	4	10	16
Oil Merchants and Dealers	13	12	27	29
Colour Manufacturers and Dealers	—	—	12	5
Artists' Colourmen	—	5	4	4
I. *Tobacco*				
Tobacconists	17	43	87	130
Cigar Dealers and Importers	—	4	8	16
J. *Miscellaneous*				
Drysalters	41	47	67	80
Furriers	6	12	8	19
Pawnbrokers	62	146	148	164
Tallow Chandlers	10	16	17	14
Toy Warehouses and Dealers	—	8	17	30
Jewellers and Silversmiths	12	20	17	24
—Working	1	7	7	17

TABLE A:4. Numbers of Tradesmen—Leeds

TRADES	1822	1834	1841	1848
A. *Book and Stationery*				
Booksellers and Stationers	21	24	30	42
Stationers—Wholesale	—	2	3	8
B. *Chemists and Druggists*				
Chemists and Druggists	20	40	49	72
—Manufacturing	8	11	18	21

TABLE A:4 *cont.*

TRADES	1822	1834	1841	1848
c. *Cloth and Clothing*				
Boot and Shoe Makers	38	115	108	256
Clothes Dealers	12	25	13	18
Milliners and Dress Makers	13	85	71	176
Tailors	44	150	71	240
Linen and Woollen Drapers (and Haberdashers)	38	57	75	103
Smallware Dealers	—	—	5	9
Hosiers and Glovers	22	14	22	36
d. *Pottery*				
China, Glass and Earthenware	7	8	7	24
Earthenware Manufacturers	—	8	10	13
e. *Food Trades*				
Bakers (and Flour Dealers)	17	26	20	39
Confectioners	25	34	37	44
—Wholesale	—	—	1	2
Corn and Flour Dealers	14	38	46	93
Butchers	—	199	180	253
Fishmongers	—	4	8	11
Fruiterers and Greengrocers	—	13	18	26
Grocers and Tea Dealers	65	79	77	74
Tea Dealers	27	17	27	30
Poulterers		8	6	12
Provisions Dealers (Bacon and Cheese Dealers)	10	41	43	38
Shopkeepers	—	313	362	620
f. *Metal Goods*				
Cutlers	7	7	7	8
Hardware Dealers	—	16	14	14
Ironmongers	12	19	16	24
g. *Leather Trades*				
Curriers and Leather Sellers	10	77	27	40
Leather Dressers	—	3	9	6
Leather sellers	—	8	10	12
Tanners	—	8	5	7
Saddlers	13	20	23	23
h. *Oil and Colour*				
Oil Merchants and Dealers	13	15	17	22

TABLE A:4 *cont.*

TRADES	1822	1834	1841	1848
I. *Tobacco*				
Tobacconists	29	32	29	49
J. *Miscellaneous*				
Drysalters	19	19	26	19
Furriers	4	4	6	6
Pawnbrokers	11	19	31	24
Tallow Chandlers	7	8	10	12
Silversmiths and Jewellers	9	4	7	14
Jewellers—Working	1	2	7	7

TABLE A:5. Numbers of Tradesmen—Norwich

TRADES	1822	1839	1851
A. *Book and Stationery*			
Booksellers, Stationers, Printers and Binders	23	15	21
Stationers	—	10	12
B. *Chemists and Druggists*			
Chemists and Druggists	17	32	30
—Manufacturers	—	—	1
C. *Cloth and Clothing*			
Boot and Shoe Makers	56	99	167
Clothes Dealers	11	25	29
Milliners and Dress Makers	22	46	129
Tailors	53	85	97
Linen Drapers	10	—	—
Woollen Drapers	9	9	4
Linen and Woollen Drapers	16	28	35
Silk Mercers	2	6	—
Haberdashers and Hosiers	22	20	36
Glovers and Breeches Makers	1	4	11
Hatters	15	13	14
D. *Pottery*			
China, Glass and Earthenware Dealers	16	18	16
E. *Food Trades*			
Bakers (and Flour Dealers)	89	134	150
Confectioners	9	24	28

TABLE A:5 *cont.*

TRADES	1822	1839	1851
Corn Chandlers and Flour Dealers	—	10	10
Butchers	—	62	70
Fishmongers	—	16	24
Fruiterers and Greengrocers	5	36	20
Grocers and Tea Dealers	51	68	85
Tea and Coffee Dealers	4	13	16
Tea Dealers and Drapers—Travelling	—	—	10
Shopkeepers	—	133	228
F. *Metal Goods Trades*			
Cutlers	4	4	12
Hardwaremen	2	6	6
Ironmongers (Oil and Colourmen)	11	15	22
G. *Leather Trades*			
Curriers and Leather Sellers	16	18	25
Tanners	4	4	3
Saddlers	15	21	20
H. *Tobacco*			
Tobacconists and Manufacturers	7	9	14
J. *Miscellaneous*			
Furriers	—	5	8
Pawnbrokers	12	13	15
Tallow Chandlers	15	11	15
Toy Dealers	4	4	14
Silversmiths and Jewellers	7	7	6
Jewellers—Working	1	—	—
Jewellers	—	6	6

TABLE A:6. Numbers of Tradesmen—Bolton

TRADES	1822	1834	1851
A. *Book and Stationery*			
Booksellers, Stationers, Binders and Printers	6	8	20
B. *Chemists and Druggists*			
Chemists and Druggists	7	14	29
—Manufacturers		3	9

TABLE A:6 *cont.*

TRADES	1822	1834	1851
c. *Cloth and Clothing*			
Boot and Shoe Makers	8	33	79
Shoe Warehouses	11	9	—
Clothes Dealers	4	—	9
Milliners and Dress Makers	—	38	74
Tailors (Drapers)	—	41	74
Linen Drapers	13	11	15
Linen and Woollen Drapers	9	12	11
Woollen Drapers	6	—	—
Linen Drapers and Tea Dealers—			
Travelling	—	—	9
d. *Pottery*			
Glass, China and Earthenware	3	4	4
Earthenware Dealers	—	4	11
e. *Food Trades*			
Bakers and Flour Dealers	43	30	19
Corn and Flour Dealers	5	6	28
Butchers	—	39	63
Fishmongers	—	3	1
Fruiterers and Greengrocers	—	3	3
Grocers and Tea Dealers	18	25	50
Tea Dealers	5	8	14
Poulterers	—	3	—
Shopkeepers	—	145	294
f. *Metal Goods Trades*			
Cutlers	1	1	—
Hardware Dealers	—	—	2
Ironmongers	5	8	10
g. *Leather Trades*			
Curriers and Leather Sellers	4	6	12
Saddlers	5	5	10
h. *Tobacco*			
Tobacconists	5	4	5
i. *Miscellaneous*			
Drysalters	—	—	2
Pawnbrokers	7	16	21
Tallow Chandlers	5	7	3
Toy Dealers and Jewellers	—	5	—

TABLE A:7. Numbers of Tradesmen—Leicester

TRADES	1822	1835	1841	1850
A. *Book and Stationery*				
Booksellers and Stationers	14	16	19	20
Stationers	—	—	—	5
B. *Chemists and Druggists*				
Chemists and Druggists	11	22	27	34
C. *Cloth and Clothing*				
Boot and Shoemakers	42	188	156	238
Clothes Dealers	3	14	9	19
Milliners and Dress Makers	18	60	34	160
Tailors	28	95	68	151
Linen and Woollen Drapers	22	25	28	34
Lacemen	—	—	—	8
Haberdashers	—	6	4	26
Hosiers	—	4	—	17
Hosiers and Glovers, Hatters	9	9	8	9
Glovers	—	4	2	6
D. *Pottery*				
China, Glass and Earthenware	5	16	16	24
Earthenware Dealers	4	—	—	—
E. *Food Trades*				
Bakers and Flour Dealers	56	99	101	120
Corn and Flour Dealers	—	40	23	29
Confectioners	7	16	15	29
Butchers	—	90	84	131
Cheesemongers	9	7	—	—
Fishmongers	3	3	2	5
Fruiterers and Greengrocers	—	15	—	30
Grocers and Tea Dealers	57	82	72	76
Tea Dealers	3	3	—	—
Tea Dealers and Linen Drapers—				
Travelling	—	—	—	8
Poulterers	—	5	3	5
Shopkeepers	—	176	81	257
F. *Metal Goods*				
Cutlers	4	10	8	11
Hardwaremen	—	—	—	6
Ironmongers	9	9	8	14

TABLE A:7 *cont.*

TRADES	1822	1835	1841	1850
G. *Leather Trade*				
Curriers and Leather Cutters	5	15	9	18
Tanners	2	3	3	3
Saddlers	5	10	9	12
H. *Oil and Colour*				
Oil and Colour Dealers	—	3	3	5
I. *Tobacco*				
Tobacconists	1	2	2	8
J. *Miscellaneous*				
Furriers	1	—	—	6
Pawnbrokers	9	8	9	11
Tallow Chandlers	15	12	13	8
Toy Dealers	—	2	—	7
Jewellers and Silversmiths	5	11	8	14

TABLE A:8. Numbers of Tradesmen—Nottingham

TRADES	1822	1835	1841	1850
A. *Book and Stationery*				
Booksellers and Stationers	13	16	22	33
B. *Chemists and Druggists*				
Chemists and Druggists	17	51	56	63
—Manufacturing	—	—	—	4
C. *Cloth and Clothing*				
Boot and Shoe Makers	47	295	203	349
Clothes Dealers	—	21	18	21
Milliners and Dress Makers	29	191	104	260
Tailors	50	159	117	213
Linen and Woollen Drapers	34	37	39	42
Silkmen	—	3	3	6
Smallware Dealers	—	21	24	43
Hatters and Hosiers	9	15	26	47
Lace Dealers	—	—	15	24

TABLE A:8 *cont.*

TRADES	1822	1835	1841	1850
D. *Pottery*				
China, Glass and Earthenware	8	7	11	15
E. *Food Trades*				
Bakers and Flour Dealers	73	146	137	164
Confectioners	12	26	27	30
—Wholesale	—	3	2	3
Butchers	—	213	235	293
Cheesemongers	5	10	7	11
Fishmongers and Poulterers	3	18	14	27
Greengrocers	—	25	—	—
Grocers and Tea Dealers	84	82	87	74
Tea and Coffee Dealers	7	6	4	10
Tea Dealers and Linen Drapers—				
Travelling	—	6	17	20
Provisions Dealers	—	7	5	18
Shopkeepers	—	343	292	428
F. *Metal Goods Trades*				
Ironmongers	6	11	13	18
G. *Leather Trades*				
Curriers and Leather Cutters	8	12	11	18
Tanners	—	—	2	14
Saddlers	6	14	12	22
H. *Tobacco*				
Tobacconists	—	3	4	17
—Manufacturers	2	4	5	3
J. *Miscellaneous*				
Furriers	—	7	6	7
Pawnbrokers	11	13	13	14
Tallow Chandlers	18	12	13	14
Toy Dealers	—	5	3	6
Silversmiths and Jewellers	8	9	7	17
Jewellers—Working	—	4	6	3

TABLE A:9 Numbers of Tradesmen—Merthyr Tydfil

TRADES	1822	1835	1850
A. *Book and Stationery*			
Booksellers and Stationers	3	3	10
B. *Chemists and Druggists*			
Chemists and Druggists	2	7	16
C. *Cloth and Clothing*			
Boot and Shoe Makers	3	18	79
Clothes Dealers	—	4	6
Milliners and Dress Makers	2	4	14
Tailors	—	10	76
Drapers (andgrocers)	24	10	17
Hatters	1	1	1
D. *Pottery*			
China and Glass Dealers	1	4	12
E. *Food Trades*			
Bakers and Flour Dealers	—	3	9
Confectioners	—	3	10
Butchers	—	16	108
Fruiterers and Greengrocers	—	—	9
Grocers, Drapers, Shopkeepers	4	84	191
Tea Dealers—Travelling	—	11	16
F. *Metal Goods Trades*			
Hardware Dealers	—	2	4
Ironmongers	3	3	12
G. *Leather Trades*			
Curriers and Leather Sellers	4	4	7
Tanners	2	2	1
Saddlers	4	6	10
H. *Miscellaneous*			
Tallow Chandlers	4	4	9
Tobacconists	—	—	1

TABLE A:10. Numbers of Tradesmen—York

TRADES	1822	1834	1841	1848
A. *Book and Stationery*				
Booksellers and Stationers	15	15	20	23
B. *Chemists and Druggists*				
Chemists and Druggists	20	28	24	30
—Wholesale	—	7	6	6
C. *Cloth and Clothing*				
Boot and Shoe Makers	45	86	109	168
Clothes Dealers	—	—	20	17
Milliners and Dress Makers	—	29	47	64
Tailors	35	53	71	101
Linen Drapers	30	24	32	29
Woollen Drapers	17	8	7	6
Lace Dealers	—	—	—	2
Hosiers and Glovers	7	12	9	10
Hat Makers and Dealers	9	11	12	14
D. *Pottery*				
Glass, China and Earthenware	14	12	12	15
E. *Food Trades*				
Bakers and Flour Dealers	52	39	36	40
Corn Merchants and Dealers	5	9	11	11
Confectioners	8	14	16	19
—Wholesale	—	—	2	5
Butchers	—	87	85	125
Fishmongers	—	9	9	11
Fruiterers and Greengrocers	17	4	4	13
Grocers and Tea Dealers	72	52	44	40
Tea Dealers	—	16	20	18
Tea Dealers and Linen Drapers— Travelling	—	—	3	15
Game Dealers	—	6	5	9
Shopkeepers	—	88	123	229
F. *Metal Goods Trades*				
Ironmongers	11	12	13	10
G. *Leather Trades*				
Curriers and Leather Cutters	9	13	13	—
Curriers and Leather Sellers	—	—	—	29
Tanners	4	3	2	2
Saddlers	13	16	22	21

TABLE A:10 *cont.*

TRADES	1822	1834	1841	1848
H. *Miscellaneous*				
Paint, Oil and Colour Dealers	—	—	—	4
Pawnbrokers	11	4	3	5
Silversmiths and Jewellers	8	7	6	6
Jewellers—Working	—	—	1	3
Tallow Chandlers	7	6	5	5
Tobacconists	1	5	12	11
Toy Makers and Dealers	10	7	5	4

TABLE A:11. Numbers of Tradesmen—Carlisle

TRADES	1834	1848
A. *Book and Stationery*		
Booksellers and Stationers	8	9
B. *Chemists and Druggists*		
Chemists and Druggists	11	16
C. *Cloth and Clothing*		
Boot and Shoe Makers	64	81
Clothes Dealers	8	9
Milliners and Dress Makers	13	45
Tailors	37	48
Linen and Woollen Drapers	—	24
Hosiers	6	6
Hatters	9	10
D. *Pottery*		
China, Glass and Earthenware	5	10
E. *Food Trades*		
Bakers and Flour Dealers	14	37
Confectioners	7	15
Butchers	41	45
Fishmongers	4	7
Fruiterers and Greengrocers	1	2
Grocers and Tea Dealers	44	30
Game Dealers	—	3
Tea and Coffee Dealers	8	7
Shopkeepers	71	157

TRADES	1834	1848
F. *Metal Goods Trades*		
Ironmongers	7	8
G. *Leather Trades*		
Curriers and Leather Sellers	7	10
Tanners	7	7
Saddlers	9	9
H. *Miscellaneous*		
Drysalters	2	2
Pawnbrokers	4	4
Tallow Chandlers	4	7
Tobacconists	—	2
Toy Dealers	3	6

APPENDIX II

Table Series B:1 to B:10

TABLE B:1. Population per Shop Outlet—London

TRADES	1822	1834
A. *Book and Stationery*		
Booksellers	3 439	3 018
Stationers—Retail	4 740	4 322
B. *Chemists and Druggists*		
Chemists and Druggists	5 491	5 066
C. *Cloth and Clothing*		
Boot and Shoe Makers	1 820	1 090
Clothes Salesmen	—	6 932
Slopsellers	22 036	26 655
Dress Makers	—	4 265
Milliners and Dress Makers	9 648	2 757
Tailors	1 442	910
Linen and Woollen Drapers	2 326	2 751
D. *Pottery*		
China, Glass and Earthenware	6 296	5 344
E. *Food Trades*		
Bakers	3 288	1 010
Confectioners	8 488	6 624
Cheesemongers	2 486	2 116
Fishmongers	10 728	5 112
Grocers and Tea Dealers	1 803	1 316
Tea and Coffee Dealers	17 534	11 973
Shopkeepers	—	1 021
F. *Metal Goods Trades*		
Cutlers	18 119	12 942
Hardwaremen	32 619	37 316
Ironmongers	5 277	5 280
G. *Oil and Colourmen*		
Oil and Colour Dealers	3 371	3 249

TABLE B:1 *cont.*

TRADES	1822	1834
H. *Miscellaneous*		
Tobacconists	9 213	2 965
Tallow Chandlers	4 492	7 270
Toy Dealers	22 968	12 649

TABLE B:2. Population per Shop Outlet—Liverpool

TRADE	1822	1834	1846	1851
A. *Booksellers and Stationers*				
Booksellers and Stationers	3 139	2 705	2 416	2 225
B. *Chemists and Druggists*				
Chemists and Druggists	2 777	2 010	2 056	2 000
C. *Cloth and Clothing*				
Boot and Shoe Makers	1 444	874	1 689	624
Clothes Dealers and Slopsellers	4 813	6 682	3 065	2 646
Milliners and Dress Makers	3 072	1 625	3 152	1 175
Tailors	1 875	812	1 779	921
Drapers	1 375	1 690	2 878	2 440
Smallware Dealers	8 000	3 112	2 606	2 410
D. *Pottery*				
China, Glass and Earthenware	4 376	4 544	7 523	5 770
E. *Food Trades*				
Bakers	—	1 748	1 576	1 345
Confectioners	3 072	2 989	3 310	2 870
Grocers and Tea Dealers	1 585	1 465	1 607	1 547
Tea Dealers	2 490	3 550	6 490	8 744
Provisions Dealers	4 126	2 840	650	1 160
Shopkeepers	—	398	—	510
F. *Metal Goods Trades*				
Hardwaremen and Cutlers	13 127	12 662	12 259	8 952
Ironmongers	3 358	3 785	4 243	4 321
G. *Miscellaneous*				
Tobacconists and Cigar Dealers	4 658	2 989	2 735	1 948
Tallow Chandlers	7 220	6 491	7 195	8 744
Toy Dealers	14 440	22 720	22 066	16 348

TABLE B:3. Population per Shop Outlet—Manchester

TRADES	1822	1834	1841	1851
A. *Book and Stationery*				
Booksellers and Stationers	5 982	4 602	4 519	3 695
Stationers	—	7 916	—	2 504
B. *Chemists and Druggists*				
Chemists and Druggists	2 531	2 105	1 620	1 554
C. *Cloth and Clothing*				
Boot and Shoe Makers	3 209	875	633	436
Shoe Warehouses	6 580	14 135	13 055	16 833
Clothes Brokers and Dealers	5 982	4 943	7 121	8 189
Milliners and Dress Makers	—	1 434	1 327	640
Tailors	3 290	951	738	704
Drapers	1 356	1 319	1 305	1 860
Smallware Dealers	7 741	2 748	2 098	1 870
D. *Pottery*				
Glass, China and Earthenware	4 874	3 598	3 175	3 787
E. *Food Trades*				
Bakers and Flour Dealers	—	1 832	1 217	1 030
Confectioners	4 874	4 038	4 051	2 424
Cheesemongers	11 964	19 790	23 500	30 000
Grocers and Tea Dealers	1 430	1 608	1 350	946
Tea and Coffee Dealers	5 720	6 384	6 350	4 330
Shopkeepers	—	182	225	205
F. *Metal Goods Trades*				
Cutlers	43 866	15 220	13 055	13 175
Hardwaremen	—	21 764	19 585	15 150
Ironmongers	5 485	5 350	4 895	4 195
G. *Miscellaneous*				
Tobacconists and Cigar Dealers	7 625	4 210	2 475	2 075
Tallow Chandlers	13 160	12 370	13 825	21 640
Toy Warehouses and Dealers	—	24 735	13 810	10 100

TABLE B:4. Population per Shop Outlet—Leeds

TRADES	1822	1831	1841	1851
A. *Book and Stationery*				
Booksellers and Stationers	4 185	5 125	5 065	4 095
B. *Chemists and Druggists*				
Chemists and Druggists	4 390	3 075	3 040	2 390
C. *Cloth and Clothing*				
Boot and Shoe Makers	2 315	1 070	1 410	670
Clothes Dealers	7 325	4 920	11 690	9 555
Milliners and Dress Makers	6 760	1 445	2 140	975
Tailors	2 000	820	2 140	715
Drapers	2 300	2 175	2 025	1 670
Smallware Dealers	—	—	30 400	19 110
D. *Pottery*				
China, Glass and Earthenware	12 555	15 375	21 715	7 165
E. *Food Trades*				
Bakers	5 170	4 730	7 600	4 410
Confectioners	3 515	3 620	4 110	3 910
Grocers and Tea Dealers	1 350	1 550	1 975	2 325
Tea Dealers	3 255	7 235	5 625	5 735
Provisions Dealers	8 790	3 000	3 535	4 525
Shopkeepers	—	390	420	280
F. *Metal Goods*				
Cutlers	12 855	17 570	21 715	21 500
Hardware Dealers	—	7 680	10 855	12 285
Ironmongers	7 325	6 745	9 500	7 165
G. *Miscellaneous*				
Tobacconists	3 030	3 845	5 240	5 510
Tallow Chandlers	12 555	15 375	15 200	14 355

TABLE B:5. Population per Shop Outlet—Norwich

TRADES	1822	1839	1851
A. *Book and Stationery*			
Booksellers, Stationers, Printers and Binders	2 220	2 472	2 060
B. *Chemists and Druggists*			
Chemists and Druggists	3 005	1 930	2 265
c. *Cloth and Clothing*			
Boot and Shoe Makers	910	625	410
Clothes Dealers	4 645	2 470	2 345
Milliners and Dress Makers	2 320	1 345	530
Tailors	965	725	700
Drapers	1 460	1 670	1 745
Haberdashers and Hosiers	2 320	3 090	1 890
D. *Pottery*			
China, Glass and Earthenware	3 145	3 435	4 250
E. *Food Trades*			
Bakers	575	460	455
Confectioners	5 680	2 575	2 430
Grocers and Tea Dealers	1 000	910	800
Tea and Coffee Dealers	12 775	4 760	4 250
Shopkeepers	—	465	300
F. *Metal Goods Trades*			
Cutlers	10 275	15 450	5 665
Hardwaremen	25 500	10 300	11 335
Ironmongers	4 645	4 120	3 090
G. *Miscellaneous*			
Tobacconists	7 300	6 865	4 857
Pawnbrokers	4 260	4 755	4 535
Tallow Chandlers	3 405	5 620	4 535
Toy Dealers	12 755	15 450	4 855

TABLE B:6. Population per Shop Outlet—Bolton

TRADES	1822	1834	1851
A. *Book and Stationery*			
Booksellers, Stationers, Printers and Binders	5 500	5 585	3 050
B. *Chemists and Druggists*			
Chemists and Druggists	4 715	3 190	2 105
C. *Cloth and Clothing*			
Boot and Shoe Makers	4 125	1 355	770
Shoe Warehouses	3 000	4 965	—
Clothes Dealers	8 250	—	6 780
Milliners and Dress Makers	—	1 175	825
Tailors	—	1 090	825
Drapers	1 140	1 945	2 345
D. *Pottery*			
China, Glass and Earthenware	11 000	5 590	4 065
E. *Food Trades*			
Bakers and Flour Dealers	690	1 240	1 300
Grocers and Tea Dealers	1 835	1 790	1 220
Tea Dealers	6 600	5 590	4 355
Provisions Dealers	—	—	2 650
Shopkeepers	—	310	205
F. *Metal Goods*			
Cutlers	33 000	44 700	—
Hardware Dealers	—	—	30 500
Ironmongers	6 600	5 585	6 100
G. *Miscellaneous*			
Tobacconists	6 600	11 175	12 200
Pawnbrokers	4 715	2 795	2 905
Tallow Chandlers	6 600	6 385	20 335

TABLE B:7. Population per Shop Outlet—Leicester

TRADES	1822	1835	1841	1850
A. *Booksellers and Stationers*				
Booksellers and stationers	1 965	2 862	2 790	2 408
B. *Chemists and Druggists*				
Chemists and Druggists	2 500	2 080	1 965	1 770
C. *Cloth and Clothing*				
Boot and Shoe Makers	655	245	340	250
Clothes Dealers	9 165	3 270	5 890	3 170
Milliners and Dress Makers	1 530	765	1 560	375
Tailors	980	480	780	400
Linen and Woollen Drapers	1 350	1 800	1 890	1 770
Haberdashers	—	9 135	13 250	2 315
D. *Pottery*				
China, Glass and Earthenware	3 055	2 860	3 310	2 510
E. *Food Trades*				
Bakers	490	460	525	500
Confectioners	3 930	2 860	3 535	2 075
Grocers and Tea Dealers	480	560	735	790
Shopkeepers	—	260	655	235
F. *Metal Goods*				
Cutlers	6 875	4 580	6 635	5 470
Ironmongers	3 055	5 085	6 625	4 300
G. *Miscellaneous*				
Tobacconists	27 500	22 900	26 500	12 040
Pawnbrokers	3 055	5 725	5 890	5 470
Tallow Chandlers	1 835	3 815	4 075	7 525

TABLE B:8. Population per Shop Outlet—Nottingham

TRADES	1822	1834	1846	1851
A. *Book and Stationery*				
Booksellers and Stationers	3 155	3 175	2 365	1 710
B. *Chemists and Druggists*				
Chemists and Druggists	2 410	995	930	895

TABLE B:8 *cont.*

TRADES	1822	1834	1846	1851
c. *Cloth and Clothing*				
Boot and Shoe Makers	850	170	255	160
Clothes Dealers	—	2 420	2 890	2 690
Milliners and Dress Makers	1 415	265	500	220
Tailors	820	315	445	265
Drapers	1 205	1 370	1 335	1 345
Smallware Dealers	—	2 420	3 465	1 315
d. *Pottery*				
China, Glass and Earthenware	5 125	7 255	7 727	3 765
e. *Food Trades*				
Bakers	560	350	380	345
Confectioners	3 420	1 955	1 925	1 885
Grocers and Tea Dealers	490	620	600	765
Tea and Coffee Dealers	5 855	8 465	13 000	5 650
Provisions Dealers	—	7 255	10 400	3 140
Shopkeepers	—	120	145	130
f. *Metal Goods*				
Ironmongers	6 835	4 620	4 000	3 140
g. *Miscellaneous*				
Tobacconists	—	13 600	13 000	3 325
Pawnbrokers	3 725	3 910	4 000	4 035
Tallow Chandlers	2 280	4 230	4 000	4 035
Toy Dealers	—	10 160	17 330	9 415

TABLE B:9. Population per Shop Outlet—York

TRADES	1822	1834	1841	1848
a. *Book and Stationery*				
Booksellers and Stationers	1 495	1 795	1 450	1 475
b. *Chemists and Druggists*				
Chemists and Druggists	1 120	960	1 210	1 130
c. *Cloth and Clothing*				
Boot and Shoe Makers	500	310	265	200
Clothes Dealers	—	—	1 450	1 995

TABLE B:9 *cont.*

TRADES	1822	1834	1841	1848
Milliners and Dress Makers	—	930	615	530
Tailors	640	510	410	335
Drapers	475	840	745	970
D. *Pottery*				
China, Glass and Earthenware	1 600	2 240	2 415	2 260
E. *Food Trades*				
Bakers	430	690	805	850
Confectioners	2 800	1 920	1 810	1 785
Grocers and Tea Dealers	310	515	660	850
Tea Dealers	—	1 680	1 450	1 880
Shopkeepers	—	305	235	150
F. *Metal Goods Trades*				
Ironmongers	2 035	2 240	2 230	3 390
G. *Miscellaneous*				
Pawnbrokers	2 035	6 725	9 665	6 780
Tallow Chandlers	3 200	4 480	5 800	6 780
Tobacconists	22 400	5 380	2 415	3 080
Toy Makers and Dealers	2 240	3 870	5 800	8 475

TABLE B:10. Population per Shop Outlet—Carlisle

TRADES	1834	1848
A. *Book and Stationery*		
Booksellers and Stationers	2 210	2 755
B. *Chemists and Druggists*		
Chemists and Druggists	1 810	1 550
C. *Cloth and Clothing*		
Boot and Shoe Makers	310	305
Clothes Dealers	2 490	2 770
Milliners and Dress Makers	1 530	550
Tailors	540	515
Drapers	—	1 030
D. *Pottery*		
China, Glass and Earthenware	3 980	2 480

TABLE B:10 *cont.*

TRADES	1834	1848
E. *Food Trades*		
Bakers	1 420	670
Confectioners	2 840	1 650
Grocers and Tea Dealers	450	825
Tea and Coffee Dealers	2 450	3 450
Shopkeepers	280	160
F. *Metal Goods Trades*		
Ironmongers	2 840	3 100
G. *Miscellaneous*		
Pawnbrokers	4 975	6 200
Tallow Chandlers	4 975	3 540
Tobacconists	—	12 400
Toy Dealers	6 630	4 130

BIBLIOGRAPHY OF PIGOT AND SLATER
NATIONAL DIRECTORIES

London and Provincial New Commercial Directory for 1822–23 (1822).

National Commercial Directory . . . Counties of Chester, Cumberland, Durham, Lancaster, Northumberland, Westmoreland and York (1834).

National London and Provincial Commercial Directory for 1834 . . . of the Metropolis . . . Essex, Hertfordshire, Kent, Middlesex, Surrey, Sussex. . . . (1834).

National and Commercial Directory and Topography of the Counties of Bedford, Cambridge, Essex, Hertfordshire, Huntingdon, Kent, Middlesex, Norfolk, Suffolk, Surrey and Sussex (1839).

National Commercial Directory . . . Counties of Derby, Hertford, Leicester, Lincoln, Monmouth, Nottingham, Rutland, Salop, Stafford, Warwick, and Worcester . . . North and South Wales . . . (1835).

National and Commercial Directory and Topography of the Counties of York, Leicester, Rutland, Lincoln, Northampton and Nottingham . . . [and] *Manchester and Salford. . .* (1841).

National and Commercial Directory and Topography of the Counties of Derby, Dorset, Gloucester, Hereford, Monmouth, Oxford, Shropshire, Somerset, Stafford, Warwick, Wiltshire, Worcester. . . (1842).

National Commercial Directory of Ireland . . . [and] *Manchester, Liverpool, Birmingham, West Bromwich, Leeds, Sheffield and Bristol. . .* (1846).

Royal National Classified Directory and Topography of the County of Lancashire. . . (1851).

Royal National and Commercial Directory and Topography of the Counties of Derby, Hereford, Leicester, Lincoln, Monmouth, Northampton, Nottingham, Rutland, Shropshire, Stafford, Warwick, Worcester (1850).

Royal National and Commercial Directory and Topography of the Counties of Derby, Gloucester, Hereford, Monmouth, Shropshire, Stafford, Warwick, Worcester, and North and South Wales . . . (1850).

Royal National Commercial Directory and Topography of the Counties of Chester, Cumberland, Durham, Lancaster, Northumberland, Westmoreland and York. . . (1848).

Royal National and Commercial Directory and Topography of the Counties of Bedford, Buckingham, Cambridge, Huntingdon, Leicester, Lincoln, Norfolk, Northampton, Nottingham, Oxford, Rutland, Suffolk. . . (1851).

SELECT BIBLIOGRAPHY

This bibliography does not provide an exhaustive list of publications relevant to the subject, but is intended to provide a guide to some of the more important and interesting secondary historical, anthropological and economic works.

ADBURGHAM, A., *Shops and Shopkeeping, 1800–1914* (1964).

ASHTON, T. S., 'The Standard of Life of the Workers in England, 1790–1850', *Journal of Economic History* (Supplement IX, 1949).

BARGER, H., *Distribution's Place in the American Economy Since 1869* (1955).

BARTH, F., *Role of the Entrebreneur in Social Change in Northern Norway* (1963).

BAUER, P. T. and YAMEY, B. S., 'Economic Progress and Occupational Distribution', *Economic Journal* (December 1951).

BAUER, P. T., *West African Trade* (1954).

BLACKMAN, J., 'The Food Supply of an industrial Town'. *Business History* v (1963).

—, 'Development of the Retail Grocery Trade in the 19th Century', *Business History* ix (1967).

BOHANNAN, R. and DALTON, G., *Markets in Africa* (1962).

BURNETT, J., *Plenty and Want* (1966).

CAPLOVITZ, D., *The Poor Pay More* (1963).

CLAPHAM, J. H., *An Economic History of Modern Britain*, 2nd. ed. (1930).

COLE, G. D. H., *A Century of Co-operation* (1944).

DEWEY, A., *Peasant Marketing in Java* (1962).

DRUCKER, P. F., 'Marketing and Economic Development', *Journal of Marketing* xxii (1958).

FIRTH, R., *Themes in Economic Anthropology* (1967).

FISHER, F. J., 'The Development of the London Food Market', *Economic History Review* v (1934–35).

GALBRAITH, J. K. and HOLTON, R. H., *Marketing Efficiency in Puerto Rico* (1955).

HARTWELL, R. M., 'The Rising Standard of Living in England, 1800–1850', *Economic History Review* xiii (1961).

—, 'The Standard of Living', *Economic History Review* xvi (1963–64).

HOBSBAWM, E, J., 'The British Standard of Living', *Economic History Review* x (1957).

—, 'The Standard of Living During the Industrial Revolution: A Discussion', *Economic History Review* xvi (1963–64).

HERSKOVITS, M. J., *Economic Anthropology* (1952).

JEFFERYS, J. B., *Retail Trading in Britain* (1954).

LEWIS, W. A., 'Economic Development with Unlimited Supplies of Labour', *The Manchester School* (May 1954).

MATHIAS, P., *Retailing Revolution* (1967).

MCCLELLAND, W. G., *Costs and Competition in Retailing* (1966).

MINTZ, S. W., 'The Jamaican Internal Marketing Pattern: Some Notes and Hypotheses', *Social and Economic Studies* iv (1955).

—, 'The Role of the Middleman in the Internal Distribution System of a Caribbean Peasant Economy', *Human Organization* xv, (1956).

NASH, M., *Primitive and Peasant Economic Systems* (1966).

—, 'Some Social and Cultural Characteristics of Economic Development', *Economic Development and Cultural Change* (1959).

SKINNER, G. W., 'Marketing and Social Structure in Rural China', *Journal of Asian Studies* xxiv nos. 1, 2 and 3 (1964–65).

SMELSER, N., *Social Change in the Industrial Revolution* (1959).

TAYLOR, A. J., 'Progress and Poverty in Britain, 1780–1850', *History* xlv (1960).

TURNER, E. S., *The Shocking History of Advertising* (1952).

WESTERFIELD, R. B., *Middlemen in English Business* (1915).

WILLIAMS, J. E., 'The British Standard of Living, 1750–1850', *Economic History Review* xix (1966).

YAMEY, B. S., 'The Evolution of Shopkeeping', *Lloyds Bank Review* (January 1954).

INDEX OF TRADERS

GENERAL INDEX

Abergavenny, 8
Accounting practices, 164–5, 185–9
Advertising: clothes dealers, 140–1;
  costs, 206; development, 11, 162–
  164, 235, 237; in drapery shops,
  136; ironmongers, 151
Agricultural produce, 33–4, 36–42,
  232; *see also* Food trades and
  specific commodities
Aldermaston fair, 35
Apprenticeship, 210–12, 228
Ashford: trades association, 159–61
Ashton-under-Lyne: regulations
  against itinerants, 68
Aston: urban improvement, 7n

Bakers: growth of shops, 99; in
  Leicester market, 43; manufac-
  turing skills, 124–6; multiple shops,
  104–5; producer/retailer aspects,
  235; wages, 196
'Bargain sales', 234
Bartholemew fair, 34, 35
Bath: urban improvement, 7–8
'Bazaar' trade, 79
Bedford market, 8, 51–2
Belper, 7
Bideford market, 36–7
Billingsgate market, 16, 73
Bilston market, 52
Birkenhead market, 57
Birmingham: bakeries industrialized,
  124; development of commercial
  centre, 9; drapers, 191; fish trade,
  14, 15; fresh fish market, 17;
  market, 57, 58, 59; urban im-
  provement, 7n
Bishop Auckland market, 55
Blackburn market, 57–8
Bognor market, 52

Bolton: growth of shop retailing, 90–
  103; numbers of tradesmen in
  1822, 1834 and 1851, 247–8;
  population per shop outlet in
  1822, 1834 and 1851, 261
Bommerees, 73
Bootmakers, *see* Shoemakers
Bradford: regulations on itinerants,
  68
Brand names, 141
Bridgwater market, 8, 53
Bristol: urban improvement, 7;
  wholesale grocery trade, 116
Bury market, 52
Butchers: capital, 207, 208; costs,
  200; equipment required, 203;
  high class shops, 69; market
  trading, 43, 92, 96; premises
  needed, 199; processing and
  manufacturing skills, 121–3, 235;
  wages paid, 193, 196

Cakes and pastries, 126
Canals, 13
Candles, 115
Canterbury market, 52, 53
Capital and investment: credit
  trading, 82; industrialisation,
  effects on, 5; in markets, 45, 47,
  50–9; producer/retailer aspect of
  shop trade demanding more, 236;
  shopkeepers, 203–4, 206–25, 226–
  228; shortage encourages itinerant
  trading, 62, 70–3, 237–8; in urban
  improvement, 10
Carlisle: bakeries industrialized, 124;
  growth of shop retailing, 90–103;
  numbers of tradesmen in 1834 and
  1848, 254–5; population per shop
  outlet in 1834 and 1848, 264–5

247, Leicester, 249, Nottingham, 250, Merthyr Tydfil, 252, York, 253, Carlisle, 254; population per shop outlet in: London, 256, Liverpool, 257, Manchester, 258; Leeds, 259, Norwich, 260, Bolton, 261, Leicester, 262, Nottingham, 262, York, 263, Carlisle, 264; wages paid, 194

Street markets: Bedford, 51–2; causing traffic congestion, 52; in Coventry, 47–50; in Leicester, 47; in London, 58; relationship to shop trade, 69

Stocks, 212–20, 234–5, 237

Stourbridge market, 52

Sturbridge Fair, 32

Sugar, 113–14

Sutherst, T., 192

'Swag Shops', 76–7

Tailors, 136–8; accounts and household expenditures, 187; annual turnover and profits, 167; capital, 209; and clothes dealers, 139; costs, 200–1; in drapery trade, 101; growth, 100; in hosiery, 144; stocks, 214, 215; wages paid, 194, 197

Tallow chandlers, 102, 123; numbers in: London, 241, Liverpool, 242, Manchester, 244, Leeds, 246, Norwich, 247, Bolton, 248, Leicester, 250, Nottingham, 251, Merthyr Tydfil, 252, York, 254, Carlisle, 255; population per shop outlet in: London, 257, Liverpool, 257, Manchester, 258, Leeds, 259, Norwich, 260, Bolton, 261, Leicester, 262, Nottingham, 263, York, 264, Carlisle, 265

Tally-trade, see Credit trading

Tea dealers, 99, 112–13

Tewkesbury market, 51

Tobacco dealers: growth, 102; numbers in: London, 240, Liverpool, 242, Manchester, 244, Leeds, 246,

Norwich, 247, Bolton, 248, Leicester, 250, Nottingham, 251, Merthyr Tydfil, 252, York, 254, Carlisle, 255; population per shop outlet in: London, 257, Liverpool, 257, Manchester, 258, Leeds, 259, Norwich, 260, Bolton, 261, Leicester, 262, Nottingham, 263, York, 264, Carlisle, 265

Tolls: commodity, 54; market, 44–5, 45–7, 47–50, 53–5; town-end tolls, 54

Toy dealers, 102; numbers in: London, 241, Liverpool, 242, Manchester, 244, Norwich, 247, Bolton 248, Leicester, 250, Nottingham, 251, York, 254, Carlisle, 255; population per shop outlet in: London, 257, Liverpool, 257, Manchester, 258, Norwich, 260, Nottingham, 263, York, 264, Carlisle, 265

Trade associations and unions, 14, 15, 159–61, 191–2

Trade directories, 89–109 passim

Trade journals, 9, 67, 191

Transport, 3, 12–18, 39–42, 231; costs to tradesmen, 204–5; and fairs, 32–3, 232; public transport, 62, 190; stockholdings, 219

Truck payments, 22, 23

Turnovers, 165–9

Upholsterers, 222

Urbanization, 4–6, 39, 231; effect on wholesale fairs, 232; effect on markets, 51; effect on transportation needs, 13; urban improvement, 6–12

Wages, 24, 173, 193–8; ironmongery 153; tailoring, 137; see also Incomes

Water transport, 13, 16, 40

Weights and measures, 74–5, 142

Wholesale trade, 6, 31–4, 36, 41, 219–22, 231–3, 234; cloth and